MW00881195

#GRATEFUL:

Everything Happens for a Reason

By Annoying Actor Friend

This book was created as a work of humor and parody and it is intended for entertainment purposes only. This book makes no claim or guarantee to any of the content within. The author and publisher are not affiliated with any of the persons or corporations, living or dead, referenced in this book.

Additional characters, screen names, incidents, and dialogue are drawn from the author's imagination and are not to be construed as real. Any resemblance to actual events or persons, living or dead, is entirely coincidental.

Copyright © 2015 Annoying Actor Friend

All Rights Reserved

FIRST EDITION

No part of this book may be used or reproduced in any manner whatsoever without written permission of the author except in the case of brief quotations embodied in critical articles and reviews. For information address: contact@annoyingactorfriend.com

The author and publisher should have neither liability nor responsibility to any person or entity with respect to any loss or damage caused, or alleged to be caused, directly or indirectly by any information presented in this work.

For Mom,

because these two words have been cut from every single one of my playbill bios due to them putting me over my allotted word count.

.

INTRODUCTION

Welcome, to the first day of school. You hold in your hand *the* essential how-to-succeed-in-show-business manual that will, without a doubt, teach you how to #werk. Wait. No. That was the last book. Let me try this again…

Welcome, to *#GRATEFUL: Everything Happens for a Reason*. This book is a sequel to *#SOBLESSED: the Annoying Actor Friend's Guide to Werking in Show Business*, which was adapted from a blog that was a spinoff of an anonymous parody Twitter account that—seriously, what the hell am I doing with my life? I have way too much time on my hands.

If you have not yet read *#SOBLESSED*, then I suggest you hightail it over to Amazon and pick up a copy, providing me with a hefty royalty I can use to buy a snack at Schnipper's, Schmackary's, or whichever Broadway Elite establishment is currently in vogue at this very moment. What's playing at the old Café Edison? #NeverForget. Once you've read *#SOBLESSED*, you'll have all the skills needed to navigate *#GRATEFUL*, and the ability to master both the #ShamelessSelfPromotion and internal product placement present in this very sentence.

In *#SOBLESSED*, you discovered when you first became #blessed, and how to #werk in show business until you had learned the art of #werking/working to become #SOBLESSED. Now that you are #SOBLESSED, like any successful actor, you might be wondering, what next? Welcome to *#GRATEFUL*, a create your own show business destiny experience where

1

anything is possible…

What if you went to the chorus call that you bailed on because it was cold as balls outside? What if you booked that role that went to the person it usually goes to? What if you took a Ricola before that callback instead of a shot of Jameson? What if you *killed* someone. Show business is full of infinite possibilities, and only in *#GRATEFUL* will you have to opportunity to see every single alternative. So, like, this book is basically Laura Osnes' 54 Below cabaret *The Paths Not Taken,* having sex with a cracked out *If/Then*, while listening to *Serial.*

Before you embark on your journey back into the Mythical Kingdom of Manhattan, and all its surrounding wonder, here are a few rules to remember:

1.) Blessed or any other form of the word (i.e. blesseder, blessedest, blessederest) is dead. Sorry. We killed it. We can't have nice things. Whether used ironically or un-ironically. It's over. Never forget that you are blessed and #SOBLESSED, just like, don't talk about it, OK? Treat it how I treat my love for *The Wedding Singer*.

2.) This version of Broadway is kind of like the one in *Smash.* TO CLARIFY: It is not the one in *Smash,* but you know how in the Smashiverse, Bernadette Peters didn't exist, but her Tony acceptance speech did? And *Rent* existed, but Jesse L. Martin and Daphne Rubin-Vega didn't—and nobody in the world of the show ever commented on the parallels between Jonathan Larson and that character whose name I forgot? There will be moments when your journey through this book feels like that, but I want you to remember that this is a fantasy, and I don't give a shit.

3.) Just like real life, you're going to have a lot of false starts, and you might not reach your happy ending right away. You'll probably die a few times or worse, commit career suicide. However, unlike real life, when this happens, you'll be allowed to start over! It might get frustrating after a while, but I want you to consider it a gift. When real careers dead-end, you're screwed. Be #GRATEFUL.

4.) Have fun! Stop taking life so seriously. It's singing and dancing! Nobody ever died from either of these things—except maybe the dancers Michael Bennett used to murder in tech.

***

So, without further procrastination on my part, let's get to the *Empire Strikes Back* of the Annoying Actor Friend Saga. Sorry, it's been a while and I forget who my audience is. This is the *Sister Act II: Back in the Habit* of the Annoying Actor Friend Saga. Let's begin…

As you go forth on your voyage, I urge you to remember this: Whatever your choice, whatever the outcome, you must always be *#GRATEFUL*. Because everything happens for a reason.

WHAT CLASS ARE YOU IN?

To make certain you set out on the career path that most closely resembles your current mood, you must first decide if you are a Broadway Freshman, Sophomore, Junior, or Senior. The classes at Broadway High School are assigned not by your level of success, but by how you feel about the business at the given moment. Remember, Elaine Stritch probably never made it past sophomore year. Contrariwise, I know at least three Newsies who made their Broadway debuts as seniors. Allow me to recap in 140 characters or less:

BROADWAY FRESHMAN: You love Broadway. Social media. Fans. You do every BC/EFA event and there's at least one GIF of you on Tumblr.

BROADWAY SOPHOMORE: You love it, but pretend you're above it. You play it cool. Like, you follow Broadway people on Twitter, but don't favorite anything.

BROADWAY JUNIOR: You hate it, but pretend you love it. You want to do something else, but never learned any other skills so you lie to yourself.

BROADWAY SENIOR: Why the fuck are you reading this book? Thanks for the money, though!

So, which are you…?

Broadway Freshman. (page 12)

Broadway Sophomore. (page 454)

Broadway Junior. (page 458)

Broadway Senior. (page 6)

BROADWAY SENIOR

You're currently on Broadway, because you're always on Broadway. The Broadway Senior is only a senior because they don't remember what it's like to be anything else. Not all nominees of the Elaine Stritch Awaresie Award for Unemployment Avoidance are seniors. Many of the perennial workers of Broadway genuinely love it. You, however, are so hashtag-over-it, you literally can't even with anything remotely connected to your place of business.

That is why you make certain to arrive promptly at half hour and haven't done the stage door since before you were born. Morning press events are an inconvenience because they exist prior to noon, and even the Tonys are old hat. BTW, does anyone still wear a – sorry I forgot you hate everything Broadway. Above all other industry obligations, you find sports-involved activities to be the worst. Bowling is boring, and you wouldn't set foot near the Broadway Softball League, even if you were promised an extra week of vacation pay—however if there were an organization called the Broadway Knitters League, where you could sit in silence and ignore everyone, you might reconsider.

You've been in the biz since it was better than it is now. When people say, "Things aren't as good as they used to be," they're referring to your career. It frightens you to think you've spent most of your life living a dream with which you've fallen out of love. It happens. Sometimes you can get really passionate about something, and then realize maybe it isn't all you thought it was cracked up to be. I've been there, too. Like, I thought *Saturday Night Fever* was awesome on Broadway, and then I saw it on tour, and was like, "WTF was I thinking?" You're basically going through the same thing right now—except instead of the Bee Gees, it's your life choices.

I'm not going to tell you how to live your life, but I'm not afraid to judge it based solely off of the story you've told me online – especially if that story tells a more happy and successful one than mine. That being said, you've been pretty absent on the Internet lately, and that is a cause for concern. I can tell that you're unhappy if you're not able to at least scrounge up some kind of lie to tell all of your followers that you're not just doing OK, but hashtag-nailing-it. Maybe it *is* time for a change.

Clearly, you need to either quit the business and find a new career, or stay and discover a way to love it again. Do you…

Change careers….? (page 14)

Find the love again….? (page 270)

Choosing to give up a slot at NYMF in favor of owning a home is both a brave and noble decision, but before you can pound the pavement for a sweet pad, you need to fire off an email to the people at NYMF that is steeped in forced sadness:

Dear Whom it May Concern,

It is with kindest regrets that I must withdraw from the New York Musical Theatre Festival. Inability to find a commercial producer will make it impossible to mount a production this summer. I cannot thank you enough for the warm embrace *Pieces of Me* has received. It is, and will always be, a piece I am very passionate about. I hope to give it to the world one day soon.

All my best,

Author of *Pieces of Me*

Even I'm shocked at how easily you were able to abandon your passion project the moment real money was placed in front of you. No shade. I totally get it. It's just not something I'd expect from you at this juncture in your life. Perhaps you're at a different stage now. Ditching theatre in favor of real life luxuries can only mean one thing...

You have become a... (page 6)

You open your Facebook application and begin constructing a flawlessly funny status about falling down outside of Schmackary's. I know Facebook is retro (and meant for people who are old enough to have been in the original cast of *Spring Awakening*) but for some reason, you're the only person in the world who hasn't pissed off the Facebook Algorithms Powers That Be, and thus, all of your friends see everything you post and are about as shy of the like button on your page as Fansies are of a Newsie's personal space.

Facebook allows you to laugh brevity in the face, so you can really let loose and write a novella-length status update, which is a luxury you want to take advantage of, but don't want to abuse, because a long post might make your followers' eyes glaze over and send them scrolling ahead to someone else ranting on their feed about a satirical news article that they think is real, so you decide to keep your story succinct, because nothing is truly worse than a poorly-constructed and tediously-long run-on thought or sentence.

Once you're finished regaling anyone who will listen about your Tale from the Ninth Avenue Asphalt, you proudly press "post" and send your Stephen-Manuel Mirandheim genius out into the Ether of the Internet. Then, you condense the status for Twitter, post it on Instagram with a picture of the street where you fell (lit with the Mayfair filter), funnel all of it onto Tumblr, and then Snapchat it. This shit is going to kill! Now, it's time to sit back and wait for the likes to pour in.

The attention is pretty lackluster at first. Maybe your post bombed? That is a possibility. After all, it's between the hours of 12 p.m. and 4 p.m., and like, who's on social media at that time? People are busy with matinees, screen tests, and actor-y things like day drinking.

Just when you're about to delete everything and repost it later in the day, Cesar Rocha (CSA – Telsey + Company and CSA Associate Board Member) likes your tweet and then immediately retweets it. BOOM. Acceptance. You know it will only be a matter of minutes before you go viral.

This extra boost of confidence is really making you feel like you can nail your callback later. You have a few hours to kill before you need to go home and get ready. Where to next?

Feeling self-assured is such a rare emotion for an actor, so maybe you'll stroll up to Worldwide Plaza, grab a non-fat flat white at Starbucks, and ignore all the people you've slept with. Or, you could cut across Times Square to the H&M to see if there are any new sexy outfits you could sport at your callback. Do you...

Go to Worldwide Plaza...? (page 38)

Go to H&M...? (page 70)

BROADWAY FRESHMAN

Welcome to Freshman Year on Broadway, where every night is Saturday Night, and you always win Dollar Friday. Your Mondays are dark, but who cares? You fill them with three concerts at Feinstein's/54 Below, because everyone asks you to make guest appearances and you just can't say "no" to opportunity. This is your town. You're the belle of the ball in your own little corner of the sky known as the Great White Way.

You. Are. Supportive. If you can't get papered into a friend's show, you *actually buy* a student rush ticket. When you're not on Broadway, you keep yourself connected to the community by cheerleading on social media. You have even been known to watch an entire telecast of the Tony Awards without rolling your eyes *once*. Basically, the sun lives comfortably within your butt and shines out of it every single time someone calls, "half hour."

Today, you live in a shoebox apartment that you share with your college roommate, Carol. The two of you settled on 43rd Street between Eighth and Ninth Avenues, because that is where Telsey + Company is located, and also where the explosion sequence in *Birdman* was filmed. You are in the thick of it. This is the neighborhood that pulses deep inside the very artery that pumps blood to the heart of the American Theatre. You aren't just living the dream, the dream is living you.

You awake slowly on a Tuesday morning and take in a deep, delicious breath. The air wafting through the window that connects to an airshaft smells like warm childhood dreams and glowing opportunity—with the distant, but potent, hint of pigeon sex. Your eyes focus on the clock on the microwave in the kitchen that may also be the living room and/or bathroom—maybe all three. Who cares? You're a triple threat, and so is every room in your apartment.

The clock reads ten a.m. DAMN. Just once, you'd love to sleep in long enough to make it to your alarm. Perhaps you woke up early because you're nervous for your audition for the big new Broadway show at three. Lazily, you roll over and check your phone: ten emails, forty-seven messages in that group text, two new followers on Twitter, and a voicemail? Wow. That's retro. You check it. It's your college voice teacher. She's in town for the week and would love to meet up for coffee.

Since you have an extra hour in your day, you could squeeze in some time for your voice teacher. However, you've been neglecting the gym, and nothing warms up your voice quite like being skinnier. This is a dilemma! You know the gym is very important to Broadway success. It helps make you look like the roles you're trying to book. Still, your voice teacher molded you into the multifaceted singer you are today—and shouldn't it be about talent? On the other hand, proper breathing technique during a rigorous workout can improve the power of your diaphragm, resulting in a stronger, sexier screlt. Then again, you're anxious about your callback, and encouragement from an old friend could ease your nerves, and you'd rather die than go to the gym right now—but what about #BroadwayBody? Do you…

Go to the gym…? (page 374)

Meet up for coffee with your old voice teacher…? (page 182)

13

*

Coincidentally, your journey to self-rediscovery begins on Ninth Avenue. Bluntly penetrating the heart of Hell's Kitchen, this cozy little street has always been referred to by the Broadway community as "The Dance Belt." It's long and gay, filled with dancer girls who belt and dancer boys who wear them. On this very avenue, you finally come to the realization that it's time to retire after witnessing a fairly frequent Hell's Kitchen occurrence: two chorus kids screaming at each other across the avenue over the sound of jackhammers about heading to their respective stage doors. Upon seeing this, you promptly text your stage manager and call out of your show. Forever.

As you walk the hallowed highway of missed opportunities and unrequited callbacks, it feels as if you've left pieces of your soul along the path. To show business veterans, Ninth Avenue is the Horcrux of Broadway, but now that you've unofficially freed yourself (it's not official until you've tweeted it) from a career that often permits being asked to strip early on in the interview process, Ninth Avenue no longer feels like it holds any significance to you. In fact, as you take in the area, you find that you don't even recognize the neighborhood anymore. It's as if all of the restaurants changed overnight (because literally all of the restaurants may have changed overnight – as suddenly and without warning as the menu at Vynl).

Ninth Avenue now feels like any other street in a city that holds as many roads to travel as it does possibilities. Oh, wow—you've just been bitch-slapped by hopeful idealism. You haven't felt like this since the opening number of the 2013 Tony Awards. It's refreshing to find yourself with the potential for so much opportunity while at a significant crossroads in life. It's also refreshing to embark on this journey knowing that the movie *Crossroads* was written by Shonda Rhimes, so anything is possible. You're confident this career transition is going to be great – if only you knew what career to transition to.

When an actor quits the business, there are a handful of roads they can embark on—real estate, fitness (pilates, yoga, or personal trainer/life coach/unlicensed therapist), photographer, teacher, Internet personality, etc. Transitioning is like hitting the reset button, without your parents' bank account. It's liberating, and horrifying, and mostly horrifying. Since you have such a rock star attitude about the entire thing, however, I'm positive you'll hit the challenge head-on and find yourself happy and successful in your new career—until you find it totally boring and unfulfilling and choose to transition again. The struggle is real.

So, I guess the next choice is pretty important. I mean, not so important as the time you chose a career in the theatre over a sensible trajectory that would lead to dollars without the fear of self-loathing and regret darkening every corner. I guess any career can cause one to feel regret, but the regret of an actor is heightened because we're trained to not only closely study and understand our raw and mysteriously haunting emotions, but also harness them deep within our psyche, so at any moment we can unleash them proudly on stage for a role, casually at a prescreen, or randomly on a date. What I'm saying is, choosing your second career is more important than choosing your first, because you're older now.

If you want my two cents (because I've literally done everything, or at least googled it), I'm going to be upfront and advocate against choosing a career in real estate because I watch *Million Dollar Listing* and that world looks even more doucherific than the Broadway Prom. Fitness could be a good industry for you because you used to be an actor, and thus have always had an unhealthy relationship with body image, so it's probably a great idea for you to help others with that. I'd suggest becoming an Internet personality, but I don't know how that works. You could go into casting or become an agent, but that's a harder career within the same industry, so it'd be like breaking up with your significant other but still letting them pee on you on weekends. Going back to college is an option, but you've been funneling your weekly production contract into living an extravagant lifestyle right at your means, and the thought of student loans just seems so basic at this point in your life. Maybe you shouldn't have quit your show before figuring this out, because now you're stuck without a job and a five-year plan. Wow, your life is giving me so much anxiety I need to crack open my Audition Xanax.

I'll make the options easy for you: You can either go into the fitness industry (because every Career Transition for Dancer candidate I've ever known has spent their grant on a yoga certification) or you can become a photographer because you like Instagram. There aren't a whole lot of options for someone whose skills are limited to singing, dancing, and acting, so you should be happy I narrowed it down to the two best options. Do you…

Go into the fitness industry….? (page 18)

Become a photographer….? (page 257)

*

Holding strong to the dirge-tastic tempo set, you bravely shoulder on in an attempt to save face in front of the creative team, and for the most part you believe it might be working. It feels like you've been singing for a solid six minutes, but maybe they'll appreciate what is hopefully coming off as a balladic cover of a classic up-tempo. You're basically a *Grey's Anatomy* soundtrack right now, and back when Sara Ramirez was still doing Broadway this might have been relevant. However, if anything, maybe this accidental approach to your song will come off with a retro-edge that—

"Thank you," says the director, the moment your song finally comes to an end.

You stand there smiling for a beat.

A second beat.

A third beat.

"Thank you," the director says again, "for coming in today."

Oh.

Nodding, you say your "thank you," walk out the door, and march promptly to the nearest bar because your life is over.

THE END.

*

Having spent the last twenty minutes indulging my rant about career transition, you've autopilot-walked all the way to Columbus Circle. You don't spend a lot of time above 54th Street, but you've always found Columbus Circle to be a charming place to use the restroom or score a cheap tank top on the way to immersing yourself in Central Park's Sheep Meadow: The Real Life Tinder.

The center of Columbus Circle is a nice, calm place to sit and think, so you race across the street, dodging cars Frogger-style, and grab a seat on a stone bench facing the fountain and the statue of a man people only bother to complain about on social media on the holiday named after him. It's oddly quiet in the circle today, allowing for a brief moment of reflecting back on the illustrious career you've left behind. It's OK. The panic has begun to subside. You're happy with the change. Oh, that's right. You're supposed to make a change... Into the fitness industry? Sorry I got distracted in the middle of this section because I needed to go workout.

The most obvious choice would be to apply for a position at Mark Fisher Fitness, and then the second step after that would be to kill yourself, because why would you leave the world of Broadway to work for a company whose key demographic is a parody of Broadway? You'll need to try another fitness establishment. You're a member at New York Sports Club, but it's not exactly a place you'd like to work because you mostly just tolerate it for the few hours you spend there a week. That means Planet Fitness is out and Crunch would basically be a lateral move. There's always David Barton, but if you wanted to be a trainer in a glorified bathhouse, you could just build a time machine and go back to the 1971 Ansonia because at least their gay sex parties were accompanied by Barry Manilow and Bette Midler. That leaves Fusion Health & Racquet.

Fusion Health & Racquet is New York City's most elite luxury health establishment. It isn't just a workout club; it's a sanctuary of goodness. Even Fusion's motto is, "It's not exercise. It's existence." When people find out you frequent Fusion, they be like, "oh, you look on fleek." It's definitely a status symbol. When you're a Fusion member, you have a responsibility to continuously post online about your group fitness classes, and also, Instagram body selfies with their branded hashtag: #FusionTalkedMeIntoWhatIHaveBeenDoing. People know you're important if you got to Fusion. They also assume you're broke if you're an actor who goes to Fusion. Who cares? Fusion has really nice lotions and towels soaked in cucumber-mint water. It's worth it.

Looks like Fusion Health & Racquet is your best choice because, if anything, you'll get a free membership, and the only time you've been able to frequent that club was the summer you played fast and loose with the one-week trial gift cards you pocketed at a Broadway Bares Solo Strips event.

Armed with the courage of those people who always seem to nail their auditions without nerves because they are either drunk, or went to Michigan, you march into the Fusion club at Columbus Circle and descend in an elevator into the bowels of the building. Upon entering the lobby area, you are immediately immersed in the Fusion experience. It's cleaner than a Mormon temple and cooler than any of us will ever be. Fusion is like a high fashion runway show with treadmills. If the Las Vegas Cosmopolitan commercials threw up on a rack of free weights, that'd be Fusion. One thing you do know about Fusion, is the further uptown you go, the less intimidating the members get. At 59th Street, you're basically spitting distance from Hell's

Kitchen, and the idea of working so closely to your ex-colleagues makes you feel more uncomfortable than when people use contractions in hashtags.

Deciding that this club won't be a good fit, you make a hairpin turn in the lobby, hop back in the elevator, and head uptown to find a less trendy Fusion location. The farthest north is 93rd, but you're not that insecure. You settle on 77th Street because it's near where most of *You've Got Mail* was filmed, so it's like older, but not too old, you know?

Upon approaching the front desk, a perky Ken Doll looking guy with a nametag that reads, "Callan" greets you cheerfully.

"Welcome to Fusion!" he practically sings.

"Hi. Are you guys are hiring any personal trainers, pilates instructors, or whatever? I have no experience in the fitness industry, but I just quit Broadway, so I know how it works." You explain.

Callan leans in coldly, "You think you can just walk into Fusion with no background in fitness and get hired at one of the most prestigious health clubs in the world just because you look like an actor?"

You stare at each other for a beat.

"Because yes, you can," he continues.

Callan hands you an application that you promptly fill out. You don't have a professional resume to attach, so you just sort of wink and smile and hope that the same tricks that made you a successful actor will apply here as well. Callan then asks you to wait in the member lounge upstairs while the fitness manager looks it over.

While seated on a chair in the lounge, you take in your surroundings. It's magical in here. If waiting areas at auditions calmed you with free wifi and the scent of eucalyptus, you might still be an actor.

After a few short minutes, you are greeted by a menacing figure.

"New applicant?" he asks.

This guy is huge, but has a thoughtful demeanor. Like the Incredible Hulk in Lululemon.

"I'm Stuart Ray. Fitness Manager. Welcome to Fusion. Follow me."

Stuart leads you to his office – a little glass fishbowl in the center of the main floor, surrounded by stretching mats filled with members doing warm-ups that are so inexplicably strange, you're offended on behalf of your years of dance training (or at least watching other people dance. I can't remember exactly what your theatrical strengths are, OK?).

You take a seat opposite Stuart in his office. Oh, no. Is this an interview? Shit. You're not sure if you've ever done a real person job interview. Your version of a job interview involves inhumane activity like…well…everything that goes into an average audition.

This interview seems pretty cool and casual. Stuart asks you about your background and why you want a career in fitness. You're able to tap dance around the hard parts by really chatting up your life experiences (i.e. talking about yourself). You have a Facebook fan page, Twitter, Instagram, Vine, Snapchat, and a Periscope, so you're pretty proficient at regurgitating the history of you.

Stuart really seems to be eating up your personality. I'll bet you've got this job in the bag. Shit like anatomy, kinesiology, and how not to carelessly and violently murder your client during a session can be taught; personality cannot.

"One last question. It's a personality one."

"In the bag," you think to yourself.

Stuart leans back in his chair and asks: "If you could be any shoe. In the entire world. What shoe would you be?"

You laugh, "Oh that's easy! I'd be – "

You freeze. This is a huge question. Not only is it the last one, but also it's about a subject that has so many possible answers that you completely draw a blank. It's like when someone asks me what my dream role is; I can't even think of a play title, so I just end up saying, "Chipotle."

There can't be a wrong answer to this, right? It's such a stupid question. You could say anything and find a way to sell it. Let's think for a minute. Fusion loves money, so any version of a Jimmy Choo, Louboutin, or Manolo Blahnik would work. However, you don't want to sound pretentious. TOMS, Vans, and Sperrys are nice and sensible, as well as sleek – but potentially boring. Are you...

An extravagant shoe....? (page 32)

A simple shoe....? (page 34)

*

Stopping abruptly, you turn to the accompanist and say, "Like, what the actual fuck are you doing? That's *not* the tempo I gave you. Didn't you understand me when I snapped it out for you?"

"I'm sorry," apologizes the pianist. "I'll do it right for you now."

"That's what I thought," you state proudly. "Now, give me a bell tone and let's get this shit done."

The accompanist nods his head, taps a B flat, and you sail into your song, taking the room with you into oblivion.

I'm serious! You're really nailing it! "Slay" can't even begin to describe what you are doing in this room, but I'll say it anyway –

"Slay! SLAY! SLAAAAAAAAAAY!"

You're hitting *all* of the notes—notes that haven't even been invented yet. You're turning this Pearl Studios into mother-effing church, and I am converting to the religion of You.

When the song ends and you return to earth from the heavenly heights to which you leapt, you're not at all surprised by the satisfied looks on the creative team's faces –

"Well, shit," says the director, "that was fucking epic."

"I know, right." You state.

The music director stands. "Randy over there," he says motioning to the accompanist. "We ask him every now and then to put on a pair of proverbial oven mitts and play an actor's audition, just to see what they do.

"Now, mostly they'll just plow through and pray. Sometimes they politely stop and blame the tempo on them. But never do they acknowledge that he is actively trying to destroy them. It's a test we've been administering for years, and you're the first one who's ever passed."

"Whoa," you say.

"I know, right?" he asks.

"That's why," the director stands, "we've no other choice but to offer you a leading role. We don't even care if not one of them is right for you. It doesn't matter. You've proven yourself. You saw through our bullshit and called us on it."

"Congratulations," nods the music director.

"Well done kid," laughs Randy at the piano.

The director walks over to you and places his hand out for you to shake. You take it firmly in yours. He smiles. "Welcome to Broadway."

EPILOGUE (page 465)

*

"I love your shit!" cheers Corey over text. "Of course I'll read your script!"

With great expediency and enthusiasm, you send a PDF of *Metamorphosis: the Hilary Duff Musical* to Corey, and eagerly await his response.

A day passes.

Two.

Three.

"Hey, you get a chance to read yet?" you inquire in an email to Corey.

Another day passes.

Two.

Three.

You'd assume Corey was dead, but he's been active on Twitter, and you're pretty sure you can't tweet without a pulse (however much it seems some still do.)

After another brief bout of silence, Corey explains that something crazy came up at his show and it set him back a bit, but he hopes to get to it soon. I guess it's onto Paige.

Paige doesn't read it either.

OK, this is going about as smoothly as a post-opening night booze poop. Although they might not be your first choices, your friends Ashley and Ellyn are always good for a laugh. Maybe one of them will be willing to read your script. Do you…

Send your script to Ashley….? (page 336)

Send your script to Ellyn…? (page 343)

*

This really isn't your scene. Maybe it's the party talking, or the chocolate fondue, or the fact that in the five seconds you spent inside the clubhouse, you heard more *Frozen* references than were used in this very sentence. You politely pivot-turn, open the door, and box step yourself right out of there.

While strolling up Ninth Avenue, you think maybe it's not too late to meet up with your voice teacher. You shoot her a text, but she explains that she made plans with your rival from college. You always figured she liked them more, anyway—especially since they're on their sixth Broadway show, and you aren't. Trying not to feel down about your flatlining career, you take a breath, and say to yourself, "Shake it off. Time to book."

As you stand in the street, a dude on a Citi Bike missiles past you, forcing you to the ground. Sprawled out in the middle of Hell's Kitchen, you look up and catch a glimpse of the vigilante's face, then hear what sounds like a muffled, "Sorry!"

Furious that you nearly blew out your knee on the most important audition day of your life, you jump to your feet and scream back, "Suck it, Kyle Dean Massey!"

He doesn't hear you. Oddly enough, this isn't the first time a Fiyero has brought you to your knees (I'm talking about being genuinely affected by a performance, guys. Some of the Fiyeros can really *sing*).

Ego bruised, you sulk to the side of 45th and Ninth. Having suffered a major endorphin crash, you could really use some comfort food to replenish your emotional energy, and take your mind off being embarrassed. Face planting in the middle of a neighborhood where everyone *and* the ghost of Gwen Verdon can see you is worse than that time you busted out the wrong audition song after the accompanist gave you a bell tone.

Luckily, you're just steps away from Schmackary's, the only place to go when you are a Broadway person who needs cookies. This could be just the sustenance you require to forget what happened. However, you're also next to Juice Generation, and maybe a healthy Hail to the Kale will give you the proper vitamins required to propel you to a powerful performance at your callback. You're thinking kale's the answer—but cookies, though. Do you...

Go clean with kale...? (page 207)

Commit to cookies...? (page 234)

*

Feeling the need for a sentimental conversation with a person who actually matters, sitting down with Carol is a much better idea than trolling Glass House for validation. Any attention you get there will be as empty as a Twitter like. Carol has been a solid friend since college, and even though she's suffering mad depression from not having worked since the first Obama administration, you're positive she can put all that aside and genuinely congratulate you on this job that you wanted more than anything in the world.

After a sensible costume change at your apartment, you hit the streets to head down to the East Village for some free well booze that's been poured from top shelf liquor bottles. Since you're in an exceptionally Broadway-loving mood, you throw on #Hamiltunes Radio and shuffle through all of your favorite idealistic anthems: "Lullaby of Broadway," "Let Me Be Your Star," "Organ Prelude" from *Sweeney Todd*, etc.

Even though you're underground on an Orange Line train below West 4th (thus out of reach of a wifi signal) iTunes Music still manages to work because it's the #Hamiltunes Radio station and anything that begins with "Hamil" is indestructible (tbh there was a brief moment in December of 2015, when I got so Fa-Hamil-tigued, the only thing I was Hamil-interested in was *Mark* Hamill because *Star Wars: Episode VII*).

As you exit your train car at a stop in a neighborhood named after a lyric in *Rent*, you are met with a wall of people who are not moving. Ugh. It's crammed like a post-workout tuna can down here, and smells worse. You have to get around this. There's always a way for someone like you to get out of situations as basic as pedestrian traffic. People who haven't figured out how to work their way around a crowd moving upstairs at a subway stop are seriously non-Eq.

Trying to cage your frustration as you stand in a gridlock on the platform as the train pulls away, you look around to see if there's a thin bypass on the edge that could be used as a walkway to fast track you to the staircase, where you can cut in and get to the top before everyone else. I call this express lane, "Michigan Avenue." After a moment, you spot an opportunity to slide by on the right of the crowd, using the narrow, yellow line that separates the tracks from safety. Feeling fearless, you squeeze around the masses and breeze up the edge of the platform, toward the stairs. Thank goodness you have such great balance from years of experience—balancing in ballet, *and* balancing your sanity within this career.

As you confidently progress to the stairs, you notice that your #Hamiltunes Radio has ceased shuffling through music. Perhaps it stopped because it's gone a significant amount of time without playing an actual song from *Hamilton*. You are well aware that the daily running power of #Hamiltunes Radio cannot be satisfied unless it has shuffled at least thrice to "Satisfied." Knowing this important fact, you look down at your iPhone and begin hastily skipping through the frozen songs that refuse to play, until you reach Hamil-topia.

After what seems like the amount of time you spent listening to *Hamilton* when it was first available on NPR, you finally land on a track from the show— "Schuyler Defeated." Huh.

"Oh, well, I guess that'll do," you think to yourself, not noticing that you are teetering dangerously close to the edge and about to—

You fall off.

Now, years of dance, and gym, and fitness things *should* make it fairly easy to quickly get back on the platform again. Hell, this isn't your first time trolling train tracks. You've dropped your phone on them before, and when confronted with the fresh horror of seeing your first born in peril, you weren't afraid to put your life on the line to protect the keeper of your social media presence and soul.

This previous experience flashes through your brain as you fly through the air, leading you to believe, for a moment, that you can recover from this fall, until you hear the roar of an approaching train and catch the quick glimpse of an orange "F" shooting toward your face. Then, silence.

"Perhaps the symbolism of a large 'F' was a little literally on the nose," you think to yourself in the quiet space between, before the darkness.

It's strange how quickly it can all vanish. Not a minute ago, you were on your way to working on a new Broadway show, and now you're working on being dead—a predicament you wouldn't be in if you didn't book the job you wanted so deeply. How could positive vibes fail you so drastically?

THE END.

Let's be honest right now, when it comes to your status within the community as a composer/lyricist/librettist, you're a complete nobody. Getting your work out there is going to be tricky. How does one become a successful young musical theatre writer these days?

In the past, all you had to do was know Oscar Hammerstein, and the Universe just handed you shit like *West Side Story*. Today, there's either the festival fast track, or the slightly slower social media slog. Sending *Pieces of Me* to something like the New York Musical Theatre Festival (NYMF) is a quicker way to get a fully-realized production mounted in Manhattan, while working the YouTube route to build an audience like Pasek & Paul (*Smash* season two) or Joe Iconis (*Smash* season two), is a bit more tedious of an endeavor. Do you…

Submit to NYMF…? (page 148)

Submit to social media…? (page 457)

*

Stuart stares deeply into your glazed-over eyes.

"You'd be what…?" he asks.

"Louboutins. Sparkly black Louboutins, with deep red bottoms that match the fiery passion I have within my actual soul," you respond with a wink.

"OK," Stuart nods, as he makes one small note on your application before glancing back up and saying, "Thank you so much for coming in today."

Oof. His tone was dripping with the kind of indifference that normally accompanies a courtesy callback. Stuart escorts you out the door, and you never hear from him again.

Maybe it was your eagerness or self-aggrandizing that cost you the job. Misplaced confidence is what sold you as an actor – and those qualities are usually universally embraced in all careers, so it's mystifying they failed you today. That line about your soul was some Grade A doucheriffic nonsense, however, so maybe that's what did you in.

Anyway, you decide to call your stage manager and tell them you took some bad prednisone and were just kidding about quitting, and then you send a video of yourself singing Rihanna in Times Square as proof. They take you back with open arms and you decide never to leave Broadway again, because better the devil you know than the devil you don't, and omg who is excited for *The Devil Wears Prada: The Musical*, RIGHT?

THE END.

*

OMG! YOU'RE LAURA OSNES! You win!

THE END.

After years of time spent in costumed shoes (the majority of which you've been privileged enough to keep after the production closes – unless it's regional theatre, then they either package your company's shoes to rent to colleges and non-Equity, or charge you like eighty bucks for them. I mean, *really*) you're kind of over flashy footwear. It just isn't you anymore. Your Kinky Boot has worn its way down to a *Good Vibrations* flip-flop – and you're okay with that.

Stuart interrupts your inner monologue.

"You'd be what…?" he asks.

Without thinking another moment, you look down at the shoes you are wearing and blurt out, "Converse."

Stuart stares at you questionably. "Converse?" He asks.

"Yeah," you say. "You can dress them up, dress them down. They're gender neutral. They can do anything!"

"So, you'd be something… versatile?"

"Yep! That's me. I'm extremely versatile."

With a pensive expression, Stuart begins writing notes on your application. You think this has to be a good thing. During your actor days (which were literally forty-five minutes ago), notes were usually a positive. It takes a lot less time for someone to just write, "No." Normally, I'd agree. But… CONVERSE? Like, that was the best you could come up with? And don't get me started on your explanation. OK, fine. *I* will…

Neutral. Versatile? That answer is about as creative as writing a musical based on a movie that came out in the Nineties. Don't get me wrong, I enjoy Converse. They have a legacy spanning from *West Side Story* to NBC's *Chuck* (which I only watched because I loved Zachary Levi in *First Date,* and *Tangled* is better than *Frozen*). I realize this was a "real world" bullshit interview question that non-actors went to college to learn how to master the perfect answer for, but you've made your friends attend at least one Upright Citizens Brigade show of yours, so I know you understand improv. You could have done better than "versatile."

If it were me, I would have said something like: "Converse were featured on the show art for *big: the musical*, and they define playful passion and hopeful idealism. I am the Converse shoes dancing on the FAO Schwarz piano of life." But yours works too, I guess, because despite that *Lestat*-level train wreck of an interview, you manage to book… I mean, get hired, as a personal trainer at Fusion. Congratulations! Career successfully transitioned.

I can't go into much detail about what the employee training process at Fusion is like, but needless to say, it's more of a ball-buster than a *La Cage* cooter-slam. They make you memorize a lot of text. It's like doing *Wolf Hall*, but instead of *Wolf Hall*, it's really hard shit. Did you know there are actually four different names for your quads? You thought your theatre background would give you a "leg-up" in understanding anatomy because you're always talking about how you have tight hip-flexors, but you're surprised to find out that the thing aggravating your back is called a "piriformis." Fitness is hard, y'all.

Much like summer stock, there's sort of a fly-by-the-seat-of-your-pants vibe at Fusion. You learn everything you need to know within about a week, and whether you're ready or not, you're presented with potential clients to train. It's the kind of thrown-to-the-wolves experience that makes you empathize with Allison Williams in *Peter Pan Live!*. Before you know it, you're performing consultations (which Fusion has branded as a "Fusion-alysis") and complementary sessions (where you work for free. SEE ALSO: 29 Hour Readings, SETA tours, and 90% of Feinstein's/54 Below shows) on various members. After a few failed attempts to land a client, the familiar lack of confidence that used to plague you as an actor seeps back in. You're not quite sure if personal training is where you're supposed to be. You haven't really made any progress and it's beginning to make you feel helpless. Even though you're surrounded by kettlebells, battle-ropes, and heavy weights, none of them can be used as weapons against self-doubt.

When you were in a production that wasn't great, you could at least fall back on the support of the cast members who agreed that it sucked. Right now, your proverbial show is a disaster *and* you're not clicking with your colleagues. The other trainers are pleasant, but kind of stoic and quiet. They keep to themselves and don't really know a lot about Sondheim. The other day you saw Mandy Patinkin humming softly to himself on the elliptical, and when you ran to tell all the trainers that the guy from *Sunday in the Park with George* was doing cardio, you were greeted with nothing but blank stares. The fuck? I don't know if it's possible to survive in an environment that can't appreciate rich chord progressions, internal rhyming, or *Pacific Overtures.* I mean this is pure agony.

Feeling the need to get talked off the ledge, you head to Stuart's office for a chat. Once there, Stuart mentions that a prominent casting director has just joined the club, and is looking for a trainer. Well, this is somewhat convenient timing isn't it? You're not looking to get back in the business, but it would be nice to work with someone with whom you share something in common. This particular casting director was unfamiliar with you during your time as an actor, so it won't feel like a conflict of interest. Maybe you guys will hit it off and you'll consider staying? Or, maybe it'll get really awkward and make things worse for you, causing you to quit. Do you…

Take the appointment with the casting director…? (page 41)

Pass on the casting director…? (page 256)

Worldwide Plaza it is! Nestled in the heart of Broadway campus, this one block abyss of awkward encounters is kind of like the high school quad. It sits above New World Stages, and is host to everything an actor needs in one place. Between Blockheads, Just Salad, Ricky's and Petland Discounts, you could spend an afternoon in one location getting wasted on cheap margaritas, grab a sensible salad that won't soak up your booze and ruin your buzz, toss on a wig and score a pair of pasties, then pick up a toy to make your dog less pissed at you for spending all of Cinco de Mayo buying tequila labeled "Gold." Worldwide Plaza is really where it's at, unless you're trying to avoid someone.

OK, look, if you're trying to avoid someone in the business, move to Nebraska or the Upper East Side. Making it through Midtown without running into someone who doesn't know you hate them is about as likely as Jason Robert Brown giving himself a constructive criticism. If you embrace this inevitability, you can move on and play with fun alternatives of how to handle dealing with the daily douche. Ignore the possibility that *you* might be the douche. You are never the douche. Your BFA program raised you better than that.

As you enter the Starbucks to grab a flat white— let me stop you for a minute. Why are you getting a flat white again? You know you can't have flat whites before an audition because a.) calories b.) dairy c.) Starbucks adopted the flat white in an effort to stay current with what is happening in Brooklyn. Like when Broadway tried to stay current with what was happening in Brooklyn by creating *BKLYN*.

Now that flat whites are off the table, might I suggest a sensible hot tea with lemon? Good. Get in line and order that. I don't care which tea you choose. Pick the one that lubricates your chords the best. Speaking of lubrication, your ex is in front of you in line. Quick! Distract yourself with your phone!

Diverting your eyes from your ex, you refresh your email and all of your social media applications. You're happy to see that the tweet from earlier is doing nicely, but UH-OH... Buried in your DM alerts, you spot an email from your agent that includes all of the callback information as well as an additional eighty pages of sides that are completely different from the ones you were asked to prepare for the audition. Between the limited time you have to learn this material, and the presence of your ex who looks more than slightly better than you do today, maybe you should take your cue and leave.

As you turn around to back out faster than an investor for *Rebecca*, you're mortified to see your *other* ex coming through the door. Well, this certainly is a pickle, isn't it? Here you are, sandwiched between two evils, trying to decide which is the lesser among them.

This might appear to be a negative thing, but you must remember that you are an idealistic Broadway Freshman, and the positives will always outweigh the negatives because there are no such things as negatives. You're positive about this. Make the current dilemma a fun acting challenge. How good are your people ignoring skills? Are you able to engage yourself in an independent activity long enough to deter both of these ex-lovers? If you cringed when I used the word, "lovers," then good, that's exactly the kind of reaction that should accompany the heightened uncomfortable situation you are in at this very moment.

Now, it would be easy to just continue to fumble around on your phone, but that's a fairly basic independent activity for a seasoned actor such as yourself—and eventually you'll have to do things that expose your eyes, like looking up and ordering. If you want to really exercise your craft, you could open up a dialogue with one of the exes. I suggest the less successful of the two, so when you ask them, "What are you up to slash working on?" they'll immediately lose their power. Or, you could slip out of line and talk to Mary Testa, who is seated right by the door.

A while back, you and Mary Testa did one of those 29 Hour Readings (they're called this because 29 hours is the exact amount of time the industry cares about the shows presented in these readings before they forget about them entirely) and it would be pretty easy to use her as a buffer because it gets you out of line, and both of your exes will think you're important because Mary Testa did Broadway before you were even born. Still, I think it would be fun to see your unsuccessful ex try to come up with a way to make, "Oh, you know. Just auditioning," sound like progress. Do you…

Ask what are up to slash working on…? (page 59)

Talk to Mary Testa…? (page 421)

*

"Sure. Why not?" you tell Stuart.

"Great," Stuart smiles, "He's requested seven tomorrow morning."

"Awesome. Just enough time for me to freak out," you groan. You're stressed out and it shows.

Stuart looks at you pointedly and asks, "Remember your interview with me?"

"Yeah?"

"I asked you if you could be any shoe, what shoe would you be?"

"Uh-huh."

"And you said Converse," Stuart laughs. "Boring as shit. Worst answer I've ever heard, in fact. Spectators. Louboutins. Beatle Boots—those are shoes. Christ, I'd have taken a Croc."

"But you hired me."

"I read your Twitter; I saw that you could be spontaneous. That's all this is. Stop thinking so hard."

"I majored in theatre, thinking too hard was part of the curriculum."

"You'll be fine. Just remember: you aren't auditioning for him; he's auditioning for you. You don't *need* to take him on as a client."

"Huh," you exhale. That might be the best advice you've ever received, and you didn't need to go through four years of B.F.A. training to attain it.

Stuart's words are comforting, but they don't stop you from spending all night poring over fitness articles and functional movement screen material with the same neurotic meticulousness you used to apply to audition preparation. You're lucky you have that kind of discipline to fall back on, but you really thought this shit was going to end when you hung up your LaDucas. I guess when Shakespeare said, "All the world's a stage," he was being fucking literal.

41

You try to get a good night's sleep, but your mind is racing faster than the hands in Deaf West's *Spring Awakening*. Eventually, your alarm blasts at six a.m. and you're like, "There's this entire world that exists before noon and I don't know how I feel about it."

You're still not quite used to these early morning start times. Usually, you only have to be awake before dawn if you're doing the *Today* show. This week, you've seen the sunrise more than a Michigan kid has seen a final callback for the creative team. In fact, you've seen the sunrise almost more than I've made a catty comment about kids who went to Michigan. Needless to say, we're all very tired.

You patiently wait at the front desk for the arrival of your prospective casting director client (whom I'll refer to from here on out as Jay Bernard Carnarubin). Jay's career revolves around scheduling appointments for other people, so you know he's not going to disrespect you by being late. Time is really important, but you only began to understand this after you saw the obscene amount of dollars people are willing to pay for an hour of yours. Even though you haven't booked a client yet, the fact that you cost like $1.50 a minute makes you wish all the minutes you spent practicing audition material would have rolled over into a fully loaded bank account. Can you imagine if actors got paid for auditions? LOL. Obviously that idea is as insane as my talent – but what if actors were at least *treated* like they were being paid to audition? I just think more fucks would be given about us if the Powers That Be were constantly aware of the service actors are providing when we grace them with our presence.

Right on time, Jay Bernard Carnarubin breezes through the revolving doors. You're not quite sure what kind of personality to expect, because as successful as you were as an actor, he wasn't your casting director, you know? He wasn't the guy whose name you'd casually drop while having drinks with friends. Like, you've never said the sentence, "Carnarubin loves me." Telsey? Duh. Of course Telsey loves you—not as much as they love me, but they wouldn't kick you out of bed for eating Schmackary's.

"Jay?" you ask, as you stop him at the front desk.

"Hey! Nice to see you," he politely responds.

Well, shit. He said, "nice to see you." Prominent people in the business tend to say, "nice to see you," instead of "nice to meet you." It's more ambiguous than a "great news, wish I could share" tweet. This alternate phrase eschews them from an awkward situation like introducing themselves to someone they've already met. It's an inspired trick, but you're uncertain if he's saying it here to be polite, or if he actually remembers you from that one audition. While this "nice to see you" curveball is throwing a wrench into your introduction, it's a good thing to remember the next time you run into someone with whom you may or may not have had an entire drunk conversation at Glass House. In fact, when in doubt, anyone you ever meet, you've probably already met at Glass House.

"Nice to see you, too," you calmly reply, like this entire meeting is a big fat #NBD, and not a possible make or break it moment in your career as a fitness professional. Just play it cool, boy. Real cool. Don't turn your life into a production of *Stressed Side Story*.

First sessions with clients are always kind of weird. They're like a first date within a job interview, which may be the second worst thing in the entire world after an open non-Equity chorus call. There's a lot that goes into the first session. You're trying to be impressive, show off your personality, work them hard (but not too hard), and then hope that by the end of it they'll give you money to do it again. So, I guess it's more like a first date

43

on a job interview set within an escort service – at an open non-Equity chorus call.

The entire thing is kind of a blur, but as your session with Jay comes to an end, you really feel like you clicked. Before you can say another word, Jay asks when you can meet again. You did it! You've landed your first client! Suddenly, you're overcome with a familiar euphoric feeling – the one that used to fill you up after you nailed a final callback. Remember it? The one where you feel as if you've just run a sprint. Endorphins race through your body with such exhilarating force, that you understand for a fleeting moment why someone would be dumb enough to run a marathon. This is the high. You've missed it. And somehow, it's better now than it ever was on Broadway – because for some reason you finally, for the first time, feel in control of something.

Things for you at Fusion make a turn for the better, and you're immediately thrust into an extensive movie montage set to "Suddenly I See" by KT Tunstall, looped over scenes of you getting more clients, more education, and more promotions, before a title card is laid across the screen that reads, "Two Years Later." Life is almost too perfect, and you start to wait for the shoe to drop – and when it does, you hope it isn't as boring as Converse.

As you enter your third year as a successful Fusion trainer, you start to feel like a character in *Into the Woods* at the top of an act – foolishly wishing for something else. You don't know what it is, but something is missing. You love your job, and your clients, but you find your life reaching a state of plateau not much different from when you were in a long running show. Here you thought you'd found new happiness – some kind of control over a life that was teetering off balance due to boredom. But you're a creative, theatrical person, and the kind of control you're attempting simply is… it's not possible. If there is one thing the history of theatre has taught us, it's that creative life will not be contained. Broadway breaks free, it expands to new territories and crashes through barriers, painfully (*In My Life*), maybe even dangerously (*Spider-Man: Turn off the Dark*), but, uh… well, there it is. You can't deny what is in your blood, and to try to ignore it, or think you can move on, is painfully naïve.

It's frightening to think you might never find a status quo you're comfortable living within. Are you destined to lead an unfulfilling existence? On paper, you have nothing to complain about, but you're also a New Yorker, so you have everything to complain about. You're currently standing in the middle of the gym floor, surrounded by members whose form is hurting your feelings and it's not helping to ease the profound irritation of everything that is bubbling-up inside of you. Do you…

Ignore your feelings…? (page 53)

Do something about it…? (page 56)

*

"You're right," you tell Daniel, "we should change the title to *Broadway Debut*."

"I'm proud of you," he says. "That took a lot of courage and self-edit."

"Um. OK…? I didn't realize the title was that bad."

"It was," nods Daniel. "So, do you want to write the press release now?

"Yeah, sure," you respond somberly.

There's a part of Daniel's personality that borders on douchebag, but he's managed to rein it in the past month, so you're a bit discouraged to hear he'd been respectfully managing some deeply-rooted animosity toward one of your ideas. It makes you wonder what else he's been hiding from you.

Trying not to mourn the loss of *Pieces of Me*, you quickly draft a press release stating that a "private industry reading" of your new musical *Broadway Debut* will be held this week starring, "a cast of Broadway favorites that include: Corey Michael Cooper, Ashley Marie Smith, James Tyler Doyle, Brittany Beth Adams, Holden MacGroyne, and Ellyn Marie Marsh." You then toss in a few buzzwords like, "a creative team has not yet been announced" and "Broadway-bound," before firing it off to your friends who work at Playbill and Broadway World with the subject line, "Should Be Fun."

Within a few hours, the press hits the interwebs, and you start getting "Congrats!" texts from "friends" you haven't spoken to since you thought the second syllable in Laura Benanti's last name was pronounced with an open-your-mouth-and-say "AH" vowel. People are really coming out of the woodwork due to your perceived success. There's even a small thread starting on the Broadway World message board—and those

46

always end positively. You can't wait to not read that shit!

When the day of your Broadway-bound-informal-industry-read-thru-in-your-shoebox-apartment-with-a-case-of-cheap-wine finally arrives, you are *psyched*. Unable to control your enthusiasm, you decide to open up the message board thread on Broadway World and WHAT ARE YOU DOING DON'T DO THAT STOP!

The first couple of posts are fairly harmless, and even optimistic! There's the typical back and forth about which theatre *Broadway Debut* will take, a few casual comments about the relatively unknown cast involved (which some are excited about, some imagine will change, and some are like, "but will they sell tickets?") and then user "Quarter2_9" barges in to take a drive-by-dump on your dreams…

> "**Quarter2_9:** Sad news. And bad news. *Broadway Debut*? I can just smell the creators' forced idealism dripping from that insufferably saccharine title. As if Broadway needs the development of yet another masturbatory Millennial creative abortion for the *Newsies* generation to sink their fascinated-with-skinny-gay-boy fangs into. Obviously the Klout score and Twitter verification status of the writers has swayed the click-bait-obsessed mods of our "trusted theatre news sources" into posting this poppycock. It'll only be a matter of time before fifty inept producers latch on to what's "hip and buzzy" by producing this pretentious bore on Broadway, where it will no doubt take the place of a deserving revival. And am I wrong in believing that this asinine attempt at art dredged from a sewer will prove to be something that the

critics will swoon over?

You know the answer.

We all do.

Bad, bad news."

The posts after "Quarter2_9" follow suit in tone and overall meanness. It's all really discouraging, and now you're more depressed than when you paid full price for *Hamilton* and then didn't think it was "all that." (Yeah, that's right, bitches! You're in my world now, and in my world, you might not think that *Hamilton* is all it's cracked up to be. That's not necessarily my belief; so don't get mad at me for your opinion in this universe.)

More importantly, what have I told you about reading crap online? Only people who hate you write crap online! You aren't supposed to take any of it seriously! Have I taught you nothing!? Clearly I haven't, because you waste no time in taking all of that shit as fact, getting emotionally wrecked by it, and then channeling that hurt into a text conversation with Daniel where you rip him a new one for pushing to change the title…

DANIEL:
why r u yelling at me

YOU:
you made me change the title. now we're screwed!

STFU we aren't screwed.

everyone has already made judgments

48

about the show based off the title. we r DOA.

it was your decisikn

decision*

you suggested it!

but it was YOUR choice to change the title.
and tbh it was only ONE of a few ideas that
I disagree with. I was just keeping my
other issues quiet until after the read cuz I
wanna give the script a chance to breathe with
actors.

WTF. WHAT other issues?

we can talk about it at the debrief.

NO. I have you the respect of considering
changing the title. the least you can
do is give me the respect of telling me what I ask.

UGH. GAVE*

I don't want to ducking talk about it.

Daniel, it's not 2010, you can make a
shortcut in the settings so "duck"
changes to "fuck."

what if I need to say "duck"

WHAT DO YOU THINK
IS WRONG WITH MY SCRIPT

the concept's cool. but the dialogue
and the characters? come on -- I can't
be the only one who sees this.

WHY DIDN'T YOU SAY ANYTHING

it's only been a month! I've been busy
trying to write music and shit! I figured
we could work it out later.

so all the good stuff u said about
my book? all the nights drinking
and laughing and spiraling down
YouTube wormholes? that was
all a lie?

I figured we could talk about it eventually.

I can't trust you anymore.

sure you can. you still bae.

no... no. it's different now.

what r u saying?

I thought I knew you. I thought
I knew us. but none of it was real.
who I am with you is a lie and I don't
love myself like this.

how about we go apple picking,
leave the iPhones, get you away

from work, you'll see that you're
a different person. u are.
you're great.

but our problems would be waiting
for us when we got back.

we'll write somewhere else,
and hopefully our problems
won't follow us.

Daniel, please don't joke.
we're far apart. we're different.
we have nothing in common.

sure we do. we love writing with each other…

we love writing with each other…

don't we?

I want a creative divorce.

***

Whoa. That was the most heated argu-text
you've ever had with Daniel. It's a shame because you
honestly believed everything in your relationship was
fine. To hear that Daniel had been holding back
valuable critiques made it impossible to trust him ever
again. You'd always wonder if he was just humoring you
when he complimented your work. Sure, hearing nice
things is nice and all, but not when the intention is false.
Better to get rid of fake people now, because they are not

51

the kind of personalities you want to be surrounded by as you embark on a career in commercial producing.

While you think it was a healthy decision in the long run, parting ways with Daniel due to creative differences leaves you back at the start of your creative venture. There's no way you can further develop *Broadway Debut/Pieces of Me*, because Daniel's mark is all over it. It's a tainted concept right now. You'll have to think of something new to develop, and that unfortunate truth is becoming increasingly depressing the farther away you get from breaking up with Daniel.

But you know things now. Many valuable things—like that for a relationship to succeed there needs to be strong communication one hundred percent of the time, and hopefully you can carry that with you should you decide to embark down this path again.

As for now, there's nothing left to do but consult the Universe…

YOU:
Well, universe… What next?

UNIVERSE:
new phone. who dis?

THE END.

*

You decide that these feelings will pass, and eventually you'll feel whole again. Instead, the repression makes you go crazier than Broadway Internet when there's an iPhone controversy during a performance. After a few weeks of suppressing these emotions, and trying to remain sane while simultaneously being proud of what you do at work, but also wanting more, you crack like Patti LuPone seeing someone on an iPhone during a performance. It's possible to hold two conflicting thoughts in your head that are both truths, but you don't give a fuck about trying to figure that out, because you literally can't even with anything anymore.

While stewing in a fit of rage during your workout, that really annoying member who just sucks walks up to you and asks if she can work in, and you're like, "There are three other machines you can do this exact exercise on, you stupid bitch," and then you grab a yoga strap and strangle her to death. Huh. That escalated quickly.

So, now you're incarcerated because you didn't bother to deal with your feelings. You thought your career was a prison, and now you're in a literal one. Smooth move, Ex-lax. Yeah, I know that's a lame retort from the Nineties, but the content here is dictated by the shittiness of your decisions. Just because you got Crazy Eyes on that *Which Orange is the New Black Character Are You?* BuzzFeed quiz, does not mean you're going to fare well where you're going. I hope you're able to find yourself in prison, because I'm positive *many* people are going to be able to find themselves in *you* (ICYMI: I'm talking about shower sex).

THE END.

"I'm sorry," you say to the accompanist, as he continues to play, completely unaware that you've stopped.

"Randy," says a guy behind the table whom you assume is the music director. "Randy! *Stop!*"

The accompanist (Randy) finally stops playing and glares at you. Well, this is awkward.

"I think," you go on, "I think… I gave you the wrong tempo…? Can I try the right one?"

Randy nods, and you dance-ily jog over to the piano to tap out instructions for your up-tempo again – but this round you request double-time, hoping that Randy's general gravitation toward playing at Christina Perri-pace will find a way to level out if you over-shoot the tempo.

It works. The performance of your song is great, and your execution of the sides is even better. All in all, it's a solid audition that any actor would be proud to post about on Facebook about when that was appropriate in 2011.

"Thank you so much," smiles the director. It's crazy that you don't know any of these guys' names. "Can you wait outside for a minute?"

Oh, hell yes you can!

"Sure!" you say, as you grab your book and exit the room.

Waiting in the hallway, the time ticks by long enough for you to Insta-stalk two exes and a new crush – so somewhere on the better part of a solid minute. Once this proves boring, you switch over to Twitter and scroll through the engagement on your most recent tweet to see who liked it and OMG YOU ACCIDENTALLY CLICKED "FOLLOW" ON SOMEONE RANDOM

—

The door opens revealing one of the casting assistants, who quickly pulls you aside.

"You were great," he says.

"Thanks!"

"But that's all we need to see today."

"Wait, what—

The casting assistant quickly smiles and skips back into the room.

Well, I guess there's always hope you'll receive a callback later.

You don't.

This sucks. You did everything right. You were calm, polite, and really damn good. The only thing you got out of it was the awkward moment of following a random person on Twitter, and then hoping you clicked "unfollow" before they got the notification.

"Why do bad things happen to good people?" you ask yourself as you sit alone in your apartment watching an episode of *Mysteries of Laura* and wondering what Debra Messing did to deserve that. After a few hours of trying to block out the sadness stemming from what transpired at your audition by watching unfortunate television, you decide to take solace in knowing that while someone always has it a little bit better than you, someone always has it a little bit worse.

You keep thinking this as you reflect upon the poor soul who recently had the passing privilege of you following them on Twitter, only for it to be ripped from their hands more traumatically than your chances of booking that show. Remembering this brings you great comfort. Things are already beginning to look up. The sun *will* come out, tomorrow—or, maybe the day after tomorrow if you're having a fat day.

THE END.

*

You know that part in *Honeymoon in Vegas* where
– never mind, of course you don't. Anyway, you decide
to *do something*. I'm proud of you for taking action. Now,
what are you going to do? No, seriously. You think I
have a clue? I still have no idea what I'm doing with *my*
life. You'd never know this, because perception is
everything, but if you think I have it together, joke's on
you because I'm the biggest disaster of them all (and I
know this because I saw *The First Wives Club* in San
Diego.)

Anyway, you decide to take action and do
something about the life plateau you've been cruising on
for two years. You're not sure what will fix the feeling of
indifference you have towards everything, so you decide
the best way to deal with it is by wasting an exorbitant
amount of time online. Whenever you're feeling down,
the best thing to do is go onto the Internet and see what
other people are WHAT ARE YOU DOING, STOP
READING THAT.

After a few minutes of regret, you stumble upon
some online content that is somewhat interesting. A
friend has retweeted a tweet written by a parody account
based on those *On the Town* flyer boys in Times Square.
It's funny, and unique, but you're over here like Cathy
thinking, "I can do better than that." No disrespect to
the person who runs that account – you genuinely love it
– but you've never had a single tweet of yours ever
retweeted, and you're somewhat envious of this person's
perceived success. Why don't you try your hand at it? It
could be a fun distraction.

Given that you've quit show business, and there
are more Theatre Problems Twitter accounts out there
than actual problems in theatre, you decide to make an
account geared toward satirizing personal trainers and
how they feel about members at their gym. It's shocking

how much shade you can throw at someone with bad form in under 140 characters. You set up the account and promptly fire ten to fifteen zingers off into cyber space. Too bad nobody's reading them. After tweeting shit like, "You think I charge too much for personal training? Have you listened to yourself for an hour?" and "It's not called a Turkish fall-over," you're kind of bummed that only thirty self-promoting personal trainers have bothered to follow you back (and they don't even *like* your tweets). Shit. You had no idea that Twitter would be harder than the dancing in *A Chorus Line* is to girls auditioning for Maggie.

Rejection is as natural to life as sexual desire and *Smash*, but it's how we deal with it that defines who we are. You were met with plenty of rejection as an actor, and the last thing you need is to encounter it online. The Internet is no place to feel badly about yourself. Even though this casual creative hobby of yours is anything but serious, you wish people paid attention to it. It's disheartening to think that nobody is finding your cultural commentary on the behavior of fitness instructors and gym enthusiasts even remotely entertaining. Why are trainers so boring, and the people using our equipment so completely unaware?

When you were acting, you continued to follow your dreams regardless if the Universe was telling you to pack your show-embroidered-dance-bag and give in to defeat. Show business dreams are only fulfilled when pursued under the influence of a lot of drugs or misguided confidence. Sometimes both. When it comes to your afterschool activity on Twitter, the stakes aren't nearly as high. Knowing that what you're playing with is about as serious as that song in *Legally Blonde* called "Serious," you start thinking maybe Twitter is not where it's at, and you should find another avenue to unload your creative energy.

As you contemplate where to stick your talent, you receive a somewhat disconcerting text from your close friend David. It's a screen capture of someone's Facebook status. You receive so many of these a day that 75% of the pictures on your phone are screen captures, and when you visit your photo collection for the past year, it's a mosaic of status updates that form the face of Anne Hathaway in 2013.

This particular status update is so bad; it's like other level shit. Like Steven Boyer in *Hand to God* other level, but instead of being brilliant at playing two roles, it's brilliant at infinite ways of sucking. Its crappiness is so inspiring, a tiny kernel of an idea forms in your brain and you're as taken aback by this kernel as Carol Channing was that time she found one in the toilet.

This idea is kind of weird, and it involves going back to Twitter again. You aren't happy with your previous experience on this platform, so to go back with a different idea could be a huge blow to the ego. Do you…

Take the risk…? (page 62)

Try something else…? (page 252)

*

You turn around to face Ex #2, who came in behind you (and this wasn't the *only* time!).

"Oh, hey," sighs Ex #2.

You smile. "Hi!"

"How are you?"

"Oh, you know. Just auditioning," you say proudly.

Ex #2's eyes turn cold. "That's not what I asked."

You ignore. "What are you up to slash working on?" you ask.

Ex #2 chuckles and sighs, "If I wanted to know about your career I'd un-mute your Twitter."

Perhaps jumping right into "the biz" talk might have been a little "premature," and being "premature" is exactly why your relationship with Ex #2 ended lol—whoa, get your mind out of the gutter…I was referring to when you talked about sharing Seamless accounts after the third date.

"Don't listen to the lies that social media tells you. It's all perception," you say earnestly, knowing full well that the only lie you're telling is this one about telling lies on social media, because if there's one thing you're honest about, it's what you put online. Your life truly is as it is presented on social media, because you present everything on social media. It's not your problem if people choose to focus on the highlights.

"I told you," your ex says with an eye roll, "I muted you. You don't exist to me online."

WHOA. WHOA. WHOA. You are nothing without an online persona that everyone can see. If your exes, or the people who've wronged you, aren't forced to see your successes on a daily basis, does your social media presence even exist? All of this is too much to handle, so you just kind of awkwardly say "goodbye" and walk out of Starbucks. That was rough.

It's understandable how upset that encounter made you. Your ex wasn't even fazed by your presence. Is it possible they're over you? How could *anyone* be over you? You're so amazing! You try to give yourself this validation as you wander slowly through Midtown, but it's hard to believe your self-affirmations without a floor length mirror.

The fresh horror that anyone would think poorly enough about you to not at least find some sort of joy in your online character has really cut you deep. You're so thrown by all of this that you're only able to mildly commit to learning all of the new audition material you just received. You feel deflated, like the ego of a, wait a minute... is this what a deflated ego feels like? Bummer.

Your emotions the rest of the day are colored with a sense of emptiness. As you wait at Pearl Studios to go in for your callback, you feel nothing—like you're on a bobsled and it's snowing out and it's cold. The sweet sound of Tara Rubin's voice calling you in doesn't even register. The callback is a blur. You def didn't book. Everything seems wrong. For the first time since you've become a Broadway Freshman, you feel a hint of negativity toward the business that has brought you such bliss. What does this mean?

Many things about show business can spark jadedness. Luckily, up until now, you've managed to avoid all of them. However, this horrible truth that someone would mute your social media presence is leading you to second guess everything you've ever known. Could it be that you're not as interesting as you thought you were? Have you been lying to yourself this entire time? Are you even a real live person, or just a trendy plot device in someone else's story? Whatever the case, you're definitely in a transitional period, and the question is, "how much does your tweets being ignored matter to you?" That will determine the level of disillusionment you're feeling toward the Broadway industry. Are you…

Really upset…? (page 454)

Like really REALLY upset…? (page 458)

Theatre would be nowhere without risks. As much as it may seem like I enjoy ripping flops apart, I'm actually celebrating their unabashed ballsiness. Nobody sets out on a venture to fail, so I can't help but respect all shows for trying. As a card carrying Millennial, I'm obligated to give a participation trophy to everyone just for showing up – but that doesn't mean I don't honestly respect them. Confidence is sexy. Like, I have a hard-on-lady-boner for every new show that was brave enough to open in the same season as *Hamilton*.

Everyone is always talking about the next big thing, and nobody ever knows what that "thing" is going to be. Sometimes Broadway is ahead of its time. If *Dance with the Vampires*, *Dracula*, and *Lestat* came out in 2008 during the *Twilight* craze (which I hope we're all feeling solidly walk-of-shamey about right now), those shows could still be running. I mean, they wouldn't be, I promise you – but it's nice to think that they could be. Risks, people. Take glorious risks.

Your risk is born in the same magnificent and blissfully unaware place that makes people start a web series. It's a half-baked idea that involves you using Twitter to spoof the way actors behave online, all while hiding behind a cloak of anonymity. I guess keeping your name out of it sort of negates this being much of a risk, but that might be a good thing for now, because what if what you say isn't very funny—or insightful—and people get mad at you? Being yelled at online is the worst! Better not sacrifice your reputation until you're absolutely ready – and who knows how long *that* will take?

After settling on the name Irritating Performer Pal, you quickly set up the account, tweet a few stock actor phrases, and then text all of it to David for his approval. You're worried he might not find it as funny as you, and that the summer heat is giving you an unrealistic view of your own creativity. When you were an actor, everything you did was perfect; writing, however, (like personal training) is a new frontier, so there's plenty of concern over how good – never mind, David just texted back an "LOLOLOL," and even though that might have been an autocorrected "lol," you'll take it as an endorsement, and head back to Fusion to train your next client, Julie (a friend from your acting days who you're making look hot for her first network television role).

It's weird that you aren't in the least bit envious of Julie. In another time, perhaps nine or ten years/minutes ago, you might have harbored insane and misdirected anger toward a friend for being more successful than you, despite them being a different type or gender. I'm really happy you grew out of that bullshit.

When you meet-up with Julie at the gym, she's carrying a fancy silver water bottle with the logo of her TV show on it.

"Wow. You might as well be wearing a show jacket," you joke.

Julie smiles, rolls her eyes, and says, "You know I hate this shit, but you told me I needed to drink water, and this was all I had. Do you want me to be dehydrated, or embarrassed? You're going to say dehydrated."

"Yep."

You share a laugh. Julie is probably the most socially aware actor friend you have, so this water bottle exchange is just a fun bit. Julie would only ever do something douchey to be ironic. You guys moved to New York around the same time, and while you've maintained a friendship, there definitely was some distance that grew between the two of you when Julie was more successful. She was always cool, but you were sort of a dick. Someone is always doing better than you, and someone is always doing worse, but that truth should never dictate how one behaves in a friendship. Still, the career of an actor encourages envy, even among close friends, and that just sucks.

When you moved on to training, you and Julie reconnected because you decided not to have a stick up your ass for once, and actually be happy for your friends for real, instead of posting online about how you are happy for your friends, when you're actually just trying to show all your other friends how many successful friends you have. It's fun to train Julie, because she's a friend and that makes the hour go by quicker, but also because you get to talk about "the biz" with someone and silently reflect on how the topic interests you, instead of making you want to stick needles into your urethra. I imagine kidney stones and urinary tract infections feel pretty much like talking about show business when you don't want to talk about show business – so I'll bet Julie is in a lot of pain right now.

In an effort to not make Julie feel too annoyed or uncomfortable by talking about the business, you redirect the focus back to you and your new creative venture. Wow. You sure do put the "personal" in personal training. You tell her about your parody account and scroll through some of your tweets.

"Like, is this even funny?" you ask.

Julie smiles and says, "Yeah, I think it's great."

A second endorsement! You question further: "You don't think people will get mad at me?"

"Who gives a shit? You're not in the business anymore. You could literally do or say anything."

Julie has a point. And it's this important observation that lingers with you as you pour a stiff Tanqueray and soda in your kitchen later that afternoon (sometimes these early ass mornings get to you, and if you're up at 4:30 a.m., isn't it only natural to allow happy hour to commence before five? If you were still on a Broadway schedule, waiting more than twelve hours to drink would be like one in the morning.)

This cocktail hits you pretty hard, so the safest and smartest choice now would be to pull out your laptop and start doing shit while utterly inebriated, right? You open up your Twitter browser and are saddened to see that nobody has followed you yet. Ugh. Why is getting this started just like trying to acquire your Equity card all over again? Maybe you should just blindly follow a bunch of actors and see if anyone returns the favor. Meh. Actors are soulless shameless self-promoters (you know this from experience so it's not a dig) and there's no guarantee any of them will notice. Worse, you're pretty toasted, so who knows what you'll do if you don't close the laptop soon. You could end up un-muting your ex and liking a bunch of their tweets. What should you do?

Follow People… (page 66)

Close the computer… (page 248)

*

Continuing down the path of Not Giving A Shit About Anything, which has become your direction of choice as of late, you decide to follow a bunch of random actors on Twitter. Starting with David's profile, you scan through the list of who he is following and follow all those people. Then, you click on a Keenan-Bolger and follow everyone they are following. This continues for about seven minutes, until you've followed around five hundred people in the show business universe. Feeling satisfied with your work, you retreat to your bedroom and pass da fuck out.

You wake up bright and early the next morning and excitedly roll over and pick up your phone to see if you have any Twitter notifications. This isn't behavior normal to you, as you never imagined Twitter being the first thing you check on your phone every morning. Hopefully you won't make this a habit because that would be so sad!

Upon refreshing the notifications, you are completely gob smacked by the tiny icon that says, "20+" over the little picture of the bell at the bottom of the application. You've seen a "1" there before, and maybe even a "2" that one time a million years ago when Max von Essen retweeted your #SIP, but never have you ever seen double digits followed by a plus sign. What does this mean? Are you viral? Is this what Iain Loves Theater feels like? This is unprecedented and unexpected. The thrill of this attention is somewhat addicting and you haven't even checked to see if those "20+" notifications are people yelling at you.

Much to your delight, you find that you've been followed back by thirty actors. It's crazy to think that yesterday you were nobody, and today you have thirty bonafide fans. Never mind that they might only be following you for networking purposes, or out of morbid curiosity—they are following you and thus, they are your fans. Furthermore, the remainder of the notifications are either likes (standard), retweets (retro, so they mean double now), and comments that seem pretty positive. It looks like the reviews are in, and in your tiny corner of the Internet, you're a buzzy invite-only reading, and the thrill of this tiny amount of attention is seducing you to push for an immediate transfer.

Throughout the course of the day, you continue to tweet trite social media statements from Irritating Performer Pal, and with each 140-character quip, you garner a follower, and then ten followers, a hundred. By the end of two days, you're at a thousand. After a week, you've reached two thousand. People seem to be connecting to what you have to say, even though you're not really creating any original content. Right now, you're just tweeting stock phrases, and if you don't find something different to do with this account, it's going to get old pretty fast.

Since you're behind a mask of anonymity, you have the power to be somewhat of a social media police, without having to weather any personal backlash. It might be fun to wield that power. You could subtly go directly after offenders, and maybe they'll learn a thing or two about how to operate like a human being on the Internet. All you need is a muse – someone with a Karen Cartwright level of fame and unawareness, who could benefit from your assistance.

You close your eyes, and bow your head over your Lin-Manuel Miranda prayer candle and ask the Gods of Creative Genius to send forth a muse of fire. Within seconds, a beacon of hope appears on your Twitter feed in the form of an irritating tweet. Wow, that was fast. I guess *The Secret* really does work. Either that, or Lin-Manuel Miranda really can do everything. (Seriously, people, we need to get our shit together. We have the same amount of hours in the day as him and Beyoncé combined, or something like that. I spend most of my hours either questioning the purpose of my existence or watching Netflix, and sometimes both at the same time. Meanwhile, Lin-Manuel has written sixteen eloquent rap pieces in the amount of time it took for me to finish this sentence, and did you know Lin-Manuel raps?)

Please accept my apologies for that unexpected rant. Passionately productive people make me uncomfortable because I feel like they're hiding something – specifically some sort of device that alters space and time. Anyway, back to your Twitter muse. She is fairly prominent in the business, you respect her work, but you found her tweet somewhat questionable. You decide to essentially do a straight cut and paste of what she posted, and tweet it out as Irritating Performer Pal. You get a bit of traction, and also, your first negative tweet:

"There's a difference between cheeky humor and blatant mockery."

Huh. You never thought of it that way. They might have a point. Is this the direction you want to go? It's risky, but it could really pay off. People might be more cautious about what they post, making you responsible for changing the landscape of social media, and how cool what that be? I mean who is this random nobody to tell you how to run your anonymous parody Twitter account, anyway? But what if they are right... Do you...

Continue down the path...? (page 74)

Change directions...? (page 77)

*

"Um, duh!" exclaims Paige when you randomly run into her outside Physique 57. "Send me your script like yesterday!"

A week following yesterday, it becomes clear that Paige was not leaping to read *Metamorphosis: the Hilary Duff Musical* in quite the way she implied.

"I am literally the worst," she explains. "I'm doing this web series thing, and a concert, and something else, and it's taking up *all of my time*. I can't even—whatever."

OK, looks like Paige is out. Onto the understudies and swings. Do you…

Send your script to Corey…? (page 289)

Send your script to David…? (page 76)

*

In form completely uncharacteristic to the healthy, normal behavior of a seasoned Broadway professional, you've decided to voluntarily walk through Times Square. What's even stranger (and somewhat disconcerting) is that you haven't yet blown through your last unemployment check on drinks at Glass House in a vain attempt to look employed—so you actually have expendable income to put toward some sweet new threads at H&M.

You head east, bisecting the Epicenter of People Who Walk without a Purpose. I'm positive Midtown Manhattan has a magnet buried fifty feet below the TKTS booth that was designed solely to attract pedestrians with no real objective. This disease is not unique to tourists. Depending on the time of day or week, even staunch New Yorkers are known to do what I call the "Fade on a Diagonal." It's that thing where someone is walking ahead of you, and just when you're about to pass them, they sort of fade diagonally in front of you right when it's too late to negotiate yourself around them, and you end up stumbling straight into a Bootleg Elmo.

Oh, the Bootleg Elmos. They are the 1980s Times Square prostitutes and porn shops of today. Sure, we find them tacky, potentially dangerous, and a threat to the culture of Times Square, but I guarantee you that in thirty years, we will all be complaining about how much better it was back in the days when walking to the stage door included the fear of molestation from a furry.

That being said, even the furry culture has evolved since the Times Square Pedestrian Mall opened in 2009. It used to just be a handful of Elmos (or the occasional Cookie Monster) standing on street corners seducing tourists into taking pictures with them, before politely demanding a donation. Now the Elmos move in large herds. They've also multiplied into Doras, Hello Kittys, and, most recently, Elsas who apparently thought "letting it go" applied to themselves.

The cartoon characters tend to stick together up by Duffy Square (that's the north part near those stairs where you spent countless hours after auditions at the Equity building, dreaming of your future and all the possibilities). South Central Times Square is home to the super heroes, and they're even more abrasive than the Woodys. A costumed superhero can sense a tourist six blocks away. I strongly urge you not to walk near them while wearing an "I Heart NY" shirt, or while looking up.

Spatially unaware pedestrians. Grabby furries. Scary super heroes. All of these fears pass through your head as you enter Times Square and prepare to dodge them with the stealth agility of a dancer who has never needed physical therapy. Left. Right. Up. Down. You leap. You bound. You turn. Times Square may be the closest anyone will ever get to feeling like they're in a 1980s Nintendo game.

Keeping your eyes ahead and firmly on your end point, H&M is almost within reach. You can smell the savings. After limbo-ing under a sea of selfie sticks, you reach your hand out toward the H&M door and –

"HOTCHA!"

A flash of red. An inverted bevel. A crooked bowler hat. Fuck. Game over. She got you. You've been sniper-hotcha'd by Roxie Red Tights: Times Square's Famous *Chicago* Flyer Girl.

Nobody forgets the first time Roxie Red Tights jazz-squared into his or her life. It's an Instagrammable moment. Every Roxie Red Tights is so committed to the cause, I've actually considered buying a ticket to *Chicago*, but—hahaha sorry I can't finish this sentence with a straight face because I don't buy tickets to anything. But seriously, the *Chicago* flyer girls are werking those Capezio heels within an inch of their lives—because an inch is all those shoes are giving them. And the red tights? Pretty genius marketing, considering the costume color pallet for the actual production is black with undertones of black. This sets them apart from their counterparts slumming it over at the Ambassador. Roxie Red Tights' decision to include a pop of red has truly helped define a brand for the "off-stage" company of *Chicago*.

Many have tried to replicate the flair and unabashed not-giving-of-a-shit that is Roxie Red Tights. However, from *Catch Me If You Can* flight attendants, to *Pippin* ladies in purple and *On the Town* sailors, they have all failed. The only possible flyer-flinging entity that has rivaled Roxie is the *Follies* Ghost Girls. The *Follies* Ghost Girls were six feet tall with mascara running down their faces, decked out in a Gregg Barnes showgirl masterpiece made of silver, diamonds, mirrors, and ghosty looking things.

The *Follies* Ghost Girls weren't as playful as Roxie. They just kind of slowly lurked around Times Square, avoiding eye contact. Instead of hotcha-whoopee-jazz-handing out flyers directly to a tourist, they hauntingly groped the walls of the McDonald's on 46th and Seventh, and then presented a flyer to the open air. I hands down believe the *Follies* Ghost Girls provided the most entertaining Times Square flyer-giving experience—except they never existed. I made them up. Sorry. I really wanted them to be a real thing in like 2011.

So here's the big dilemma, and probably your hardest decision of the day. Do you engage with Roxie Red Tights?

You look at her, pensively. She's standing in releve´ with a bent leg hiked up on a scaffolding bar. Her left arm shoots high up in the air, with every finger on that Fosse-hand in a full split. The flyer reaches out toward you with such forward momentum; you feel it could go on forever. Her smile is so bright and big, it dwarfs the American Eagle jumbotron behind you. Her eyes are wider than legs on a casting couch. She's desperate. She needs this. She needs you. What do you do?

Take Roxie's flyer....? (page 318)

Ignore Roxie....? (page 81)

Deciding to ignore the thoughtful advice of your followers, you continue forward, abrasively lambasting the Broadway community by posting their tweets as Irritating Performer Pal. I mean, you like *really go for it*. Nobody is off-limits. You even throw shade at Audra McDonald and NOBODY THROWS SHADE AT AUDRA. This single act basically seals your fate. You don't really come back from that.

If I may... Um, I'll tell you the problem with the social media power that you're using here: it didn't require any discipline to attain it. You read what others had written and you copied it. You didn't earn the knowledge for yourself, so you don't take any responsibility for it. You stood on the shoulders of social media offenders to accomplish something as fast as you could, and before you even knew what you had, you patented it, and packaged it, and slapped it on a plastic lunchbox, and now, you're tweeting it.

Let this be a lesson: you can change a few words in a tweet (or even in an extended passage from your favorite movie) and most people won't notice – but you'll know, and that knowledge will bring you great guilt that will ultimately grind your creativity to a halt (unless you're making an extended *Mean Girls* reference. Those are always okay, and often encouraged).

Unfortunately, your lack of individuality and borderline trollish approach to Irritating Performer Pal has created a brand that is equal parts polarizing, off-putting, and just plain sucky. Unable to attract a larger audience (let alone keep the one you have), your fun after-school activity fizzles faster than a musical based on the Russian revolution, or any sort of cries-and-dies European musical written after 1989.

I suppose you want a happy ending to all of this, but tbh, if you fail on Twitter, it sort of means you fail at life, so the rest of your existence is going to be somewhat pointless… like entering your name in the *Hamilton* lottery.

THE END.

Screw Paige. David has always been a quicker texter anyway.

You shoot a message off to David, asking if he'll give *Metamorphosis: the Hilary Duff Musical* a quick pass and some notes. He doesn't respond immediately, and that gives you pause. David always responds. He's also one of those rare entities who uses the "Read Receipts" option, so you always know when he's opened a text. Your message is still marked as "delivered," so he's either not opened it, or stopped using that function. Either way, since it's been an hour since you sent it, all signs point to him being dead.

Alas, David is not dead. You randomly remember that he was just put into *Finding Neverland* after a long stint in *Chicago*, and has been finding himself in the process. After indulging heavily in the Kool-Aid at the Lunt-Fontanne, it'll some time before he gets to your text. Best to send your script to Corey.

Corey doesn't read it either.

Three up, three down (just like in a half an inning of baseball—you think.) Your next best bet is to try your less reliable friends, Ashley and Ellyn, because they might surprise you. Ashley is more of a dancer and Ellyn is more of a singer. This could seriously affect the type of feedback they provide. Do you…

Send your script to Ashley…? (page 336)

Send your script to Ellyn…? (page 343)

*

In an effort to actually take constructive criticism in a way that doesn't make you spiral down the self-loathing wormhole you discovered after your first faculty review at your BFA program, you gracefully take the note from your follower, and decide never to directly troll another actor again. I'm sure there will be times when it'll *appear* that you're going after a specific performer, but I promise you, it's all in their head.

Pondering the purpose of your social media presence is dangerous. The Internet is an extremely scary place, so the last thing you want to do is spend too much time analyzing your existence when that time could be better suited making memories… and memes! Inspired by the complete randomness of the World Wide Web (like how shit actually goes down on Reddit despite it looking even more dated than All That Chat), you start writing jokes in the voice of Irritating Performer Pal (whom I'll refer to from now on as IPP, because I went to college for musical theatre and can't spell "irritating" right on a first try).

The new direction for IPP buys you some more time to fully figure out what the eff you're doing in the first place. I'd like to tell you that one day you'll come to a grand understanding of what this all means, but LOL. Who cares? Just go with it. Have I ever led you astray?

After a few months of cracking jokes confined to Twitter only, you're itching to write something in longer form. 140 characters is so constricting. You feel like you're in a Los Angeles 99-Seat Theater production, just dying to transfer to a real contract where you can get paid.

Twitter really is like a 99-Seat Theater Plan. You work for free, providing content in exchange for a platform to share your gift. Wow. Twitter and the 99-Seat Theater Plan kind of suck. I probably just turned off a lot of you Hollywood people – but if you're going to get all butt hurt about my very New York opinion of your struggle, you should have identified as a Broadway Junior, because that trajectory is about pilot season, and you'd probably feel safer out there with your In-N-Out, and your kale, and why doesn't In-N-Out use kale— God, I want In-N-Out right now.

In an effort to break the boredom, you could start a blog. Blogs are big, right? Everyone has a Tumblr. Even my Right-wing Uncle's racially-insensitive jokes forwarded from an AOL email address are being adapted into a Tumblr. You could also transition to an Instagram account. Social media offers bountiful ways to waste your time. How would you like to spend the minutes in your life that you'll one day ask for back?

Make a Tumblr… (page 97)

Make an Instagram… (page 240)

Working up the nerve to reach out to your parents about money is always difficult, especially when it's been an unacceptable amount of time since you last spoke to them (that could either be one day, a few months, or a year, I DON'T KNOW YOUR LIFE). Anyway, once you finally find the courage, you pull out your phone and text your mom…

YOU:
Hey do you guys have 25 – 75k lying around
to produce my musical?

YOUR MOM:
new phone who dis

Who is your mom, Linda Benanti?

After a lengthy back and forth where the conversation is communicated mainly through Bitmojis, your mom agrees to loan a substantial amount of money to help produce *Pieces of Me*, if the rest of the money comes from the sale of all the crap you left behind when you went to college.

"There are more Beanie Babies than you'd expect," she says to you over the phone. "I'll put them up on eBay. They should cover about twenty bucks of expenses."

Worried that you won't have enough signed window cards in the world to make up the other half of the cash needed to produce your show, panic begins to set in. Here's the thing about panic though, it's so boring and expected. You don't have time to indulge in trite emotions. Not when there's a show to put on. Lucky for you, the Internet is about to save your ass.

Nobody knows what makes something go viral. I've been trying to go viral for three years, to no success.

Yet, somehow, your mom's witty and endearing eBay listings of all your Beanie Babies gets picked up by BuzzFeed and blows up the Internet.

Apparently, everyone in the world got rid of his or her Beanie Babies except for you, and because of Nineties Nostalgia, your collection becomes highly coveted. Isn't it funny how the Universe has a way of showing up with gifts when you least expect it? As sudden as it seems, this event was set in motion years ago. Way back when the first Waves the Whale was tossed in the trash, it set off a chain of events that would lead to the global purging of every Beanie Baby, except for that trash bag filled with TY treasures in your parents' attic.

"It's crazy!" your mom squeals on the phone. "They're selling like *Hamilton* tickets!" (Your mom is sweet, but not very original.)

By the time the auction ends on your collection of Beanie Babies, you've raised over $75,000, and will not need a loan from your parents to produce *Pieces of Me* at NYMF.

OK, I'm going to step in and suggest an alternative usage for your sudden financial success. How about—and hear me out here—how about instead of spending it on art, you use that money for a down payment on an apartment. I know it sounds crazy! I'm asking you to choose between dreams and reality! You can either make your dreams a reality, or have the reality of everyone else's dreams. Do you...

*Throw NYMF under the bus
and buy an apartment...?* (page 8)

*Produce Pieces of Me with
Beanie Baby blood money...?* (page 119)

*

Overall, you're pretty good at feigning being busy in an effort to ignore someone. However, Roxie's sniper-hotcha was a bit too well executed for you to completely divert her eye. Still, you're able to awkwardly fake a phone call while pencil turning around Roxie with the precision of an ensemble before a long run sets in.

As you head toward the entrance to H&M, you hear Roxie call out, "Talking on a phone? Haven't seen someone use that as an excuse since Alexander Graham Bell! Whoopie!" Her voice is a surprisingly accurate impression of Anne Reinking as Gwen Verdon.

Impressed by her blunt calling out of your bullshit (more so than her forced attempt to make a period appropriate joke about how talking on the phone is so dated), you turn and throw her a bone by proclaiming in your best Roxie Hart voice, "I gotta pee!"

Roxie Red Tights giggles, and spins on her one inch character shoes while squealing, "Skidoo!"

I must admit, even I am in awe of how well you nailed that Roxie voice. It's a deceptively nuanced warble that only Broadway dancers over the age of sixty-five can truly execute correctly. That's because I'm pretty sure that once a dancer hits that age, they just naturally start talking like Gwen Verdon. It's like she saved her voice in Ursula's seashell necklace as a gift for any gypsy who can still kick their face with two titanium hips. I also think that once you turn sixty-five you're allowed to refer to Fosse simply as, "Bob."

Feeling great about your quick comeback to Roxie (and flattered that I complimented your voice talent) you proudly prepare to enter H&M. As you approach the door, it swings open and out walks the last person on the island of Manhattan that you would want to see right now. No, it's not your ex, or that acting teacher who said you weren't ready to be successful in the "field." It's Taylor T. Thomas, the dick who books everything over you.

"Oh, heyyyyy!" Taylor says with a forced, sappy-saccharine tone.

"Hi, Taylor! How are you?" you falsely smile back.

NO! Why did you engage?! I was supposed to give you a choice of whether or not to engage with this fuck-nut and you blew right through it! Why is this what everyone ends up doing?! Whenever you run into a person who is so terrible, you'd rather voluntarily binge-watch a supercut of just Lea Michele's scenes from *Glee* than get caught in a fifteen second exchange with their fart-face—yet, when put in the situation, what do you all do? Get caught in a fifteen second exchange with a fart-face! Sorry to come off as juvenile, but like, I hate fake people. Oh, well, you're on your own now. Have fun.

"So, what are you working on?" Taylor asks (OF COURSE. They *always* ask that).

"Oh, just auditioning," you respond, way more cordially than you should.

"Hmm. Me too. But aren't we all always auditioning?" Taylor laughs.

You pause; hoping maybe the remainder of this fifteen-second meeting from the hells of Nola Studios can be filled with an uncomfortable silence.

Taylor continues, "Yeah, just picking up a last minute outfit for this callback I have."

"Oh. Cool."

Taylor doesn't even take a breath to wait for you to speak. The diva-dickhead just keeps plowing on, "Yeah, it's that new show with a bunch of Broadway people. I don't know. Should be fun."

Yeah. You know. You can now assume that Taylor is called back for the exact same show and role that you are. Now instead of focusing on your callback, you're focusing on Taylor, and how the creative team probably wants to have sex and make Tony babies with motherfucking Taylor. DAMMIT.

Taylor is what we call a Type Troll. Someone who is exactly your type, always manages to get cast over you, and often throws you off your game in an audition setting by trolling you with awkward small talk, or just by existing. You can have more than one Type Troll in your life, and all of them are douchebags.

Type Trolls are not to be confused with actors who are just your type. Many actors who are just your type can become friends. Some will probably be in your wedding party because you've spent the majority of your time in New York together at chorus calls, appointments, callbacks, and gypsy runs for the shows you lost to the Type Troll. If your preferences gear toward the same sex variety, you may even date someone who is your type, because they are also *your type*. I strongly urge against this, because once you breakup, you will be stuck with this person at every subsequent audition, adding to your already extensive lineup of Type Trolls.

Remember: the Type Troll only wants to bring you down. Never engage them. Ever. This altercation between you and Taylor will most likely have a negative effect on your callback. So, I hope you learned your lesson the next time you start jumping off script and making choices before I present them to you.

During my rant, I neglected to notice that you completely ignored me, and got right up in Taylor's face.

"Taylor?" you say with guttural anger. "Nobody gives a *shit* about your callback."

With that, you swing your fist back and punch the asshole in the face. My. That escalated quickly.

This random act of meanness is incredibly liberating, causing you to laugh as Taylor stumbles backwards and rolls to the ground with an amateur, melodramatic technique that seems pretty Liberal Arts for someone with the solid BFA training this douche undoubtedly earned from Michigan, CMU or CCM.

What happens next materializes a bit too quick for you to process, so I'll give you the highlights:

First, Frank DiLella of NY1 (who was filming a feature on which *Gypsy* revival tourists have liked best) races over to scoop out the scene. He puts you on camera and asks you what happened. You explain that Broadway's Taylor T. Thomas (who is currently blacked out on the sidewalk) threatened your safety, and you had to defend yourself. You continue defaming Taylor's character, and Frank is really eating it up. He wants to turn this into an entire segment celebrating you and what goes on in the brutal behind-the-scenes battles of Broadway. This could make you a star!

Just when you're about to burst from all this excitement, you hear a familiar voice behind you.

"Officer, that's who threw the first punch. I saw it all myself."

You turn to see Roxie Red Tights standing with a cop, pointing right at you. You look at Roxie, then to the cop, and then back to Frank, who is looking down at Taylor. You're completely perplexed as to why you're being thrown under the bus.

Then you see it. Sticking out of Taylor's back pocket is none other than a flyer for *Chicago*.

"And I got it all on my phone," says Roxie Red Tights.

"Why are you doing this to me?" you plead.

"Because none of us got enough love in our childhoods," she snickers with a kind of chilling awareness of humanity's darkness. It makes you curious as to what she's seen in her life.

Frank smirks and asks, "Mind if we use that footage?"

"Not at all."

Of course Roxie agrees. And, of course, the story hits Broadway Internet before you make it to your callback. So, naturally, the creative team can't decide if you have sociopathic tendencies, or just had a moment of weakness fueled by booze or a burning desire to stage an immersive revival of *West Side Story* in the middle of the Times Square Pedestrian Mall. Needless to say, they decide to go another direction—preferably one in the opposite way of you.

At night, as you lie in bed, you can't help but wonder if you'll become one of those stories that people talk about in a dark corner of Shubert Alley when someone asks, "Whatever happened to so-and-so?" Are you destined to be a footnote in a deleted chapter from *The Untold Stories of Broadway Volume XXI*?

The anxiety over your choices today becomes too overwhelming to bear. Had you engaged with Roxie, she wouldn't have turned you in, and nobody would know you assaulted another actor because you didn't want to hear about their callbacks anymore. Being the first person to take to violence in an effort to put an actor in their place should be grounds for some kind of honorary Tony award. However, it has actually done the exact opposite for your career.

Your future has never been more in flux than it is at this very moment. When you close your eyes to sleep, you ask the Universe for positive vibes in an effort to fix what might have been a career-ending choice you made today. This fear and uncertainty causes your stomach to turn into an iron cavern of self-loathing and regret, twice the size of a normal actor's. Then, as you drift into that place between sleep and awake, Roxie Red Tights appears to you through the misty fog of Times Square manhole steam, and whispers knowingly into your ear, "And that's show biz, kid."

THE END.

*

"I… think," you continue, with mild trepidation, "I think that it's a great idea if you write both the music and lyrics."

"Cool!" smiles Daniel. "When do you want to start?"

"When are you free?" you ask.

Thus begins a creative relationship for the ages. Over the course of the next month, you and Daniel are inseparable. When you're not collaborating in person, you're connected through rolling conversations over text, email, Voxer/HeyTell/whatever you use for voice messages, etc. There is such an instant creative chemistry between Daniel and you. It's a shame you weren't closer friends in college because now you're, like, a decade behind Pasek and Paul.

The thing about close writing partnerships is that they function similarly to romantic relationships, except without the Netflix and chill part. After a week of working together, Daniel's significant other began to think the two of you were having a thing, and you were like, "Eww. It's *Daniel*." Nope. The connection you and Daniel share is purely platonic. The raciest thing you two have engaged in was a late-night dinner party where the two of you were supposed to be brainstorming ideas for act one, but instead provided live commentary to the 1963 *Judy Garland Christmas Special* to three people on Periscope after crawling to the bottom of a Beefeater bottle. This must be what it's like to be Kate Wetherhead and Andrew Keenan-Bolger.

At the end of thirty-one short days, you and Daniel have a completed first draft of your musical *Pieces of Me*. It's crazy what can be accomplished in such a short amount of time when you actually commit to being productive. The last time you approached a project with this much dedication was when *Felicity* was first available

87

for streaming— and you completed this endeavor in half the time. Perhaps it was your closeness to the source material (your literal life experiences) that made it easy to construct three-dimensional characters into a compelling narrative (or maybe your show sucks. I don't know, because you haven't asked me be in it).

When the two of you are finally satisfied with your first draft, Daniel suggests inviting over a group of friends for an informal table read.

"And we can replace them with bigger names for the workshop, right?" you ask.

"Duh," agrees Daniel.

There are six parts in the show, and neither of you will be playing the roles based on yourselves (because it'll just hit too close to home, you know?) nor do you want to invite anyone else to the reading who may have been the inspiration for one of the characters. You keep this in mind as you scroll through your contacts searching for six friends who will come and read your work with no judgment, in exchange for wine (this takes about four minutes).

Once you assemble a strong cast of reputable Broadway ensemble members, and a date for the reading, you start to wonder if it might behoove the two of you to shoot a press release over to Playbill and Broadway World.

"Why?" asks Daniel.

"Because," you urge, "if we get press for doing an informal 'industry reading' of our new musical, people will start to take us seriously as writers. It's all about perception."

Daniel rolls his eyes. "But this is a read-thru in your apartment with a case of Trader Joe's three-buck-chuck."

"What do you think *industry* means?!"

"OK, but if you're going to put this out there for everyone to see, then we have to talk about the title again."

UGH. Daniel's been nagging you about the title since Panera. It's really been the only disagreement you've had with him during this entire process (besides the time he demanded he write the lyrics, too) and you don't want to budge on it.

"I'm just saying," Daniel continues, "if you're putting a press release out there, then that's the official title of our show and we can never change it."

"That's not true," you state. "We wouldn't be the first musical to change the title while in development. *West Side Story* was once *East Side Story*, *The Sound of Music* was once *Love Song*, *Oklahoma!* Was once *Away We Go!*, and *Glory Day* was actually called *Glory Days* when it opened and closed on May 6th, 2008."

"So, why don't we call it *Broadway Debut* now, and if we don't like it later, we can go back to *Pieces of Me*?" suggests Daniel.

"*Or*," you say. "Why don't we call it *Pieces of Me* now, and if we don't like it later, we can call it *Broadway Debut*."

"Look," exhales Daniel in frustration, "this was your concept to begin with, and I'm going to respect that, and let you make the final decision here—but I really believe *Broadway Debut* is a better title. I thought it was before I grew invested in this project, and I still think it is now."

Hmmm. This is hard. Collaborators are meant to challenge each other, and Daniel has definitely held strong to this opinion ever since he was an objective outsider. The last thing you want to do when writing your first musical is fall in so deep that you block out all constructive criticism. That being said, *Pieces of Me* is what first spoke to you. Can you really abandon the basis of your initial inspiration? Do you…

Change the title to Broadway Debut…? (page 46)

Keep the title Pieces of Me…? (page 223)

*

Hopping on the 101 again, you drive to the 170 and hightail it north toward the 5. Just as you're about to merge, traffic comes to a grinding halt. You glance up ahead to see what's going on, but the last mile before your off-ramp is more slammed than The Grove parking structure on a weekend.

Feeling that it's safe to check your phone because you aren't moving, you scroll through Twitter to see WTF is going on. According to the trending hashtag, #LAlpacas, a herd of designer alpacas escaped from a farm in Sun Valley where they blocked traffic on the southbound 5 for more than an hour, before wreaking havoc on the 170 north, where you sit chained to your car.

"The news says it could be hours before they detain this herd," you whine to your agent over the phone.

"Oh, yeah," he sighs, "these alpacas are a real pain in the ass. I've been moving appointments all day."

"What am I supposed to do?"

"Sit tight. I'll make a few calls," he says. "Try to get to the rest of your auditions, and whichever ones you miss, we'll figure it out."

In an effort to take your agent's advice, you attempt to relax by watching the entire first season of *Difficult People* on your iPhone while sobbing because there's finally a TV show that celebrates *Smash* jokes and you didn't get to it first.

After a solid two hours of waiting, the alpaca herd is safely corralled, and traffic on the 170 finally begins to move, allowing you to make it to your auditions for *Evener Stevens* and *This Will Get Canceled* (you do quite well at both, considering the recent stressful circumstances).

On your way to Burbank for your last appointment of the day, you receive a call from your agent while you're stopped for gas.

"Good news and bad news," he says. "Your audition for *My Eight-Year-Old Son* was moved to the primary casting office down by Wilshire. There's no way you'll make it in time."

"No!" you cry. "That was for NBC! I want to be the next Megan Hilty!"

"CBS is really interested in you. How about being the next Neil Patrick Harris?"

"Pass."

"They want you to test for *2 Friends & Their Job*."

"What does this mean?!" you scream with joy.

"It means," he explains, "that we gotta talk contract. Salary. Billing. The whole nine yards."

"But I didn't book it yet."

Your agent laughs. "Some of you New Yorkers can be so green."

He goes on to clarify that before you can test, your entire contract for the series has to be agreed upon. This is serious shit. You could be at upfronts in a matter of months. But, don't get ahead of yourself. You still have to test, get cast, shoot the pilot, and then have the pilot get picked up, and before any of this, you need to do a work session with the entire creative team to make sure you don't blow it in front of the network executives.

"And that's basically everything that goes into your first big TV screen test!" says your agent.

"Wow!" you shout in excitement while accidentally overflowing your tank, spraying gas everywhere. "I don't believe it!"

When you recount the events of the day to your roommate Ally, she is congratulatory and supportive.

"Like," she says, "so cool."

"I know, right?" you smile.

"And what's great about those work sessions is, if they love you, you'll feel it in the room," she explains. "You can tell when you're the one that they want."

"OMG," you laugh, "remember *Grease: You're the One That I Want!* on NBC?"

"No," Ally says blankly. "Anyway, it's good to remember when they like you, because you won't be getting positive reactions from anyone during the actual test."

"Good to know," you say.

Ally never told you that she acted, but you gathered that since she's a bartender in LA, she was at the very least an aspiring Vine star.

Before your work session, your agent sends you some additional scenes to learn because there's a sociopathic side of the character that wasn't present in any of the materials in your original packet. Making sure to devote every single waking moment to *2 Friends & Their Job*, you pour your heart into being the most prepared and marketable actor to ever grace the CBS screen.

Proud of the unusual amount of discipline you've dedicated to landing this role, you confidently enter your work session, believing that whatever happens next is out of your control, and to just be grateful for the opportunity and—lol, jk, if you don't get this pilot you are legit going to go full Shia LaBeouf on the place.

"Thank you for coming in," the director says with a faint smile.

"Thank you for having me!" you grin.

That's really where the pleasantries end. As you work through the sides, there is a hue of indifference coloring any feedback from the creative team. It's like they don't really care that you're here.

While trying to ponder if there's anything you're doing differently from your initial audition, Ally's cautionary words race through your brain.

You can tell when you're the one that they want.

Oh my God. Could it be? Are you… callback fodder? You experienced this horrible fate a few times back in New York, but you never imagined it happening at the hands of the fine people in Hollywood.

This unfortunate outcome only occurs when the creatives or casting directors in charge of a project want a specific actor for a role, so to sway the network (or whatever Powers That Be) in their favor, they stack the deck with people who aren't right in an effort to manipulate everyone into fighting for the person that they want. It's a really shitty way to waste an actor's time, and after countless unpaid hours spent focusing on a job that was never going to be yours, it's time to get real…

"Let's not do this," you say with exasperation as you drop your sides to the floor.

"Beg pardon?" asks the director.

"*This,*" you emphasize with rage. "It's obvious that I am wasting your time, but the true irony is, you have no clue that you've wasted mine."

The casting director looks perplexed. "What are you talking about?"

"You don't want me. You never wanted me. You want one of those other actors out in the waiting room, and the rest of us are here to make them look better for the network executives."

The creative team sits in silence, allowing you to continue.

"I just signed my life away on a forty-five page contract. I'm going to be on hold for this pilot for at least ten days. When you finally release me, I'll have lost valuable time. Irreplaceable time. Time that very well could have earned me millions of dollars. But do any of you give a shit? No. And that's fine. I get it. So, instead of making me jump through sixty more hoops, why don't you do me a solid and admit that I'm right by letting me go when there's still time to book something for Amazon Prime."

The director looks to the casting director. She nods. He looks back at you.

"Sure, that's fine."

"Thank you," you say as you move to leave.

The casting director stands up. "Before you go."

"Yeah?" you ask as you turn back around.

"I think I have a costar you'd be great for on *The Big Bang Theory*."

"Thank you for your time," you politely smile, and respectfully leave the room.

As you drive back home to Studio City, you begin to question your decision to move to LA. In the past few weeks, you have been chewed up and spit out in a way that redefines what it means to feel used. At least New York looked you in the eye before it took a dump on your chest.

These thoughts turn circles in your brain as you sit in traffic for what could either be the first or eighth hour today. You've spent so much time in your car since you arrived here, that you don't even know the difference between it and your bedroom. Moreover, your own thoughts have become your only friends ever since your social life was confined to the whims of LA traffic.

You sort of hate to admit it, but you miss running into friends on the streets of New York. You miss having anything you'd ever need within a few miles' reach. You actually miss the MTA. Scratch that. You miss the MTA allowing you to drink whenever you want, and not worry about having to drive home, or spend an obscene amount of money on an Uber. Most of all, you miss the people.

In a strange twist of fate, something quite unexpected has happened. You moved to LA to escape your past, and ended up finding yourself in the process—and the person you found is all the way back on the other side of the country, waiting for your return.

It is in this moment when you realize that it's time to hop on a plane to New York and—

Embrace who you've become... (page 12)

Tumblr is a great place for people who are younger than you to connect and curate content that they can share with their network. In short, it's a lot of GIFs. So. Many. GIFs. Broadway Tumblr is made-up solely of *Newsies* and Aaron Tveit GIFs, often with both parties present in the same GIF. The goal with Tumblr is to get your content pulled from somewhere else and shared on it, or whatever, I think. You've made it when you make it to Tumblr. I'm not sure if it's the place you should be originating your material, but it is pretty hip, and you want to stay trendy with the kids so they'll like your stuff—and oh my God, high school never ended.

I'd like to explain why branching out into multiple social media arenas too quickly could be dangerous, but my advice is somewhat irrelevant considering I only gave you two choices and they both had to do with social media. I may be a douche, but at least I'm a self-aware douche. We'll just have to see how well you take on this challenge before I decide if you die or not. I mean it: Social media is life or death. Literally. The Internet kills twelve careers a minute.

You jumped from Twitter to Tumblr because you wanted to write extended content. So, what to write about? You could write journal-type entries from the perspective of IPP. That could be fun. Why don't you try one? Go ahead, I'll wait.

***

Meh. I appreciate the effort, but I have a few notes. Mainly one: try something else. It's nauseating reading a character who talks in that voice for such a *long* period of time, don't you think? You're better at commentary. I don't suggest reviewing shows, because you still have friends in them and you don't want to get blood on your hands. If only there were some sort of theatre-themed television show you gave zero shits about. If only *Smash* were still around. Wait. Remember when I said this was a fantasy? Well, it's about to get more unrealistic than *Smash* itself when I tell you that Netflix has decided to reboot the series after its successful Actor's Fund benefit concert of *Bombshell*. Holy shit, my dreams—I mean—*your* dreams just came true.

Season three of *Smash*'s thirteen episodes will be available on Netflix next week, and you're going to binge harder than you did that time that person booked that thing over you. In preparation for the event, you post a drinking game on your Tumblr, and one of your followers is like, "Is this Tumblr going to be a real thing? Because it should." Compliments! People like you! You love positive attention! Validation from one person means you should probably spend hundreds of hours recapping *Smash*!

You decide to move to a proper blog because Tumblr is so other level Millennial you literally can't even. Remember: you're trying to share your *gift*, not your GIF, AMIRIGHT ladies?

Now that you've transitioned from Tumblr to a blog, you feel safer – like whenever *Cabaret* is at Studio 54. It's time to recap *Smash*!

You've never recapped a TV show, which means you have absolutely no fuck of a clue what you are doing. On the flipside, you're recapping *Smash*, so that kind of works. Developing a framing device for your weekly recaps comes to you while running in Central Park (oh yeah, I forgot to mention that for some random ass reason, in this universe you're a distance runner). The thing you loved about *Smash* was that it appeared like it didn't give a fuck how the business of Broadway was depicted on screen. I'm 100% certain it actually did give a fuck, because those episodes cost like six million dollars to make. Still, you've come up with the concept that *Smash* gives zero fucks about being realistic to Broadway, and that you love them for it. Titling your blog *Smash Gives Zero Fucks* – wait, is that really what you're going to call it? Don't you think using an expletive in your title will be somewhat off-putting to readers? No? OK...*Smash Gives Zero Fucks* it is.

Season three of *Smash* is the show-tune-dripping fever dream we've always wanted. It's Netflix, so the writers genuinely give zero fucks how far they take it. Kyle returns as a ghost that gives friendly advice to the incarcerated Jimmy, who has like four prison husbands. Eileen doesn't throw martinis anymore; she just has people whacked in Shubert Alley. The Chinese baby adoption plotline is back and it is *pissed*. Tom is casually written off the show without explanation because Christian Borle was like, "No." Karen finally does Derek for a role and Ivy isn't even mad, because she's involved. Why Karen or Ivy, when you can have Karen *and* Ivy? I mean, basically, *Smash* on Netflix is like what *Smash* looked like before it was taken from Showtime and produced for NBC. Also, Ana wins five Tonys and PSM Linda runs Broadway now. That's season three of *Smash*.

Your recaps are pretty rough in the beginning. I think when you look back you'll realize your readers were watching you learn how to construct a sentence in real time. Either way, you somehow manage to amass a following that inspires you to take risks in your writing, and you really love that you've found this unique creative outlet. You never thought you'd say it, but, "Thank God for *Smash*!"

And then *Smash* ends. Again. I guess season three was meant to be a limited engagement, like the original network run, or a Wildhorn musical. Now what? You were on such a roll there for a bit. *Smash* was awesome because it gave you an opportunity to indirectly poke fun at the industry under the guise of making fun of *Smash*.

You could continue on blogging without the *Smash* framing device, or you could try saving that content for a book about how to succeed in show business. The blog doesn't pay, so you might as well try turning your stupid hobby (sorry, but it really is a stupid hobby tbh) into actual cash dollars. However, you don't want to lose social media steam by ditching the blog to devote all your time and energy to a book that nobody could bother buying – and also, books are hard to write, and I'm not so certain you'll ever figure them out. Do you...

Write a book....? (page 102)

Continue the blog...? (page 237)

OK, let me get this straight: I'm giving you a big opening to potentially sexually arouse a powerful person, and you chose instead to stand next to them on the off chance you get the opportunity to make small talk about *How to Get Away with Murder* in between sets of plyometric exercises? WTF! Did you wear your shorty-shorts *only* for the personal fulfillment of staring at yourself in the mirror? They're good for more than that!

I'm not saying that Ashton Reed is a shallow enough director/choreographer to give you a role in their next show solely based off of how you perform at Mark Fisher Fitness today, but your chances would have been a hell of a lot better had you been standing in front of them. Taking the passive, prudent approach is fine for coffee shops and callbacks, but this is Mark. Fisher. Fitness. You're in an actual porn, with occasional functional movement exercises. This is no place to be sensible. There was an opportunity in front of you, and you didn't take it, so instead, you get nothing. You lose. Good day, sir.

As angry as your life choices are making me right now, they aren't offensive enough for you to get killed off with a kettlebell or something. That being said, you're certainly dead to me... so...

THE END.

I'm proud of you for taking on the insurmountable stress of writing a book about pursuing a career on Broadway, while not actually pursuing a career on Broadway. I've known you longer than anyone, and I'm aware that even with your experience, you kind of don't know shit about what you're talking about. You'll have to source your successful and savvy friends if you're going to try to tell a bunch of people how to "work" and "werk" in show business.

Looking over the various chapters you plan to write, it becomes clear which friend should assist you on each one. For college, you choose your friend from high school who now runs a prominent youth theatre in Manhattan. She has a student in every reputable BFA program in the country except Michigan, which she's never been able to figure out. Your friend who hasn't been unemployed since, like, *Bombay Dreams*, helps you with the Broadway section, while the person you're currently sleeping with who can't seem to ever get *off* unemployment (or tour) serves as your aid in those subjects. For the chapter on pounding the pavement, you rely on your own experience because you were a disaster in the audition room, so it should be real easy writing that. The same goes for social media. You've now spent more time online, learning about shit like "fleek," "squad goals," and "post AOL acronyms," than you ever did in a rehearsal studio. In fact, you could teach a master class in how to make a meme in less than sixty seconds using picfont.com and a prayer. As far as the chapter dedicated to pilot season, it never pans out because you don't ever synch up with Julie to fill you in on what the hell that's all about. Maybe you can get it together for the next book – if you ever decide to be foolish enough to write another one.

Once you've conducted all of the interviews necessary to provide your readers with a well-rounded, yet totally-tunnel-vision-and-potentially-biased view of the world of Broadway, you take the summer to write the book in your own words. Because summers are swampy in New York, you leech off of the free air conditioning/wifi at Fusion and write the entire thing in the member lounge. It's a wonder you've never been fired for that type of shit.

The book launches in the fall, and I don't want you to get too big of a head about it, but it's the best book that has ever been written. Your book is the shit. It demands to be seen. There's so much #truth in it, that people are losing their minds on social media. Your risk paid off.

While your book is popular in a niche, indie way (just like Broadway), there's an important element in the text (where you blatantly troll Actors' Equity) that you wish could reach a larger audience. You think it's important for everyone to be able to read what you find to be a very important analysis of union contracts, but to put it on your blog for free won't pay your rent. Do you share your gift for the good of the cause? Or do you save it for those who paid?

Save it... (page 107)

Share it... (page 108)

*

You've chosen a Shameless Selfless Option in Shameless Self Promotion world. I'm proud of you. Every now and then you have to come back to reality and remember that you have friends who were friends before you had kickass credits. Carol is a good girl, and she deserves your attention. Sometimes it's easy to forget that you are a truly #SOBLESSED actor, and learning this new callback material will be a breeze. Besides, shows open and mostly close, but friends are forever until they aren't because they become more successful than you.

"Hey, girl. Are you OK?"

Carol throws a blanket over her face. "Nobody loves me."

"That's not true."

"What do you do when nobody loves you?" she asks. "I'm a disaster."

"Carol. *Nobody Loves You* was a Second Stage disaster. You're not even a first stage disaster."

"What does that even mean?"

"Life beats you up, Carol. It doesn't matter if you get taken by a cult or you've been rejected over and over again at auditions. You can either curl up in a ball and die, like we thought Cyndee did that time, or you can stand up and say, 'We're different. We're the strong ones, and you can't break us.'"

"You're right! I need to remember why I love and respect Broadway, and the only way to do that is to win the *Hamilton* lottery tonight."

"Carol," you say, "there are like forty other shows on Broadway."

Ignoring you, Carol dusts the Parmesan cheese off her sweats and marches out the front door.

TIME OUT. Did you just use a line from *Unbreakable Kimmy Schmidt* to get yourself out of this awkward situation? How did that even work? Everyone has seen that show four times. I'm watching it right now.

I guess poor Carol has been unemployed for so long she can't afford Netflix, and you have those really strict morals against sharing passwords. You should kneel at the altar of Elphaba and thank the Gods of Forward Placement that Carol bought your little act because she believes Mark Fisher Fitness *is* a cult and there really *was* a girl named Cyndee there who curled up in a ball after forty-five minutes of kettlebell swinging to just the *Smash* songs from *Hit List*.

OK, moving on. Now that you feel energized by selflessly inspiring Carol (isn't being a blessing to others a real self-motivator?), you take a few minutes to glance over your new sides before heading to the bathroom to get camera ready for your callback.

Remember, it's always best to apply your favorite Instagram filter to your face before every audition (especially if the audition is for stage). Up close, you must always look exactly how the role should look. Just because the front row in most theatres is yards away doesn't mean the creative team is required to understand that.

You hop in the shower and get a good steam going by setting the water to hotter than under Tony Danza's collar every time they published the weekly grosses for *Honeymoon in Vegas* (is this dated?). After a sensible forty-five minutes of belting a montage of completely random songs, you retreat from the shower to commence whatever industrial light and magic witchcraft it takes for you to pull your shit together physically. By the time you are done, you almost resemble the hotness showcased in your headshot (if you squint while holding it at an angle under a dark light after an afternoon of bottomless mimosas).

Now it's time to make a very important decision... Probably the most vital choice you have made today... Do you... go with the simple colored top or a sleek and sensible black ensemble? The role is pretty neutral to either options and you look great in both. WHICH DO YOU CHOOSE...?

Colored top. (page 111)

Sensible black. (page 335)

Not deciding to do something isn't really a choice. Choices usually involve an action, so this misguided restraint is kind of lame. I mean, you want to generate the most buzz for your product, and that occasionally comes with offering up free material. You've been doing it on Twitter and your blog for over a year, so spreading a little controversy at no cost to the readers could actually benefit you. Also, if you were really all that passionate about your concerns with Actors' Equity, wouldn't you want them known?

If this is the kind of passive approach you intend to apply to the rest of your life, then I literally don't have time for you. I wasted enough time in my past not doing what I should, and I don't have the patience to sit around and watch someone else make the same mistakes. I'm going to catch up on *Veep,* or something, bye.

THE END.

*

Like the Broadway performance papering
process, this decision is a well-intentioned risk that could
pay off. Some producers are more guarded than others,
so I appreciate you publishing such a large portion of
your book on your blog for free. When it comes to
papering, I think that somewhere around "thank you,
five," all empty seats should be offered up to company
members to help generate word of mouth. We all know
our friends are going to wait as long as humanly possible
for a free ticket before they bother to try to the lottery,
and by that time, the show will probably be closed.

Seeing friends in Broadway shows is a pain in
the fucking ass. Yeah, I love Broadway, I love my
friends, and I'm always super stoked about what I'm
going to see before the show curtain goes up – but I'm
not nearly as psyched about all that positive shit as I am
about a positive balance in my bank account. If you
want to see a Broadway show for free, either become
friends with a press rep or get a job at BuzzFeed. Your
actor friends are seldom going to get you shit because the
cast is always the last to have access to free tickets. Your
grandmother's podiatrist who loves *Phantom* will get
papered into your Broadway show before your parents. I
was at the opening night of *Follies* because my friend was
a dresser on *Priscilla Queen of the Desert* and his wardrobe
supervisor got a block of tickets. That shit makes about
as much sense as the plot of a NYMF show.

While you were entertaining my rant about
papering, your rant about Actors' Equity has gone semi-
viral. You're thrilled, and very proud of the accidental—
but surprisingly opportune—timing in which you chose
to post the blog: Thanksgiving. It's amazing how many
people would rather read a pointed essay about the
declining pay of a once-bountiful Equity contract, than
spend time conversing with their family.

The blog draws attention to your book, but, more importantly, to your cause (which I can't really specify because I feel like our concerns with Equity rotate faster than shows at the Brooks Atkinson). The community is fired up, and people are looking for the straw to break the camel's back—and/or the tequila shot to tank that one Broadway Bares dancer who spent a day too long on the master cleanse.

In another epic case of lucky-as-fuck-timing, two huge Broadway franchises post a casting notice for their shows under the contract that you find questionable. It's now a few days after Christmas, and these announcements (partnered with the holidays providing more time for people to focus on their phones) make for a special social media opportunity. Throwing it back to when you first created IPP, you grab a spiked beverage (margarita this time, because you're in Southern California – sorry, I forgot to tell you that) and write a call-to-action blog as quickly as possible, because you have some kickass Mexican food waiting in the kitchen, and you don't want it to get cold. I seriously don't think I can talk enough about how much you love authentic Mexican food.

You go to bed satisfied with yourself because honestly, it's the ingredients that they can't seem to get right in New York City (specifically the tortillas), and also, you feel good about your blog. When you wake up, your phone has blown up. The notifications on your Twitter seem countless, and that's nothing compared to the stats on your website. This might be your most viral moment. The community wants change, and you have inspired that desire for change.

You're not used to this kind of attention directed to your silly parody Internet personality. I must say, I'm pretty shocked, too. You're the person who makes memes of Rachel Berry pushing over Karen Cartwright and Ivy Lynn. Are you actually prepared to Mockingjay a revolution? I guess, at the very least, you know how to make some inspiring graphics for future blog posts. But, seriously... People are calling on you to lead. *You.* Nobody even knows who or *what* you are. Even I'm not entirely certain if you're human, or just what happens when Professor McGonagall *piertotum locomotors* my recently used emojis.

By abrasively calling to action union members behind the cloak of anonymity, you're essentially poking Actors' Equity like it's a badger (because some badgers are just asking to be poked, right?) but badgers bite back – I've read *The Wind in the Willows*, I know this. So, do you continue poking the badger? Or, do you quit poking the badger? Things could get really messy if you start playing with fire, but it could be worth it just to ...*become* the girl on fire. Do you...

Poke the badger...? (page 112)

Don't poke the badger...? (page 236)

*

Feeling fun and festive, you slip into a colored top that makes your eyes pop. With a spring in your heart, and in your step, you bounce down to one of the Pearl Studios for your final callback with the creative team. You're confident that there's no possible way you won't land this job given the amount of preparation you have devoted to both the callback material and to your appearance. Time. To. Book.

You totally don't book.

Looking back on what happened, you can't think of anything that went wrong in the room. By all intents and purposes, you nailed every aspect of that callback. Each choice made was the right choice. You wouldn't change a thing about your performance— which is rare in cases like these where you can always think of some way that you sucked.

The only decision to question is your outfit choice. Maybe it was too bright and cheery for this show. Perhaps it set the wrong tone for the direction you went with the material. The fear that you didn't look your best is lingering in the pit of your stomach as you ponder how things would have turned out had you chosen to wear your sleek black ensemble. I guess you'll never know, but will forever believe that the outcome would have been different had you picked the other outfit. Remember this as you go forth unto your next audition.

THE END.

*

Due to the fact that you might want to save this hotbox of crazy story for the memoirs on the off-chance someone ever cares enough about your life, I'm not going to go into too much detail about the utter shit-storm that follows you poking the badger. No... Not poking. Poking is for Facebook in 2006. You more or less tried to bitch slap the zeitgeist with your rep book—and not a regular rep book. I'm talking about the one *before* you took out the fifty pounds of music your college vocal coach swore you would need for your future, when you pretty much just sang the same song for every audition whether it was a Gershwin or jukebox musical, which, FUN-FACT, are the same thing.

In short, after doing your best Norma Ray impress—sorry, I don't know what came over me... After doing your best *Jack Kelly* impression, Broadway Internet gets really, really yelly. Grassroots organizations are founded, the New York Times gets involved, your mom gets involved, the *Broadway World message board* gets involved. The entire Equity community is ignited with conversation, and you're having a blast being a part of it (primarily because of the sweet *Hunger Games* memes you made to accompany each mouthy blog post.)

The union hears their members' call to action (which, still, I have no clue what you all are yelling about because I had rehearsal) and offers up meetings at the Equity Building that draw lines leading all the way down to the non-Equity Chicago Flyer Girl dangling from the scaffolding outside of the McDonald's. Equity even holds a town hall at the same hotel where Broadway Con takes place. I think. It's inspiring to see all the young union members, who consistently neglect to vote in elections, band together for a common cause when it involves the opportunity to publicly share their opinions on a stage in front of an audience.

No shade directed at all the under-forty card-carrying members of Equity who finally decided to show up and engage in a union discussion. I can't be tough on them, when I AM THEM. I think it was Sydney Lucas who once said, "Better late, than never," so we should feel pride in getting involved, no matter how long we dragged our feet. Full disclosure: both of those meetings were a first for me, and it was eye opening seeing just how hard our union officials work for less pay than the lowest contract Equity has to offer (because most of them literally get no dollars). It was also crazy how hard Jen Cody worked me to find out your identity. I was like, "Sorry, Jen, I signed an NDA." Anyway, whether we agree with our counselors, or not, they work harder than the *Spider-Man 1.0* cast did on a two-show day, and we have the power to vote, so if we don't like shit, it's kind of our own fault.

I'd like to say that all the hard work accomplished by these rich and meaningful discussions eventually lead to a stronger union. The positive dialogue continues briefly, until LA Equity raises a larger stink about something completely different just because they're hungry. Oh, LA. What a mess. Since you and I are both New York Equity, we are contractually obligated to have a complete lack of understanding of LA Equity. They are *Glee*, we are *Smash*, except we are like if *Smash* had *Glee's* ratings and priority over Top 40 records. Either way, both shows have been cancelled, and that's a fairly on-the-nose metaphor for how some view Equity's overall strength lately. Normally, I'd agree. But right now Equity has a smart, young, woman president, who can engage the members and also scrclt a G, so you know shit will just come together eventually, because that's how democracy works.

Your take-away from abrasively kicking the badger with a wing tipped tap shoe is this: you learned a lot about your union, you grew respect for its elected officials, and you found a side of you that loves activism. You place this passion in your pocket and wait for the chance to use it again.

After the Equity stuff dies down, you try to find new ways to reinvent IPP. Up until now, you've existed solely behind an Apple device, and you're looking to somehow bring your text to life. There are roughly sixty-eight #ActorProblems web series' out there, so you don't want to bother throwing yourself into an already over-saturated market. Furthermore, a "self-produced web series" means "friends-produced web series," AKA: crowd funding. Am I dating myself when I ask, "Remember when Jake Wilson had the audacity to produce *The Battery's Down* without a kickstarter?" Probably. Regardless, there would be nothing innovative about a web series based off your online persona, so I'm not even going to give you a choice of whether or not to do one.

Instead, I'm ordering you to stop being a selfish douche by sitting on your ass collecting book royalties, and maybe try giving a little back by finding a way to spin this crap into something that benefits Broadway Cares/Equity Fights AIDS. If anything remotely connected to Broadway has not found a way to become a BC/EFA event by its second year, it either doesn't exist or it's the Broadway Prom. You won't even need to write or do anything else, either! You could just turn your book into an audiobook, get a bunch of stars on it under the confirmation that all the royalties earned will be donated to charity, and then you could win a Grammy! While you're at it, why don't you also try adapting your book into a Feinstein's/54 Below concert, find a completely different group of Broadway performers who are willing to work for free, and give all that money to BC/EFA, too? It's amazing what you can accomplish when you stretch one joke out over the course of two years, huh?

All this sounds pretty easy in theory, but you'll have to get BC/EFA's consent, and then you'll have to find actors willing enough to put their name to your voice, while you stay anonymous. That's a lot to ask of your friends, let alone strangers. Moreover, it's at this moment when you realize how limited your connections truly are. How are you going to get big named stars you don't know to take valuable time out of their day for an anonymous person who has asked them to travel to a recording studio at Ripley-Grier (probably) for zero dollars to spend hours on end reading tedious run-on sentences, just because they're passionate about BC/EFA, whom you have yet to ask to endorse your book (btw, you just got confirmation that BC/EFA is in)? I don't even want to start talking about your concert idea. You have too many questionable ideas, and are in desperate need of an assistant, or intern, or something. You're really successful now and lol, jk, irl you're still a barely financially stable personal trainer with a fuck-ton of time on their hands after two p.m. True success is all about perception, and perception is just lying with style.

Finding a director and engineer for your audiobook is damn near impossible. Feeling defeated, you decide to distract yourself from IPP by writing an Onion-style article on your personal blog, satirizing the members at Fusion being inconvenienced by the smoke when a fire breaks out in the laundry room. Three people read it, one of which is your friend Diana who you did a national tour with, like, ten years ago. She texts you about the blog, and you jokingly ask her if she produces audiobooks. As luck would have it, her friend Anne does. She hooks you guys up, Anne agrees to direct and produce, as well as bring along her kick ass engineer, and boom, you have an audiobook in production faster than an accompanist at Nola can play your ballad like an uptempo. I guess activity does breed activity. Maybe there's something to all those motivational quotes you've been trying to block from your newsfeed.

All of these outside-social-media projects are exciting, but about as interesting to your online audience as extraneous exposition in an adventure story. You miss the spontaneous thrill of what social media can be. You've become nostalgic for the days of empowering the community through booze-fuelled rants about Equity accompanied with altered Mockingjay graphics. At its core, IPP is about spreading awareness, but you've drifted from that idea in favor of grand, public projects, leaving your Twitter feed to drown in the obscurity of live tweeting any and all live events—including sporting. WHAT. HAPPENED. TO. YOU. Hopefully you can get back to your roots soon.

***

Broadway loses beloved members of the community daily. Occasionally, someone is so beloved, the Broadway League decides to dim the lights in honor of them. It used to be a rare occasion, but lately, the dimming of Broadway has become more of a common affair. IT SHOULD BE. I'm a Millennial. I wish they dimmed the effing lights for everyone. I don't care if that means the lights never turn on. When I die, I don't just want the lights dimmed—I want them to demolish half the theatres. At some point in the life of a person who has worked on Broadway, they have changed the life of someone else for the better. The late Jan Oceans was one of those people (a ballsy comic and Tony nominated playwright who championed New York theatre on a national platform and actually *paid for tickets*) and the

Broadway League has decided not to bestow her with the greatest honor. YOU. ARE. PISSED.

There seems to be a mutual outcry on your Internet about the egregiously overlooked honoring of Jan Oceans. By the Broadway League's standards regarding this decision, Julie Andrews wouldn't receive this recognition either. This seems like a proper moment to take your passion for activism, and your opposition to the League, and do something about it.

You send a direct message to Ben, a Twitter friend of yours who doesn't know your identity but whom you've been swapping *Newsies* jokes with for going on a year, and you ask him if it's time to get online and change this Jan Oceans situation.

"I need to do a viral thing. Should we start that? Let's get yelly," you say.

"A viral campaign to get them to dim their lights?" Ben asks.

You respond with anything but confidence, "They'd never do it. And it's 4:00 p.m. Nobody follows me at 4:00 p.m."

There is a valid point you're making here about timing on Twitter. Some say early mornings and evening are the best times to post. Others stand by 5:05 p.m. being the ideal minute. Broadway Internet news sites always seem to throw out the craziest press between 2:00 p.m. and 4:00 p.m., which you've found is actually when you have the least amount of engaged followers. Weekends have proven to be a graveyard, and you've lost many a solid tweet on a Saturday or Sunday because apparently all of your followers have much more interesting social lives than you. However, you once had your most viral tweet happen on a weekend in the middle of the day, so what the fuck does anyone truly know about the nuances of social media? Just post what you want to post, when you want to post it, and stop thinking so hard, else you turn into me during my time in a BFA musical theatre conservatory program.

Ben responds with some words of encouragement, "I would help that out."

You ask, "What should the hashtag be?"

The two of you throw back and forth a few ideas. Jan Oceans first became known for quippy catchphrases like, "Can we have an extended conversation about that?" and more recently she was notable for red carpet coverage, where she originated the question, "Whose clothes are on you right now?" You could play homage to Jan by working either of those two lines into a hashtag like #CanWeHaveAnExtendedDim or #WhoseDimmingRightNow, but Ben suggests #Dim4Jan.

Which hashtag should you use? A longer one is bigger, and bigger is sometimes better – if you're a tourist who's only seeing one show. The shorter one could be easier to trend, but it came from Ben, and what does Ben know about social media activism? He has fewer than ten thousand followers, which means he doesn't have a "K" and if you don't have a "K" next to your follower count, then what are you even doing with your life? I mean it's not 2009! Do you go with...

A long hashtag…? (page 130)

A short hashtag…? (page 156)

*

You produce *Pieces of Me* using your own money, the New York Times pans it, and you lose everything—including your soul. I felt that to ease the pain, it was probably best if I delivered the news in the shortest way possible. Look on the bright side: You had a show at NYMF!

THE END.

*

Joe's Pub it is!

Just kidding, Joe's Pub is booked for the dates you want.

Do you…

Choose Feinstein's/54 Below…? (page 306)

Choose Birdland…? (page 462)

*

"Ugh," you sigh, "I have this thing later that I need to work on some stuff for. It's so stupid," you say, in an effort to sound ambiguous. The last thing you want to do is mention that you have an audition, because that would suggest you are never "offer only."

"No problem," smiles Ashton Reed, "maybe next time!"

The two of you amicably part ways on the street, and you're feeling comfortable with how that all went down, because you didn't have to literally go down. Sometimes networking is a layered and lengthy process. Your main objective in that situation was to plant yourself in Ashton Reed's head. Turning down their offer to further socialize will undoubtedly leave an impression. Like an eight bar audition cut, you want to always keep them wanting more.

With all of the endorphins from that net-workout running through your body, you skip up Eighth Avenue, filled with confidence that will surely accompany you through your audition. There's so much chemical electricity inside you right now, you won't even need to ask for positive vibes!

There are still a few hours to kill before your appointment, and since the sides were only one page, you were able to lock them down last night. So, I guess there's nothing left to do but enjoy the beautiful day—which we haven't had a lot of lately. In fact, it's been pretty basic-New-York-shit-weather the past few weeks, which means you're seriously lacking vitamin D. If you take the moment to soak up some rays, you'll not only feel better, your body will receive an increase in serotonin, making you even more likable than you are now—which will definitely show in the audition room.

So, where should you go? Bryant Park is closer, but it's smaller, and crowded with real life business people, making it somewhat awkward for you to mock their life choices by baring your body in front of them during a workweek. You could always race up to Sheep Meadow in Central Park. It's a little farther away, but bigger, and a more socially acceptable place to lie around naked in the middle of a Tuesday. Do you...

Go to Bryant Park...? (page 253)

Go to Sheep Meadow...? (page 286)

*

Nestled snuggly in the San Fernando Valley, Studio City sits just off the 101, next to Universal. It's right in the thick of it. You're surrounded by everything Hollywood. Pursuing an acting career while living in Studio City is pretty much the same as pursuing an acting career while living on Eighth Avenue and 46th Street—except you can hide from everyone in your car.

The neighborhood was originally called Laurelwood, but later earned its name after a studio lot—now known as CBS Studio Center—was established in the area in the 1920s. This is a good sign that you'll have a successful pilot season, for your main objective here is to land a show at CBS because they seem to be the only network that doesn't throw a freshman series under the bus before it can find an audience (this is probably due to the fact that CBS has consistently strong rating across all programs because 90% of their audience has grown so old, they died with the TV on, and nobody has yet to find their bodies.)

Living in Studio City will be very convenient when it comes to traveling to and from auditions. The only thing not convenient in your life right now is everything having to do with the owning and managing of a car. Having lived in New York City for so long, you've only ever had possession of an automobile when you were the head driver on tour, or during the occasional Zipcar trip to IKEA in New Jersey. You've never needed to deal with car payments or insurance before now. Being Manhattan-bound for such a large portion of your life has shielded you from this highly stressful adult experience, and now that you've gone through it, you're in constant fear that your car will break down before an audition, and you won't be able to blame the MTA for being late, because it was your fault that you ignored the oil warning light in the first place.

Traffic in LA is as horrible as you'd heard. Saying that it "sucks" is a trite understatement. Drivers have no problem throwing around large metal kill-buckets with the abrasive abandon of a NYC pedestrian, all in an effort to get someplace three minutes quicker, so they can walk slowly the moment they get out of the car. As annoying as it is, having to face death every time you commute somewhere is not really a new challenge for you. The LA traffic scene is only as dangerous as racing through cabs and tourists in Midtown while trying to compose a tweet.

By California standards, your place in Studio City is quaint, but in comparison to your New York apartment, it's an effing penthouse. It has a *washer and dryer*. It's so spacious that you rarely see your roommate Ally. She's hardly ever there anyway because she works most nights at Bar Marmont off of Sunset, leaving her cat to spend most nights on your face.

The first few weeks of January are pretty slow. There are no auditions, so you spend the time wondering if you'll ever work again, but then not giving a fuck because you're able to post an Instagram of yourself in the sun while Winter Storm Aphrodite debilitates the entire Eastern seaboard and shuts down the city for a week. You can't imagine that your friends are jealous of your scantily-clad Runyon Canyon selfies, because blizzards make for empty theaters, which mean greater opportunities to score *Hamilton* tickets.

As January comes to a close, you start to receive emails from your agent for a few pilot auditions. Having read for TV back in New York, you're fairly used to the quick turnaround between the scheduling of an appointment, and when it takes place. Typically, you don't have more than a day to prepare, but your quick memorization skills rarely ever fail you.

As things pick up in February, it becomes harder to juggle your calendar. You'll get an audition for a Wednesday that conflicts with two others, so your agent will try to move it, but they can't, because that pilot is testing on Thursday, so you scrap the other two and only go in for the one, which you end up bombing. In fact, it feels like you've bombed every audition so far because none of them have led to a screen test. Not even the one that you had today for *Exposition*, which I thought you excelled at, and I would know. There's not a moment to feel sorry about that failure, because by the time you arrive home, you have three more auditions booked for tomorrow.

After a week of this, your brain is fried, and you can't believe there's still a month left. The hectic schedule is making it impossible to have any sort of social life. You spend all day in your car, and every night with your nose in the sides you have for the next day, which will be spent entirely in your car. When you have a moment of free time, you're too exhausted to see any friends who might be in town doing a sit down at the Ahmanson or the Pantages, so you instead crash on the couch and binge-watch shows that feature actors who've managed to get out of the very position you're in now. You've only been in this town for like forty-five minutes and it has already made you jaded.

LA bitterness is different than New York bitterness. It's fueled by the same insecurities, but you're happier, younger, and prettier out here. You're not sure what causes this. It's either something in the Arrowhead Mountain Spring bottled water, or all of the kale, or maybe it's the joy of being able to drink iced soy lattes in February while wearing a scarf as an ironic fashion choice. Whatever it is, you have never looked so refreshed. It doesn't even bother you that anyone you encounter in LA has some sort of "what-can-I-get-from-you" tone coloring everything they say. None of that shit matters because you haven't had eye-bags since you landed. I'd say that having to deal with horrifyingly fake people in exchange for flawless skin is a pretty fair trade.

You ponder this thought every time you think that moving to LA was the wrong choice. You'd be pursuing the exact same goal had you stayed in New York, except without the magical benefits of vitamin D, and half of the opportunities. It's highly unlikely that you'd get six auditions in one day if you weren't in LA.

"Wait, what!?" you scream as you read the most recent email from your agent that says you have six auditions, for six different networks, in six separate locations, on the same day.

The most auditions you've had to prepare for at once are three. You're not entirely sure if you can handle learning six packets of sides in one evening, let alone be able to successfully navigate yourself between Santa Monica, Glendale, Sherman Oaks, the Valley, Burbank, and Universal City in any sort of reasonable time. Still, you're going to try, and you don't care if you have to stay up all night, you will develop a plan to make this day work, because there's a .01% chance that you'll land one of these pilots, it'll get picked up, run for ten seasons, and make you a bajillion dollars in syndication—which is a much greater possibility than earning any kind of consistent income on Broadway.

Tomorrow, you'll be auditioning for the following shows: *2 Friends & Their Job* (CBS), *Evener Stevens* (Disney), *My Eight-Year-Old Son* (Fox), *This Won't Get Picked Up* (ABC), *This Will Get Canceled* (NBC), and *That Show's Still On?* (CW).

When it comes to memorizing material, you've always relied on a method you developed when you first started out: reading it over and over again until you memorize it. This technique has seldom failed you, but you've never been presented with having to learn forty-five pages of dialogue in one night (not even for a Telsey audition). It's really a shame that soap operas died, because they would have been great training ground for this kind of bullshit.

There is an alternate approach to learning all of these lines, and it's an app that's fittingly called LineLearner. All you have to do is read the sides into the app, and it will play the scenes back to you until you've memorized your part, at which point you can recite your lines opposite yourself as the pre-recorded reader. It could be a more efficient way to get off-book, but you've never tried it before, and a high-stakes situation such as this might require you to stick with what works. Do you…

Try the LineLearner app…? (page 400)

Learn lines the old fashioned way…? (page 185)

*

After years performing in other writers' musicals, some good (*Into the Woods*, *Carousel*, *The Wedding Singer*) and some not so good (every 29 Hour Reading ever), you know you have the chops to write the next great American musical. You're ready to be the one calling the shots when it comes to who gets lines, and who sings what, and all the things that come with being in charge—like sitting behind the table at auditions and people bringing you coffee. It's going to be awesome.

OK, so now the only question is, what is your musical going to be about? Let's think about this for a minute…You could write something original, or you could adapt a book, adapt a movie, adapt a play, adapt a novella, adapt a life, adapt an Italian film, adapt an historical novel, adapt a painting on a wall, adapt a collection of cat poems, adapt a movie adaptation of an Hungarian play, adapt a nightmare you had one time at theatre camp, etc. UGH. Finding inspiration is hard.

Feeling crippled by writer's block, you make your way to the gym to clear your head in hopes of finding a bright idea while listening to motivational music on the elliptical. I think it was Sydney Lucas who once said, "Exercise gives you endorphins. Endorphins make you happy. Happy people just don't shoot their husbands." Not only is she right about that, happy people are also more likely to find inspiration to write than sad people, because how can sad people find time to write when they're busy being sad?

Hopping on a secluded elliptical, you set the resistance to a sensible "Kelli O'Hara," but make sure to browse through all of your social media accounts before beginning. Just as you're about to flip over to your music you get an alert that Keala Settle has retweeted you.

"KEALA SETTLE!" you laugh to yourself. "That crazy bitch!" You effing love Keala Settle.

As you reflect upon the sheer awesomeness of Keala Settle, you're reminded of how jazzed you are to see her in *Waitress* and that Sara Bareilles kicks ass. In fact, she's just the kind of artist you're looking for to inspire you during this light workout.

Switching on iTunes Radio, you open up the Sara Bareilles station and get that elliptical moving.

After pumping your fists to "Brave" and "Love Song," and quietly ugly crying through "Manhattan," "Gravity," and "Between the Lines," you've yet to come up with any ideas for a musical. Perhaps it's because you've skipped all of the other artists on the shuffle, and are possibly getting intimidated by Sara Bareilles' style, instead of inspired. I suggest not skipping the next song.

The next song is "Pieces of Me" by Ashlee Simpson. OK, maybe you can skip it.

No! You promised yourself you'd open up to other influences!

But really, why is Ashlee Simpson on Sara Bareilles radio? It must be a glitch, like when *The Lion King* is on the One Direction station—or so I've heard.

Better skip it.

Don't skip it!

To skip, or not to skip!

Do you…

Keep listening to Ashlee Simpson….? (page 201)

Skip Ashlee Simpson….? (page 131)

I think Cake's original lyrics were, "I want a girl with a short skirt, and a long hashtag," but they changed it to "jacket," because nobody wants a long hashtag. It makes you look like someone who doesn't understand Instagram. Anyway, since you've decided to go with the long hashtag, let's see how #CanWeHaveAnExtendedDim fares on the Twitter.com.

It bombs.

THE END.

Passing on Ashlee Simpson is no big loss to your workout because to you, her music is just… so yesterday. Unfortunately, that was the last skip you were allowed to use this hour, and you're going to be stuck listening to the next song no matter what it is.

The music begins to play. A familiar beat and synthesized whistle emanates through your earbuds, inviting an alluring hint of nostalgia into your soul. You know this song. You loved this song. During your formidable years, it was your everything…

Let's go back…
Back to the beginning…
Back to when the earth, the sun, the stars, all aligned.

The lark-like hopefulness of Hilary Duff's voice in "Come Clean" sounds all the more sweeter now than it did over a decade ago, when you first heard it ringing over the opening credits of MTV's *Laguna Beach*. Years have taken you far away from that simpler time, when the future was infinite, and Broadway was just an idea. Reality is much different now, and your perception of the career you once held high on a pedestal has changed.

'Cause perfect didn't feel so perfect.
Tryin' to fit a square into a circle was my life.
I… defy…

And as if you were defying gravity itself, you belt out at the top of your lungs, "LET THE RAIN FALL DOWN!" not giving a shit who hears you.

Overcome by an unexpected surge of endorphins, you pump the volume to max and let 2003 Hilary Duff GIVE IT TO YOU. It's invigorating. You're immediately thrown back to the time you first heard this song—before you moved to the city. Before you were tainted. When you were clean.

> *'Cause I wanna feel the thunder,*
> *I wanna scream.*
> *Let the rain fall down.*
> *I'm coming clean, I'm coming clean.*

It was a different era—an era without smartphones, social media, BuzzFeed, wireless printers, a conclusion to Harry Potter, or Sydney Lucas. If you had to pinpoint a single period in history that connects all Millennials, it would be Hilary Duff's "Come Clean." Those born in the 1980s blasted it in their cars while ditching last period to hit the beach, and the 1990s babies grew up on Lizzie McGuire. Before this song, there was nothing, but after it came the birth of *Wicked*, *Mean Girls*, *School of Rock*, and half the cast of Andrew Lloyd Weber's *School of Rock*. Hilary Duff's *Metamorphosis* album was the cultural shift that defined Millennials as they are today. It was quite literally the "metamorphosis" of a generation (and it even has "So Yesterday" on it!). Before there was Hillary Clinton, there was Hilary Duff.

You stop yourself cold on the elliptical. The thoughts permeating in your brain lead to what you believe is an exceptional idea for a show: a concept musical in the same vein as *American Idiot*, using only the songs from Hilary Duff's album "Metamorphosis," that celebrates, highlights, and pays tribute to the Millennial generation. *Metamorphosis: the Hilary Duff Musical* will be your ticket to stardom and acclaim—whether you win the big trophy, or not.

Writing a passable book shaped around pre-existing music shouldn't be too difficult—you've seen *An American in Paris*. Even talking Hilary Duff into allowing you to use her music won't be a problem because this idea is so solid. The real struggle here is going to be finding an actress capable enough to carry this important piece, while also being exactly like Annaleigh Ashford in 2007—because the best person for this job is Annaleigh Ashford from somewhere between when *Legally Blonde* opened on Broadway and when it aired on MTV. You'll settle for a Megan Hilty circa *Wicked*, but it wouldn't be ideal. Whatever. No use stressing about it now. You're confident Bernie will find you the right girl for this role that hasn't been written yet.

Trying not to get distracted and forget any of the brilliance you've discovered during your workout, you leap off the elliptical to head home and make magic with your Microsoft Word and Hilary Duff, making sure to download the entire *Metamorphosis* album on you're way out of the building.

"Oh, wait. I have it," you say to yourself as you open up your music and proceed to blast "So Yesterday" while strutting down the street and taking in the gorgeous New York sights, and even gorgeous-er Hilary Duff sounds. What a time to be alive and working in the American Theatre. Now, where should you go to write the next groundbreaking Broadway musical?

You've read a lot about where famous writers got their meager starts creating what are now classic works. J.K. Rowling wrote the names of the Hogwarts Houses on the back of an airplane sick bag, Aaron Sorkin wrote parts of *A Few Good Men* on cocktail napkins when he was working as a bartender at *La Cage aux Folles*, and Lin-Manuel Miranda wrote *Hamilton* on Twitter. There is no right or wrong place to give birth to your own creativity. It only matters that it happens.

The one thing that all the writers whom you've studied have in common, is they don't bring their work home with them. Since you're still a few more years of student loans away from affording your own office space, the next best place to work is at a random Starbucks. But which one? You'll want to avoid the World Wide Plaza locations altogether, because nothing good can come from going there.

Midtown Starbucks' in general are probably a bad idea because you'll risk getting distracted. That leaves either the Starbucks in Columbus Circle or the Starbucks by Lincoln Center. They're both pretty spacious, accessible, and safe—except for that time you saw a guy lying on his back by the barista table, flapping his arms like wings while completely naked at the Starbucks across the street from Lincoln Center, and you were *not* amused. *Kelli O'Hara* could have seen that.

While both of these choices are equal, they will directly affect your creative process. What if that crazy naked guy returns to the Starbucks by Lincoln Center and disrupts your productivity? What if someone at the Columbus Circle location drops their Venti White Mocha all over your computer before you back it up? *What. If.* It's the little decisions that make the most impact on your life, so you better pick the right one. Do you…

Go to the Starbucks by Columbus Circle…? (page 284)

Go to the Starbucks by Lincoln Center…? (page 196)

*

Pixar should have named that movie after you, because you are the definition of "brave." Taking a deep breath, you walk into MFF and navigate your way to your class through the unicorns and rain-bois, while managing not to turn into a Lisa Frank trapper keeper along the way.

The fitness phenomenon known as "Snatched in Six Weeks" (where you get snatched in forty-two days) allows ninjas to occasionally switch out of their primary group, and THANK GOD, because today *the* Ashton Reed is taking your class.

Ashton Reed is a director/choreographer who has Tonys, talent, and only works on shows that run. The name "Ashton" has always seemed cool to you, and not because "Kutcher," but because of your kickass cousin named Ashton, who introduced you to the PBS presentation of *Into the Woods*, and is so badass, she once video bootlegged the entire *Titanic: A New Musical* tour before iPhones, without anyone catching her (there's a chance Ashton isn't badass).

You've wanted to get in with the Ashton Reed team for a while now, but have yet to crack through their walls. They have a pretty strong barricade surrounding the core group of people that they work with—and I'm talking *Les Misérables* revival kind of a barricade. It's bigger, and it ain't rotating around for you. You aren't going to break through an Ashton Reed wall unless you do something special—and today might be the day to do that.

Class is moments away from beginning, and you're about to panic because you haven't figured out a casual-but-clever conversation starter to throw at Ashton Reed without talking about the business. What would that be? *The Walking Dead? Scandal? Sports?* There isn't

135

enough time to google-stalk their interests. You've got to find a way to grab Ashton Reed's attention fast.

As the room settles into their spots, you spy a few empty spaces around Ashton Reed, and there's just enough time to fill one of them. If you're quick, you can slide in next to Ashton Reed and make fun conversation throughout the workout. However, you have your shorty-shorts on right now, and you're looking tight, so it might behoove you to snag the open space in front of Ashton Reed. It's a convenient area for you to expertly execute your kettlebell swings. If you're lucky, maybe the view might pay off after class. Do you...

Stand in front of Ashton Reed...? (page 278)

Stand next to Ashton Reed...? (page 101)

Writing *Pieces of Me* alone is going to be an extremely personal experience that will require you to spend hours mining the rich, emotional caverns of your soul for inspiration that will help you find a way back to what it was like when you were first starting out – oh, wait, you can just search through your Facebook timeline for fodder. It shouldn't be long before you have enough material to adapt it all into a musical about pursuing a career in a modern day Broadway world.

After a few minutes of scrolling through your early years, you come across the somewhat grim period in your life when you were (GASP!) unemployed. This wasn't the kind of unemployment where you were on Unemployment Insurance, and thus, privy to the privileges of Funemployment. No—these were dark times, Harry, times when you had to work a Real Life restaurant job.

While you'd blocked out this truly horrific experience long ago, social media has managed to make it all come flooding back again. It's painful to remember that there was a time in your life when finding a job took a little bit longer than was desirable. Having had success straight out of college, you expected it to continue seamlessly, and when it didn't, you considered leaving the business. It was a raw and vulnerable moment that you don't like to discuss openly, but luckily, you immortalized it in this Facebook status:

> I had an audition last month. Every actor has had this audition. The one where you know the planets are finally going to align and everything is going to work out again. It is not a matter of arrogance, but a quiet confidence that assures you that it is time.
>
> Then there is the waiting. The constant eyeing of the telephone. The anticipation of the ringing of that

special music you have specifically assigned for your agent. A few days pass, and you start making excuses as to why they have not called. "It was a weekend." "The casting office was out of town with another project." "They had to take some time deliberating." Then there is that final day of desperation where the negativity sets in, and you try so hard to fight it. For me, that day was a Wednesday.

Oddly enough, I was unusually happy that morning, despite my ongoing battle with my hushed iPhone. I was scheduled to work lunch—matinée day—in the middle of December. Holiday season in the theatre district. I was in for a day of screaming children in matching red or green dresses, and spilled Shirley Temples.

New York was feigning winter—the kind of weather where it is not necessarily freezing, but the thick fog has set in, and light drizzle seems to impede your vision as you walk. I caught a Manhattan-bound N train, where I boarded the last car.

Instead of sitting down immediately, or even noticing that a fellow waiter I worked with was trying to get my attention, I traveled to the front where I squeezed in between two commuters.

I have spent hours on a subway train and seldom do I ever "see." New Yorkers are always so consumed by books, iPhones, magazines, that we never look around and actually SEE. For whatever reason, that day was different, and while I was well beyond obsession concerning my audition, I decided to turn my music off and look at the people around me.

To my right was a girl about my age. She wore a tan overcoat that hid a blue dress. Her makeup was done acutely, and in her free hand she held a few pieces of paper stapled together. At the top, in severe handwriting, read "Girl #3." She was meticulously poring over the paper (as so many of us have often done) readying herself for an impending audition for a throw away role—another hopeful in the midst of a hundred, vying for the same nameless and forgettable part.

While she was so precisely put together, her face was tired and weathered. Clearly she had been doing this for a while, and the process had become daunting. I wanted so badly to say something to her. Sometimes the mutual understanding of a complete stranger can help more than the forced encouragement of a friend or colleague.

The train dipped under the East River and pulled into 59th and Lexington Avenue, where someone vacated a seat and my fellow hopeful sat down. She put her audition sides away and opened up a day planner. She anxiously looked down at the box marked "December 9th," and read the address she had scribbled in, then sharply placed the book back in her bag. I work an avenue over from the Telsey office, and I just knew she would be getting off at my stop.

The double doors opened at 42nd Street and she very bluntly stood up, uttered, "excuse me" and rushed out of the train. I calmly followed, and vowed to myself that if we were to find ourselves together on the stairs, I would speak to her.

Fate would place us on the steps next to each other, so I turned to her (as if we were already friends) and told her, "Good luck."

The girl looked at me with complete surprise, and let out what sounded like a stress relieved laugh as she responded, "Thank you!"

"I saw you reading sides on the train."

"Oh, yes! I'm SO nervous!" she exhaled.

"Don't be," I assured.

"So, you're an actor too?"

"Yeah. I was watching you on the train and was thinking... I just... I just really want you to get it... I want ONE of us to get it."

She turned to me with what felt like immediate understanding, and said, "I was thinking the same thing. Why can't one of us little guys that takes the train in everyday get a chance."

For whatever reason, her weathered disposition seemed to lift, and all of a sudden she was glowing.

We shared a few more words before parting at the top of the stairs, where the clock outside read 9:43 a.m.

"What time is your audition?" I asked.

"10:00 a.m."

I told her that she'd better go, and then quickly blurted out, "Kick ass."

She thanked me, and we went our separate ways.

I never got the call for which I had been so hopefully, and foolishly awaiting. That night, sadly, by way of a Facebook status, I learned that the role had gone to someone else.

For whatever reason, that moment on the train marks as one of my more selfless, yet selfish encounters in recent memory. I genuinely wanted her to get that job, but I was also desperately looking for some reciprocated assurance.

It has been a common theory that an actor will book, on average, one job per every one hundred auditions. While I was blessed for my first big job to be right out of college, it was one of my first auditions in New York. I feel like I owe the universe one hundred to pay back that experience, and now an additional hundred before the next one.

Writing this has been hard because I do not want to come off as ungrateful for what I have been given. While it feels like it's been years since I've performed, I've still had many fantastic (albeit small) accomplishments. Still, this time in between -- the two hundred auditions -- has been a rough journey. It has been both a physical and emotional struggle with confidence, image, and work ethic. I think what made that specific audition particularly difficult for me was that I very sincerely felt that it had been my two-hundredth one. It was my turn. I had put in my dues, and everything was going to come together again. I wanted it.

Looking back, maybe I have not given the discipline required to be as successful as many of my peers. The problem is, I feel like I have dug so deep with only moderately trying, that I am not sure I can pull myself out.

Wow… Would you like some My Chemical Romance to go with that Facebook status? Thank God you booked a job shortly after you posted that, because whoa. Did it even get any likes?

Moreover, in the amount of time it took for me to read that, you managed to finish adapting your entire musical from the pain in that Facebook status. *Pieces of Me* is ready to take the next step.

There are many different roads you can take to getting your show produced, but deep down, you know the subject matter is not meant for grand commercial consumption. *Pieces of Me* is a niche little jewel that would, at most, fare nicely in an intimate Off-Broadway house—before gaining an unexpected following that would undoubtedly possess some brave producer to transfer it to Broadway.

It's an oddly personal piece you've written (somewhat different than you originally imagined on the elliptical), and you're feeling a little reserved about sending your baby out into the world. Perhaps the purpose of this entire process was for you to find some way to release the pain of your past. Or, maybe you're supposed to get *Pieces of Me* out there, so it can heal someone else. Do you…

Keep Pieces of Me to yourself…? (page 239)

Give Pieces of Me to the world…? (page 31)

*

Hopping on the 101 again, you drive to the 170 and then merge onto the 5 North where you notice that a herd of alpacas are blocking traffic on the southbound side. Weird. Good thing you didn't take the 405 around the other direction, because you'd be in gridlock traffic right now.

Ecstatic that you made the right decision when it came to navigating in a town that you still know little about, you proudly march into your audition for *Evener Stevens* and nail it.

Once you're back in your car, you check Twitter to see if that random group of alpacas on the 5 has been detained. Upon reading that they are still on the loose, you decide to take surface streets until you reach the 170, which leads you down to Universal City where you do an admirable job auditioning for *This Will Get Canceled*.

As you start the car to head to the last audition of the day, you notice that your gas tank is dangerously close to being empty, so you take a quick detour to fill it up, after which, you embark on the short trip to Burbank by taking Lankershim to Cahuenga to Magnolia.

Strolling into your last audition, you couldn't feel more proud of yourself for making it through the day. No matter what the outcome is, you made it to six different locations in a strange town without getting lost, or even being late once.

"Oh," frowns the casting assistant who greets you, "didn't your agent tell you?"

"Tell me what?" you ask.

"That audition was moved to the primary casting office below Wilshire," she explains. "This is the studio office."

"So, what are you saying? I have to go downtown? I'll never make it!"

"Well," she says, looking at her watch, "I'll take your name and give them a call. It's only forty minutes away. You could get there before they're finished!"

Frustrated as fuck, you begrudgingly thank the lady and race out of the building and into your car where you turn south on Olive, right on Cahuenga, right on 101 South, and into West Hollywood, where you turn on a couple other streets you remember from the score of *Sunset Boulevard*.

Magically, you succeed in arriving at your final audition for the second time. With all the stress of the last hour (combined with the events of the entire day) you enter the room disheveled and disoriented, hoping that this is the kind of tone they are going for at *My Eight-Year-Old Son*.

Unable to get a read on your audition, the only thing you can do is congratulate yourself for doing your best. If these LA phonies don't get you, it's their own problem. Who do they think they are, anyway? What kinds of monsters move an audition across town at the last minute? Are they really the type of people you want to work with? All of these questions permeate your brain as you drive home in bumper-to-bumper traffic, wondering if maybe LA is not the place for you, and if you should just call it quits and move back home to –

Your phone rings.

"Hello?" you answer through the Bluetooth hands free car thing that you had installed.

"So, *My Eight-Year-Old Son*, huh?" It's your agent. "Kinda crazy!"

"Yeah, thanks for letting me know they moved the audition."

"Don't know what you're talking about," he says smugly. "I just got off the phone with them. They want you to test."

This news comes as such a shock; you'd probably slam on your breaks if your car weren't already standing still.

"What does this mean?!"

"It means," he explains, "that we gotta talk contract. Salary. Billing. The whole nine yards."

"But I didn't book it yet."

Your agent laughs. "Some of you New Yorkers can be so green."

He goes on to clarify that before you can test, your entire contract for the series has to be agreed upon. This is serious shit. You could be at upfronts in a matter of months. But, don't get ahead of yourself. You still have to test, get cast, shoot the pilot, and then have the pilot get picked up. If this were a Broadway musical, you're still in the workshop phase.

"Wow," you exclaim. "I don't believe it."

"Believe it," says your agent. "There must have been something you brought to the room today for them to want to jump on you so fast."

"You mean unparalleled frenetic stress and anxiety?"

"Yeah, that," he says. "Bring that again."

As your agent works out your deal over the next day, you try to get back in touch with the traumatic emotions that made you a sought-after candidate for *My Eight-Year-Old Son*. To source those feelings, you attempt to remember what it was like to attend a chorus call in the dead of winter while still non-Equity. A day of reliving those types of harrowing moments in your life leads you to have a fever dream about quick changes the night before your screen test. As you awake in a cold sweat the morning of your big day, you're confident that you've succeeded in harnessing the proper amount of anxiety needed to land this pilot.

To add fuel to your already heightened nerve-fire, you make sure to choose a route to the audition that will produce the most amount of stress possible. While sitting in gridlock, biting your nails off, and wondering if you're not quite as frenzied as you were at your audition, you pull out your phone and open Twitter to see what your successful friends are up to.

As you scroll through the feed, you notice a tweet from Deadline about *My Eight-Year-Old Son*. Upon clicking it, you read that the role you're currently en route to test for has been cast. Apparently, another actor was "tapped" for the part for which you should have been the receiver of said "tapping." This is –

"Bullshit!" you scream on the phone to your agent. "Did you know about this?"

"No!" he assures. "You just told me!"

"So, what do I do?" you ask. "Do I turn around and not go to this test?"

"Yeah," he sighs, "I guess if it's cast now, you don't have to go."

While driving home, completely disillusioned with LA, you meet your friend Karen for lunch at an outdoor café. As you vent to her about the unfortunate series events from the past few days, she tries to put life into perspective...

"It's February," she says.

"I know, pilot season isn't over," you say. "There's still time."

"No," Karen shakes her head, "it's February, and we are eating outside."

She's right. You haven't fully appreciated this until now. No matter how dire things get out here, you're still provided the gift of being allowed to eat lunch outside whenever you want. In fact, you haven't taken the time to notice that even during your worst moments in LA, you've consistently found solace in dining al fresco. It's a privilege that you must always respect.

As you finish the last bite of your dry endive with cracked pepper salad, lit warmly by the perpetually-June-like sunlight, you come to terms with this being the best it may ever get for you in LA—and you're OK with that. There will never be a reality in New York quite like the one you're living right now. You remember this as the days roll by with you doing nothing but eating lunch outside.

When pilot season ends, you have zero to show for it but a stack of receipts in your sock drawer that you've saved to write-off as business meals during next year's tax season. There might not be anything to add to your resume as you journey into the spring, but you don't give a shit. Who wants to be stuck inside a stuffy studio during the magnificent month of March, when they could be enjoying a cheese plate and glass of wine under the glorious California sun?

So, yeah… Your LA existence from here on out pretty much consists of you eating lunch outside and occasionally going to auditions.

THE END.

*

Established in 2004, NYMF has presented over three hundred musicals, and three of them have gone on to Broadway! Notable shows from previous festivals include: *Kardashians in Space, Sanders! [Barry or Colonel?], Baby Hitler Unplugged, Arbor Day, Yay Hamlet, Mandatory Audience Participation: the musical, Jim Carnahan Made Eye Contact with Me and Other Scary Stories You Tell in the Dark, Literally Can't Even, Steve Jobs: the iMusical, The Mummy Returns: And He Can Dance, War and Pain, The Unauthorized Hocus Pocus Musical, Angsty Bangs, The Pumpkin Spice Dilemma, Alice in One Direction Land, Homosexual!, Jesus Was Real and Here's the Musical to Prove It, Let's Try Vampires Again, #Hashtag, The Ballad of Stephanie Tanner, My Grandparents Funded This, Emojiscal,* and *Next to Normal.*

Ecstatic to join the ranks of this prestigious group, you open up the NYMF website to see how to submit, and discover that the final deadline is today, leaving no time to beg your friends to read over *Pieces of Me* to make sure it doesn't suck. In an effort to stay positive, you take it as a good sign that you managed to finish a draft of your debut musical just in time to blindly place it in front of a panel of strangers who will judge whether or not it has what it takes to become the next *Lesbian Zombies.*

After completing the application process, you proudly click "submit" and submit yourself to great reward or greater ridicule—because if this hauntingly truthful retrospective of your rise from the gutter of unemployment doesn't get accepted by NYMF, then the Universe is basically saying that your struggle is worth less than a disco musical about Frankenstein. Surely *Pieces of Me* will make the cut.

It does.

Congratulations! You're going to have a production of your musical presented in New York City, fully produced by you!

"Wait, what?" you gasp, as you read the Producing at NYMF information on the website that you neglected to look over when you submitted your show. Apparently, the expense of putting up *Pieces of Me* will have to rest entirely on your shoulders.

Holy crowdfunding problems, you're going to go bankrupt this summer. The participation fee alone is $6,000. Expenses will also include: a production fee to cover the package of resources NYMF provides ($600 - $900 per performance), actors/stage managers (Equity performers receive a minimum stipend of $1020), director, designers, musical director, musicians, board operators, run crew, casting director, general manager, rehearsal space, set materials, construction costs, costumes, your first born, etc. When all's said and done, *Pieces of Me* will end up costing anywhere between $25,000 and $75,000 to produce at NYMF.

A financial situation as dire as this can only be solved in one of two ways: old school funding, or new school funding. New school funding is done online through websites such as Kickstarter, GoFundMe, or Panhandler.com. Old school funding is this thing where you ask your parents. Each method comes with its own pros and cons, and neither are going to help boost your ego—but once the process of jonesing up your friends, loved ones, and complete strangers is over, they'll all be thrilled you did it in exchange for what is bound to be a truly memorable theatrical experience.

So, which do you choose? New school funding is going to be a slog, and you may lose friends over it, but old school funding is only going to further lead your parents to believing you never call unless you need dollars.

Do you...

Produce with new school funding...? (page 245)

Produce with old school funding...? (page 79)

*

Van Nuys is also known as The Butthole of the Valley. Bordered on the north by North Hills and on the south by Sherman Oaks, Van Nuys sits smack in the middle of the San Fernando Valley, where it's ten degrees hotter than anywhere else. While the location may make you feel boxed in and slightly suffocated, at least there are beautiful views of the Santa Monica Mountains from your apartment, and you're within walking distance of a charming strip mall that features three different pawnshops.

The complex you live in is straight out of *Melrose Place*. There's a courtyard in the center with a pool, and that's about the only thing it has in common with *Melrose Place*. All in all, Van Nuys is less than desirable, but at the moment you're just too excited that you're in LA to notice that you live in a shit hole.

Remember how the first time you visited New York, you thought everything was magical, and looked like it was out of *You've Got Mail*? Even the guy taking a dump on the train platform at 34th Street? This is just like that. You're temporarily too blinded by the glare of potential stardom to see that things might not actually be that great. Getting back this refreshing vintage idealism is exactly why you moved to LA. Everything around you is thrilling, and filled with possibility. Your positivity is so great, there is absolutely nothing in the world that could possibly diminish it.

Five hours of sitting in LA traffic later, you want to kill yourself.

Commuting from Van Nuys is proving to be a real problem, and you haven't even hit the busy audition season yet. Between the heat, and the stress of sweating in your car all day, the only way that you can calm down is by getting mind-numbingly stoned in the middle of the afternoon at your pool, where you and your new pal

151

Easton make funny vines in an attempt to get invited to SXSW in Austin.

Since arriving in California, you've managed to stave off the temptation to sample any of the famous local cuisine you've heard so much about, because you're trying to stay LA tight. However, after a few weeks of satisfying your munchies with organic green shit, you feel that maybe there's no harm in giving yourself one cheat meal. What harm could that do?

There's really no choice of where to go when it comes to "unique-to-the-West-Coast-fast-food-that-people-won't-shut-up-about," and that place is In-N-Out Burger. There hasn't been an actor alive who moved from New York to California, and didn't think they stumbled across the Holy Grail of Hamburgers when they first dined at an In-N-Out. Furthermore, once they discover this heavenly franchise, they never cease to incessantly remind everyone that it is better than Shake Shack. Well, who do they think they are? Nothing is better than Shake Shack. Shake Shack is the shit! I challenge anyone in the world to prove how In-N-Out Burger could possibly be better than—

"Fuuuuck Shake Shack," you say after biting into a classic Double-Double at the In-N-Out just off of Ventura Boulevard in Sherman Oaks.

There has never been a burger in your entire life to ever take you to church in the way that this fresh Double-Double is doing right now. Words do it no justice. The perfectly toasted buns…the lightly salted beef patties…the more-than-special special sauce…you finally understand the hype. In-N-Out Burger is like *Hamilton*; it's impossible to describe it to someone who hasn't been.

Moments ago, you were floundering in a city that was bringing you no joy. Now, as you wipe the immaculate remnants of 100% beef (that was never packaged or frozen) off of your face, you find that you have been saved. You're home.

This new obsession causes you to google-learn everything you can about the fast-food chain that has changed your life. When you stumble across a BuzzFeed about secret items on the menu, all bets are off. There are only a small amount of "official" In-N-Out items, and you've already sampled all of them twice in the last three days. This unknown "special" menu is blowing your mind. With the option to Animal Style anything (where they cook a patty in mustard and add grilled onions and extra spread), the decadent dining options are endless. What's even crazier is that throughout your THC-induced discovery of the In-N-Out menu, you never seem to gain any weight. The place is that fucking magical.

As you sit down to indulge in your usual Tuesday delight (a 3x2 That You Designed Yourself: three patties, two slices of cheese, mustard instead of spread, grilled onions, pickles, and chopped chili peppers) you're surprised to discover that you forgot to smoke weed today. This might be the first time in weeks that you're not stoned at In-N-Out. Thinking it might be funny to make some sort of tweet out of the situation, you pull out your phone and HOLY FUCK HOW IS IT APRIL.

Where did the last two and a half months go?! Last thing you remember, you were sitting down to try In-N-Out, and now you've come to learn that you let the entire pilot season pass by while in a stage four hemp-haze—and all you have to show for it is a handful of moderately funny vines. While this is not what you set out to do when you originally embarked on your journey west to become an Emmy Award winning television star, you were able to forge an unbreakable bond with the world's greatest hamburger franchise, and for that alone, I'd say you won.

THE END.

*

"I love your shit!" cheers Corey over text. "Of course I'll read your script!"

With great expediency and enthusiasm, you send a PDF of *Metamorphosis: the Hilary Duff Musical* to Corey, and eagerly await his response.

A day passes.

Two.

Three.

"Hey, you get a chance to read yet?" you inquire in an email to Corey.

Another day passes.

Two.

Three.

You'd assume Corey was dead, but he's been active on Twitter, and you're pretty sure you can't tweet without a pulse (however much it seems some still do.)

After another brief bout of silence, Corey explains that something crazy came up at his show and it set him back a bit, but he hopes to get to it soon.

OK, then. Onto the backups. Do you…

Send your script to Paige…? (page 255)

Send your script to David…? (page 181)

*

You fire off another direct message to Ben: "#Dim4Jan is short. I don't think people will get 'Can we have an extended conversation?' as a reference, so maybe not #CanWeHaveAnExtendedDim."

Ben responds, "I like that, but I agree that not enough people will get it."

"Let's do #Dim4Joan."

"Jan."

You curse your autocorrect. "#Dim4JAN."

Armed with a hashtag, you take to Twitter and post, "If you think @TheBroadwayLeague should reconsider their decision not to dim the lights for Jan Oceans, tweet to them with #Dim4Jan."

It takes about an hour for people to start catching on. You engage a few followers right away, but if you want this to be viral, you're going to have to work at it. It's not easy. Trending shit isn't just like switching on the kitchen light, or getting into a Casey Nicholaw show when you're in his phone. This inconvenient truth is what drives you to continue pushing for your viral moment, I mean, justice for Jan. You tweet facts about her that validate why she should be honored. You retweet anyone who engages. You are *living* for this hashtag.

By 6:00 p.m., BuzzFeed has picked it up, which was damn decent of them to take a brief break from Disney Princesses as *Fun Home* replacements to support your cause. By 7:00 p.m., the hashtag has found its way to Broadway celebrities, who, for whatever reason, still don't follow you. By 8:55 p.m., "#Dim4Jan" is trending nationally just below "Dancing with the Stars," and at 9:00 p.m., Jujamcyn announces that they will dim the lights of their theaters in honor of Jan Oceans because Jordan Roth is a badass, and I feel the need to stress the

156

truth of this fact because I mean it, and not because I'm trying to get him to produce something for me.

By morning, all the theatres have agreed to dim their lights, and that convinces the Broadway league to reverse their decision. I'm kind of shocked you pulled this off, tbh. I've been holding your hand through this bizarre career transition of yours, and with all the erratic behavior and questionable life choices, it's a wonder you can still get out of bed in the morning, let alone trend a hashtag. I wouldn't get too big of a head, though. Jan Oceans was the shit, and this would have happened no matter what. You just got to the hashtag first. That doesn't mean you can't incessantly remind your friends that you had something to do with all of this.

Speaking of your friends: For the most part, you've been able to guard your identity fairly well; most of your close friends know what you do on the side, but unfortunately, none of your IPP achievements can be shared on social media, and if an accomplishment isn't noted on social media, did it even happen? Yes. You've learned that being forced to keep the shit that you're proud of to yourself does not negate its existence. Instead of blasting your successes online, whenever something cool happens to you, you out yourself to a single person. This simple act of bestowing the gift of your identity has brought you such joy over the years. Since you and Ben shared the #Dim4Jan campaign together, you're more than certain that this is the moment to "reveal" yourself to him, so you email over your ironclad nondisclosure agreement, he signs it, and you quickly respond from your personal account.

After a yearlong DM friendship, you can't wait to hear Ben's reaction. It's going to blow his mind! You open his response and it's more like, "Meh." Hey, everyone's a critic. You're still friends. Back to the audiobook—you need to find a cast.

In perhaps the most Fansie-esque moment of your life, you decide the best way to get "above the title" stars for your audiobook is by stage-dooring all of Broadway. Armed with a backpack crammed with packages containing a copy of your book and a cover letter that ever so politely begs the actor to do your project, you bravely and voluntarily venture through the theatre district, posing as a random messenger from BC/EFA.

You'd be surprised how easy it is to get into any building in this city with a backpack, coffee cup, and confidence. If you want a free membership to Fusion, just walk by the front desk with a backpack, a coffee cup, and a confident wave. People will just think you're a new trainer. If you want to get backstage at a Broadway theatre, nine times out of ten, you can pretty much just open the stage door and breeze by with a backpack, a coffee cup, and a confident indifference. People will just think you're a swing. I have a friend who has been in *Chicago* for six years because he wandered through the stage door of the Ambassador thinking it was Ruby Foo's.

The stage door stunt helps you lock down a star name and, after that, the rest of the cast is assembled by either direct messaging followers, or pestering friends. I'm making it sound like the entire process of putting together this audiobook was fairly seamless, but hahahahahah, no. The only thing seamless about this situation was the Seamless you stuffed your face with after a recording session. For someone who gets paid to construct and juggle multiple clients' life plans, you're kind of shitty with your own. To begin, you've decided to go into production without a finalized cast, choosing instead to just record people as you get them. This means that you have no idea what the final product will look like until it is finished. Furthermore, finding a way to synch the schedules of an actor, director, engineer, and studio with that of your own finally gives you respect for casting directors everywhere. #ThankYouTelsey. Needless to say, it's truly a wonder you ever found it to the Equity building after you fell out of the bus at Port Authority that clearly originated in Allentown, you naïve fuck (jk, you know I love you almost as much as I love me.)

You decide to "drop" the audiobook shortly after your Feinstein's/54 Below concert (which somehow comes together, and nobody even notices you sitting in the audience—because, for once, people were drunker than you). You're feeling pretty great about things right now. The concert was a blast, and you're really proud of this audiobook. Even I must admit that your writing sounds actually intelligible when it's being read by a Tony Award winner. Furthermore, you've somehow got an intern now (@Gratefulterns) whose sole function is to deal with your crazy. You're a big deal in your mind's eye. All of this excitement brings you yet again face to face with that relentless urge to tell someone your identity.

There's a part of you that feels like stepping out from behind the computer and being in the open with all of these public projects will naturally lead to someone exposing you. Apparently nobody really gives a shit. Even with your very public appearance at the concert, and the fairly blatant Easter egg hidden within your audiobook, no one seems to pick up on who you are. It's almost as if you were hiding in plain sight, begging for someone to notice, and everyone else was like, "you are not the most important thing in my life." It's weird to think that 100% of your followers aren't paying attention to 100% of what you are doing, 100% of the time. Isn't that the entire point of anyone's existence on social media?

Still, the fear that you would be found out while you were developing these public projects prompted you to create a contingency plan. On the off chance everything unraveled, you wrote an essay on the entire IPP process up to this point, and it's just sitting on your desktop with about sixty PDFs and memes. You look it over, and wonder if now might be the opportunity to put it out in the world. What else have you to lose? You've stretched this one bit from a string of tweets, to something, well, a lot more over-bloated than a string of tweets. Are your 140 characters of fame up? You're completely out of ideas, and the last thing you want to do is turn into that TV show that went on one season too long—like pretty much every TV show in the Nineties except for *Full House*, which has yet to explain why the fuck that horse plotline was a suitable series finale.

So, do you want to go out on top, or fizzle for another year and have to write yourself out of a bunch of bad decisions and pretend they never happened, like *X-Men 3* or the last season of *Roseanne*? (Since your age isn't listed on your IMDB, you might be too young for these references, but I'm pretty sure the same shit happened on iCarly.) Do you...

Go out on top, and reveal....? (page 192)

Stick it out another season...? (page 194)

Having grown up on social media, you're hip to the nuances that make it tick. Even though you've never used Twitter to market a concert, you recently learned a technique from *Wicked* that you're positive will work because *Wicked* has five trillion dollars, so they must be doing something right.

A few weeks ago, you received a unique tweet from *Wicked* telling you that they loved your feed, and to DM them for details about a cool new announcement. During your correspondence, they mentioned that they would be unveiling an exciting video the following Monday morning, and after BuzzFeed's exclusive of the story ended in the afternoon, they wanted you to share the link.

Receiving a personal tweet from *Wicked* made you feel very special, and when Monday rolled around, you were more than happy to fulfill their request to post that video of Aaron Tveit and Rachel Tucker doing a cover of "Defying Gravity." If *Wicked*'s method of getting the word out worked, there's no way you can fail when you try it yourself.

Positive that this is the right marketing strategy for your show, you take to Twitter to tweet a small handful of people:

@LauraBenanti Love your feed! I think you'd love my show! You should come!
@chelseanachman Love your feed! I think you'd love my show! You should come!
@QueenLesli Love your feed! I think you'd love my show! You should come!
@tellyleung Love your feed! I think you'd love my show! You should come!
@StephanieJBlock Love your feed! I think you'd love my show! You should come!

@meganhilty Love your feed! I think you'd love my show! You should come!

@BrianGGallagher Love your feed! I think you'd love my show! You should come!

@Jordan_Roth Love your feed! I think you'd love my show! You should come!

@jdawgnyc Love your feed! I think you'd love my show! You should come!

@michaelcassara Love your feed! I think you'd love my show! You should come!

@jemma22 Love your feed! I think you'd love my show! You should come!

@PattiMurin Love your feed! I think you'd love my show! You should come!

@clseeyedleap Love your feed! I think you'd love my show! You should come!

@TheNickAdams Love your feed! I think you'd love my show! You should come!

@ellynmarsh Love your feed! I think you'd love my show! You should come!

@jenndamiano Love your feed! I think you'd love my show! You should come!

@morganajames Love your feed! I think you'd love my show! You should come!

@Jen_Cody Love your feed! I think you'd love my show! You should come!

@celiakb Love your feed! I think you'd love my show! You should come!

@JeremyMJordan Love your feed! I think you'd love my show! You should come!

@kyledeanmassey Love your feed! I think you'd love my show! You should come!

@lesliekritzer Love your feed! I think you'd love my show! You should come!

@Hunter_Foster Love your feed! I think you'd love my show! You should come!

@huntbell Love your feed! I think you'd love my show! You should come!

@KeenanBlogger Love your feed! I think you'd love my show! You should come!

@PaulWontorek Love your feed! I think you'd love my show! You should come!

@thewillswenson Love your feed! I think you'd love my show! You should come!

@EdenEspinosa Love your feed! I think you'd love my show! You should come!

@sfosternyc Love your feed! I think you'd love my show! You should come!

@theebillyporter Love your feed! I think you'd love my show! You should come!

@KacieAnne Love your feed! I think you'd love my show! You should come!

@JohnGallagherJr Love your feed! I think you'd love my show! You should come!

@fdilella Love your feed! I think you'd love my show! You should come!

@pasekandpaul Love your feed! I think you'd love my show! You should come!

@TitussBurgess Love your feed! I think you'd love my show! You should come!

@leslieodomjr Love your feed! I think you'd love my show! You should come!

@AudraEqualityMc Love your feed! I think you'd love my show! You should come!

@KRYSTAR0DRIGUEZ Love your feed! I think you'd love my show! You should come!

@DanaDelany Love your feed! I think you'd love my show! You should come!

@MissLeslieG Love your feed! I think you'd love my show! You should come!

@JamesUrbaniak Love your feed! I think you'd love my show! You should come!

@michaelarden Love your feed! I think you'd love my show! You should come!

@FeldmanAdam Love your feed! I think you'd love my show! You should come!

@melanielynskey Love your feed! I think you'd love my show! You should come!

@nikkalanz Love your feed! I think you'd love my show! You should come!

@annharada Love your feed! I think you'd love my show! You should come!

@SmashKarenC Love your feed! I think you'd love my show! You should come!

@RachelShukert Love your feed! I think you'd love my show! You should come!

@NapOnACott Love your feed! I think you'd love my show! You should come!

@TheRealAnnaCamp Love your feed! I think you'd love my show! You should come!

@jnardino Love your feed! I think you'd love my show! You should come!

@MaraWritesStuff Love your feed! I think you'd love my show! You should come!

@traciethoms Love your feed! I think you'd love my show! You should come!

@JamieLSigler Love your feed! I think you'd love my show! You should come!

@remyzaken Love your feed! I think you'd love my show! You should come!

@RattyBurvil Love your feed! I think you'd love my show! You should come!

@yursar Love your feed! I think you'd love my show! You should come!

@jenashtep Love your feed! I think you'd love my show! You should come!

@JackOsbourne Love your feed! I think you'd love my show! You should come!

@alexa_chung Love your feed! I think you'd love my show! You should come!

@AlexdWong Love your feed! I think you'd love my show! You should come!

@Anthologist Love your feed! I think you'd love my show! You should come!

@billdawes Love your feed! I think you'd love my show! You should come!

@JamieDornan Love your feed! I think you'd love my show! You should come!

@JPManoux Love your feed! I think you'd love my show! You should come!

@LindsayMendez Love your feed! I think you'd love my show! You should come!

@hitchmichael Love your feed! I think you'd love my show! You should come!

@BeverlyWinwood Love your feed! I think you'd love my show! You should come!

@callmesquigs Love your feed! I think you'd love my show! You should come!

@andyfickman Love your feed! I think you'd love my show! You should come!

@kelliohara Love your feed! I think you'd love my show! You should come!

@ConstantineM Love your feed! I think you'd love my show! You should come!

@emmykinney Love your feed! I think you'd love my show! You should come!

@RoseHemingway Love your feed! I think you'd love my show! You should come!

@alexwyse Love your feed! I think you'd love my show! You should come!

@PlaybillMichael Love your feed! I think you'd love my show! You should come!

@AndrewBriedis Love your feed! I think you'd love my show! You should come!

@BenSPLATT Love your feed! I think you'd love my show! You should come!

@GooleyChris Love your feed! I think you'd love my show! You should come!

@AnnieBarrett Love your feed! I think you'd love my show! You should come!

@itsAdam Love your feed! I think you'd love my show! You should come!

@TimFederle Love your feed! I think you'd love my show! You should come!

@BrahSears Love your feed! I think you'd love my show! You should come!

@RichBrownUK Love your feed! I think you'd love my show! You should come!

@madtrum Love your feed! I think you'd love my show! You should come!

@TreyGerrald Love your feed! I think you'd love my show! You should come!

@erikpiepenburg Love your feed! I think you'd love my show! You should come!

@TheBabyGuyNYC Love your feed! I think you'd love my show! You should come!

@FLOTUS Love your feed! I think you'd love my show! You should come!

@timothydunn Love your feed! I think you'd love my show! You should come!

@RoryOMalley Love your feed! I think you'd love my show! You should come!

@SarahMJenkins Love your feed! I think you'd love my show! You should come!

@fiona_dolan Love your feed! I think you'd love my show! You should come!

@SamHarris Love your feed! I think you'd love my show! You should come!

@MarcSnetiker Love your feed! I think you'd love my show! You should come!

@drewchandler Love your feed! I think you'd love my show! You should come!

@AndrewRannells Love your feed! I think you'd love my show! You should come!

@JuliaMurney Love your feed! I think you'd love my show! You should come!

@Nick_Spangler Love your feed! I think you'd love my show! You should come!

@aaronjalbano Love your feed! I think you'd love my show! You should come!

@jdlovitz Love your feed! I think you'd love my show! You should come!

@PlaybillAdamH Love your feed! I think you'd love my show! You should come!

@jessetyler Love your feed! I think you'd love my show! You should come!

@PlaybillMattB Love your feed! I think you'd love my show! You should come!

@BroadwayGirlNYC Love your feed! I think you'd love my show! You should come!

@kealasettle Love your feed! I think you'd love my show! You should come!

@billyeichner Love your feed! I think you'd love my show! You should come!

@lindsdee Love your feed! I think you'd love my show! You should come!

@CameronAdamsNYC Love your feed! I think you'd love my show! You should come!

@meganganz Love your feed! I think you'd love my show! You should come!

@MrJoeIconis Love your feed! I think you'd love my show! You should come!

@scottbarnhardt Love your feed! I think you'd love my show! You should come!

@ChrisRiceNY Love your feed! I think you'd love my show! You should come!

@benjpasek Love your feed! I think you'd love my show! You should come!

@colindonnell Love your feed! I think you'd love my show! You should come!

@mo_brady Love your feed! I think you'd love my show! You should come!

@NeilHaskell Love your feed! I think you'd love my show! You should come!

@vrayskull Love your feed! I think you'd love my show! You should come!

@TheAndersonTab Love your feed! I think you'd love my show! You should come!

@JoshLamon Love your feed! I think you'd love my show! You should come!

@MiriamPultro Love your feed! I think you'd love my show! You should come!

@soundofmaddie Love your feed! I think you'd love my show! You should come!

@tyce Love your feed! I think you'd love my show! You should come!

@alannalacina Love your feed! I think you'd love my show! You should come!

@iammrvandy Love your feed! I think you'd love my show! You should come!

@RealCraigBurns Love your feed! I think you'd love my show! You should come!

@AlexBoniello Love your feed! I think you'd love my show! You should come!

@joshgroban Love your feed! I think you'd love my show! You should come!

@POTUS Love your feed! I think you'd love my show! You should come!

@oprah Love your feed! I think you'd love my show! You should come!

@rosie Love your feed! I think you'd love my show! You should come!

@RIPLEYTHEBAND Love your feed! I think you'd love my show! You should come!

@MikeCarlsen Love your feed! I think you'd love my show! You should come!

@coreymach Love your feed! I think you'd love my show! You should come!

@RobinofJesus Love your feed! I think you'd love my show! You should come!

@TomPhelan9 Love your feed! I think you'd love my show! You should come!

@Rebeccasername Love your feed! I think you'd love my show! You should come!

@jackieburnsnyc Love your feed! I think you'd love my show! You should come!

@pizzarat Love your feed! I think you'd love my show! You should come!

@groffsauce Love your feed! I think you'd love my show! You should come!

@alanhenryTO Love your feed! I think you'd love my show! You should come!

@PattynEmily Love your feed! I think you'd love my show! You should come!

@mattrosell Love your feed! I think you'd love my show! You should come!

@CiaraRenee8 Love your feed! I think you'd love my show! You should come!

@Daryl_Roth Love your feed! I think you'd love my show! You should come!

@JK_Ready Love your feed! I think you'd love my show! You should come!

@KHopTXST Love your feed! I think you'd love my show! You should come!

@CteenDryer Love your feed! I think you'd love my show! You should come!

@tonymarion Love your feed! I think you'd love my show! You should come!

@lisagoldbergpr Love your feed! I think you'd love my show! You should come!

@JakeOdmark Love your feed! I think you'd love my show! You should come!

@TimMurray7 Love your feed! I think you'd love my show! You should come!

@garretdillahunt Love your feed! I think you'd love my show! You should come!

@nikkireneesings Love your feed! I think you'd love my show! You should come!

@IainLovesTheatre Love your feed! I think you'd love my show! You should come!

@MJSchulman Love your feed! I think you'd love my show! You should come!

@FrankWildhorn Love your feed! I think you'd love my show! You should come!

@Uncle_Bres Love your feed! I think you'd love my show!
You should come!

@Racheldoesstuff Love your feed! I think you'd love my show!
You should come!

@m_shingledecker Love your feed! I think you'd love my
show! You should come!

@jennyjaffe Love your feed! I think you'd love my show! You
should come!

@ClayThompson Love your feed! I think you'd love my show!
You should come!

@SaintyNelsen Love your feed! I think you'd love my show!
You should come!

@melissaanelli Love your feed! I think you'd love my show!
You should come!

@KaraLindsay1 Love your feed! I think you'd love my show!
You should come!

@HBlix Love your feed! I think you'd love my show! You
should come!

@TovahwithaV Love your feed! I think you'd love my show!
You should come!

@ColleenB123 Love your feed! I think you'd love my show!
You should come!

@TheVintageMommy Love your feed! I think you'd love my
show! You should come!

@Susan_Blackwell Love your feed! I think you'd love my
show! You should come!

@MrMattRodin Love your feed! I think you'd love my show!
You should come!

@jphilzZz Love your feed! I think you'd love my show! You
should come!

@TheRealDratch Love your feed! I think you'd love my show!
You should come!

@LenaRockerHall Love your feed! I think you'd love my
show! You should come!

@sara_chase Love your feed! I think you'd love my show! You
should come!

@divarobbie Love your feed! I think you'd love my show! You
should come!

@noahrobbinsman Love your feed! I think you'd love my show! You should come!

@TheIntervalNY Love your feed! I think you'd love my show! You should come!

@ChrisMzCarrell Love your feed! I think you'd love my show! You should come!

@stephenoremus Love your feed! I think you'd love my show! You should come!

@LouisPeitzman Love your feed! I think you'd love my show! You should come!

@michaelurie Love your feed! I think you'd love my show! You should come!

@broadwaynosh Love your feed! I think you'd love my show! You should come!

@jheimbrock Love your feed! I think you'd love my show! You should come!

@theaterppl Love your feed! I think you'd love my show! You should come!

@drewmw Love your feed! I think you'd love my show! You should come!

@Joey_Taranto Love your feed! I think you'd love my show! You should come!

@BWWMatt Love your feed! I think you'd love my show! You should come!

@TheEnsemblist Love your feed! I think you'd love my show! You should come!

@iamMJScott Love your feed! I think you'd love my show! You should come!

@Megan_Sikora Love your feed! I think you'd love my show! You should come!

@AdamSKaplan Love your feed! I think you'd love my show! You should come!

@DerekKlena Love your feed! I think you'd love my show! You should come!

@jakewil Love your feed! I think you'd love my show! You should come!

@chad_hodge Love your feed! I think you'd love my show! You should come!

@LILLACRAWFORD Love your feed! I think you'd love my show! You should come!

@airstreamrally Love your feed! I think you'd love my show! You should come!

@RySteele Love your feed! I think you'd love my show! You should come!

@imsarahmoore Love your feed! I think you'd love my show! You should come!

@cerveris Love your feed! I think you'd love my show! You should come!

@kateshindle Love your feed! I think you'd love my show! You should come!

@caseyhope53 Love your feed! I think you'd love my show! You should come!

@itsdlevy Love your feed! I think you'd love my show! You should come!

@arianerinehart Love your feed! I think you'd love my show! You should come!

@TASTiSKANK Love your feed! I think you'd love my show! You should come!

@ALNL Love your feed! I think you'd love my show! You should come!

@thehaleywebb Love your feed! I think you'd love my show! You should come!

@MelissaJoanHart Love your feed! I think you'd love my show! You should come!

@AdamJacobsNYC Love your feed! I think you'd love my show! You should come!

@erichbergen Love your feed! I think you'd love my show! You should come!

@JoshuaFerri Love your feed! I think you'd love my show! You should come!

@JimCaruso1 Love your feed! I think you'd love my show! You should come!

@HeleneYorke Love your feed! I think you'd love my show! You should come!

@liza_weil Love your feed! I think you'd love my show! You should come!

@RestingPlatypus Love your feed! I think you'd love my show! You should come!

@AndrewAndrew Love your feed! I think you'd love my show! You should come!

@carlylewarren Love your feed! I think you'd love my show! You should come!

@TayeDiggs Love your feed! I think you'd love my show! You should come!

@MollyEphraim Love your feed! I think you'd love my show! You should come!

@jbsibley Love your feed! I think you'd love my show! You should come!

@KateRockwellNYC Love your feed! I think you'd love my show! You should come!

@BrynnOMalley Love your feed! I think you'd love my show! You should come!

@RobMcClure Love your feed! I think you'd love my show! You should come!

@gidglick Love your feed! I think you'd love my show! You should come!

@torre_roma Love your feed! I think you'd love my show! You should come!

@craigzadan Love your feed! I think you'd love my show! You should come!

@lindsayabaire Love your feed! I think you'd love my show! You should come!

@PiperGoodeve Love your feed! I think you'd love my show! You should come!

@christophergurr Love your feed! I think you'd love my show! You should come!

@Amanda_Trusty Love your feed! I think you'd love my show! You should come!

@RyanSerhant Love your feed! I think you'd love my show! You should come!

@jennirach Love your feed! I think you'd love my show! You should come!

@lomo212 Love your feed! I think you'd love my show! You should come!

@BenVereen Love your feed! I think you'd love my show!
You should come!

@stephenwallem Love your feed! I think you'd love my show!
You should come!

@frankrichny Love your feed! I think you'd love my show!
You should come!

@joytea Love your feed! I think you'd love my show! You
should come!

@ChadBeguelin Love your feed! I think you'd love my show!
You should come!

@telseyandco Love your feed! I think you'd love my show!
You should come!

@tararubincasting Love your feed! I think you'd love my
show! You should come!

@donnavivino Love your feed! I think you'd love my show!
You should come!

@phloella Love your feed! I think you'd love my show! You
should come!

@denisevasi Love your feed! I think you'd love my show! You
should come!

@patrickhealynyt Love your feed! I think you'd love my show!
You should come!

@Alancumming Love your feed! I think you'd love my show!
You should come!

@JennColella Love your feed! I think you'd love my show!
You should come!

@JaredGertner Love your feed! I think you'd love my show!
You should come!

@MarkPeikert Love your feed! I think you'd love my show!
You should come!

@neilmeron Love your feed! I think you'd love my show! You
should come!

@Jadomian Love your feed! I think you'd love my show! You
should come!

@abobrow Love your feed! I think you'd love my show! You
should come!

@DavidCote Love your feed! I think you'd love my show! You
should come!

@sojoey Love your feed! I think you'd love my show! You should come!
@katieroseclark Love your feed! I think you'd love my show! You should come!
@CaissieLevy Love your feed! I think you'd love my show! You should come!
@Lin_Manuel Love your feed! I think you'd love my show! You should come!
@OfficialBPeters Love your feed! I think you'd love my show! You should come!

"That ought to do it!" you say proudly to yourself after crashing Broadway Internet for a solid twelve seconds.

When the servers that run your tiny little corner of Twitter finally come back online, the blame for the breakdown is focused squarely at you. Not only did your form-letter method of marketing cause Broadway Internet to freeze for a period of time that made many feel helpless, there was a clever tweet sent out into the ether by @Lin_Manuel that didn't post because of this technical tragedy caused by you. There are now words that were written by Lin-Manuel Miranda that will never be read, and you're the one at fault. Having committed accidental career suicide, there's no way anyone will be coming to your Feinstein's/54 Below show now.

It's a shame that your decision to emulate *Wicked*'s marketing brought upon your own demise. *Wicked* is one of the biggest brands in the business, so they can afford to hire a social media manager whose only credentials are "being under twenty-five." It never really seems to matter to any higher ups if the person they put in charge of their Twitter doesn't actually know how it works. Corporations have been part of the Twitter landscape for nearly a decade, yet I promise you, every day at least one reputable company tweets a mention without putting a period in front of it first, or tries to get someone to DM without having followed them—and don't get me started on spell check. Bottom line: it's expected for something like *Wicked* to slip up like this because there might be someone from an older generation who assumes that any Millennial can create a strong social media presence. Well, not everyone can run their shit like *The Book of Mormon* does.

It seems that many social media managers these days think that the way to develop an online brand is by asking other people to do their work for free. It now becomes painfully apparent that *Wicked* was doing this to you when they requested several people to tweet that link. You feel so used! You're like, "Why did I try to imitate their social media marketing when I actually have a solid presence myself?! I should have consulted with someone!"

Wicked recovered from their marketing misstep because they're *Wicked*. You, however, managed to throw your entire brand under the bus in one small series of tweets.

THE END.

There are many different ways to be an humanitarian: volunteering for the New York Restoration Project, donating to Doctors Without Borders, developing a support group for people who have lost a friend to their current cast. One of your favorite humanitarians, animal trainer Bill Berloni, has dedicated his career to the rescuing of animals.

Bill Berloni is the shit. He got his start at Goodspeed Opera House, where he was hired to find and train the original Sandy in the pre-Broadway tryout of *Annie*. To fill the role, Berloni visited a shelter and saved a mutt (who was just moments away from being put to sleep) and made him a star. Since *Annie*, Bill Berloni has been the go-to trainer for every animal on Broadway, and each and every one has been a rescue. From Sandys to Bruisers, Totos to Helen Mirren's corgis, Bill Berloni has saved the lives of hundreds of animals and given them illustrious careers. I wish Bill Berloni could save *me*.

As you reflect upon how awesome saving animals is, it dawns on you that you can be a budding Bill Berloni by adopting a dog from Bernadette Peters at Broadway Barks.

This annual summer event presented by Broadway Cares/Equity Fights AIDS has always intrigued you. Held in Shubert Alley, Broadway Barks raises awareness and funds for the Mayor's Alliance for NYC's Animals by showcasing cats and dogs available for adoption from various shelters around the city. This is absolutely the right place for you to find your new friend.

You arrive at Shubert Alley and it is crammed with the most adorable cats and dogs. Their cute factor prompts the only circumstance where you'd ever choose to walk through this wind-tunnel-of-tourists unironically. The main event of Broadway Barks is the parade of adoptable pets that are partnered with various figures in the community. Each one is more loveable looking than the last, but you hold out for whichever lucky dog accompanies Bernadette Peters. While you put up a valiant effort, your restraint goes out the window when *Fun Home*'s Beth Malone take the stage with the sweetest dog you've ever seen.

"Each and every little set of eyes that looks back at you from these shelters is having a huge emotional life," says Beth Malone into a microphone. "They have little broken hearts until somebody loves them. And once you know the love of a stray, it's this very intense bond and they are forever grateful."

"I'll have that one," you tell yourself as you gaze at the dog in Beth Malone's arms, your face frozen in an emoji-with-heart-eyes expression.

When you want something, you get it, and this dog is no exception. Before you know it, you're sitting at home with a precious new pup, and nothing else in the world seems to matter. Within minutes, you feel a kind of acceptance that you've never once experienced in an audition room. The unconditional love of this sweet soul makes you not care if you never book another job again. As your new dog sleeps softly in your arms, its head upon your chest, you discover that nothing else in the world will ever be better than this.

Dogs are always patient and kind. Dogs are never jealous. Dogs are never boastful or conceited. Dogs are never rude or selfish. They do not take offense and are not resentful. Dogs take no pleasure in other people's sins, but delight in the truth. Dogs are always ready to excuse, to trust, to hope, and to endure whatever comes—and now that this dog has made your life complete, so can you.

EPILOGUE (page 465)

*

"One Chocolate Telsey + Co-Coa Cream, please," You say to the Schmackary's employee.

That title is quite a mouthful—and you know a few things about mouthfuls (AMIRITE ladies?) No, really. You did a summer stock season that included titles like *How to Succeed in Business without Really Trying*, *Jacques Brel is Alive and Well and Living in Paris*, and *Precious: Based on the Novel Push by Sapphire: A New Musical Fable*.

The Schmackary's employee quickly hands you the delectable gift, which has been kissed by angels, and bears the holy namesake: Telsey. You take a heavenly bite, and quickly begin enthusiastically consuming the consecrated cookie. Once you have finished, a vibration overcomes you. Clearly, a higher power has anointed this cookie. Fuck Funfetti. Never again.

You remain in a daze for a moment, allowing the vibration to continue before realizing it's actually just your phone ringing. You promptly pull it out and see the words, "Incoming Call: BROADWAY" emblazoned across the screen.

Upon answering, your agent blurts out: "Casting just called to tell you that your audition today has been cancelled."

"My *appointment?*" You exclaim loudly so everyone in Schmackary's can hear that you have an appointment for something.

"They've decided to pass you right through to the final callback with the entire creative team," your agent continues, "Tonight at five p.m. *Sharp*. E-mailing the info now."

You thank your agent and end the call. For once, you're speechless. This is really exciting! And how coincidental that just as you bit into a cookie named after Telsey, you found out that casting is moving you forward to the final callback? Talk about a sign! Never mind the fact that Tara Rubin is casting this show—this has to be a good omen!

You're so damn thrilled, you need to post about it on social media—but how do you handle acknowledging this great fortune? You could ask for positive vibes at five p.m., but that may annoy some of your friends. Maybe you should just post a joke about how you fell down outside of Schmackary's just now. Sure, it's not at all about your cool-as-shit callback, but a self-deprecating post will get you likes, and that's really all you need right now...but what about positive vibes? Do you...

Ask for positive vibes....? (page 242)

Post about falling down....? (page 9)

*

Screw Corey. David has always been a quicker texter anyway.

You shoot a message off to David, asking if he'll give *Metamorphosis: the Hilary Duff Musical* a quick pass and some notes. He doesn't respond immediately, and that gives you pause. David always responds. He's also one of those rare entities who uses the "Read Receipts" option, so you always know when he's opened a text. Your message is still marked as "delivered," so he's either not opened it, or stopped using that function. Either way, since it's been an hour since you sent it, all signs point to him being dead.

Alas, David is not dead. You randomly remember that he was just put into *Finding Neverland* after a long stint in *Chicago*, and has been finding himself in the process. After indulging heavily in the Kool-Aid at the Lunt-Fontanne, it'll be some time before he gets to your text. Best to send your script to Paige.

Paige doesn't read it either.

Three up, three down (just like in a half an inning of baseball…you think.) Your next best bet is to try your less reliable friends, Ashley and Ellyn, because they might surprise you. Ashley is more of a dancer and Ellyn is more of a singer. This could seriously affect the type of feedback they provide. Do you…

Send your script to Ashley…? (page 336)

Send your script to Ellyn…? (page 343)

*

You die.

Seriously. You walk outside to meet your voice teacher and get knifed on the corner of 42nd and Eighth, outside Times Scare. As if that place weren't already hard enough to walk by, you have to go and die in front of it? Furthermore, when did New York City start getting violent again BILL DE BLASIO.

As you drift away into what appears to you now as the gritty Times Square of the 1970s, you think to yourself, "Patti LuPone liked it better this way. I hope she's happy now, wherever she is." And then your phone rings, and you know it's a sign from God telling you that she is.

Listen, I know this is sad, but you should have gone to the gym. Your health is everything. It's not just fitness, it's life. Think about that, as you lie there dead.

Remember how you thought you'd rather die than go to the gym? Well, if you're not careful, the Universe is bound to take you literally, no matter what you put out into it. If all the good things in your life happened for a reason, it's foolish to think that the bad things didn't as well.

THE END.

*

Being a star is something you've been trying to convince casting directors of for years, but they haven't leapt at your suggestion to headline a Broadway show, so it's your responsibility to make that opportunity yourself. One way to achieve the goal of being the main focus is by developing a solo concert starring you.

Cabarets are as natural to a Broadway performer as questioning their life choices, so it was only a matter of time before you created your own. While this is going to be an intimidating venture that will pull you outside of your comfort zone, you're super psyched to show your peers how badass you are after a two-drink minimum.

The first item of business is to decide what type of concert you want to do. This will determine the songs you'll sing and the types of personalities you'll need on your production team. There are basically three kinds of cabarets:

The Serious Cabaret: This is the one where you tell a thoughtful retrospective about your life within the business, sing a lot of lovely ballads, and then close with "Meadowlark."

The Funny Cabaret: This is the one where you tell funny stories, perform edgy and broad musical sequences, and then close with a rap version of "Meadowlark."

The Cover Cabaret: This is the one where you sing songs by a specific artist (or several artists within the same genre) and then close with Tituss Burgess' cover of "Meadowlark."

What kind of cabaret do you want to do...?

The serious cabaret... (page 33)

The funny cabaret... (page 250)

The cover cabaret... (page 456)

*

Memorizing all of this material on your own proves to be harder than expected. Normally, handling pressure comes fairly easy to you. However, some of these scripts are so wretched, you're having trouble committing the clunky and mechanical dialogue to memory. A few of the pilots are cool, but the others seem like the network was determined to capitalize on a topical subject, thus forcing a show to happen that will probably be dated by the time it premieres.

Trends are big during pilot season. Most shows this year focus on self-referential commentary, which only a handful of scripts are landing. It's a pretty hard tone to nail, and I don't know anyone who can do it. Previous pilot season trends have included: super heroes, romantic comedies, reboots, shows based on movies, and Ryan Murphy.

As the night continues on, you're distracted by anything that has nothing to do with your auditions, making it take longer to memorize your sides. While you didn't get a single moment of sleep, you managed to learn each script to the best of your ability, and you're feeling confident that you'll have a solid day of auditions, provided you don't doze off while commuting from Studio City to Santa Monica to Glendale to Sherman Oaks back to the Valley and onto Universal City and Burbank. This day is going to be a bitch.

Crawling into your car, you head toward Laurel Canyon Boulevard, where you merge onto the 101 West and then take the 405 South to the 10 West, and arrive in Santa Monica with only a minute to spare. Fortunately, you're able to find parking right outside, which of course you have to pay for.

After years of living in New York City, you're not quite accustomed to spending money when you arrive at an audition. It's not like there was a mandatory locker at the Telsey office where Rachel Hoffman made you leave your large Lululemon bag in exchange for ten bucks. Even after several auditions, you're still annoyed by this unfortunate obligation.

The casting director for *2 Friends & Their Job* is running behind, but luckily, a few of the actors are unable to find parking, so you get to go in ahead of time and sleepily bomb your first audition of the day. It might be a good idea to grab another coffee before you head out to Glendale.

With *2 Friends & Their Job* down, you jump in your car and find a Coffee Bean & Tea Leaf (you're so happy to see that they have them out here, too!) and then take the 10 East to the 405 North, where you merge onto the 101 South and take the 134 East to the other side of the fucking Valley, where you arrive in Glendale and give an average audition for *This Won't Get Picked Up*. After that, it's on to Sherman Oaks for *That Show's Still On?* which means going back through the Valley by taking the 134 West to the 101 North and getting off on Van Nuys Boulevard to do a moderately serviceable job at yet another audition. You're halfway through the day and you'd say that on the positive side, you're oh for three.

Up until now, traffic has only been its usual dickish self, so while you've wanted to kill yourself the entire day, nothing has prevented you from making it to your auditions on time. The next stop is going to require you to go straight through the Valley, and there are two routes you can use to get to it from here: the 405 or the 170. Both freeways are showing red congestion lines on iMaps and the same expected arrival time. As you know by now, traffic in LA can change faster than CBS can pick up a multi-cam pile of shit.

Which freeway do you take to your next audition?

The 405. (page 413)

The 170. (page 143)

Sitting at the Panera near Bryant Park, nervously poking at your Cobb Salad with Dressing on the Side, you try to muster up the courage to pitch to Daniel your brilliant idea, but it's proving difficult. When the premise is safely locked inside your head, you feel nothing but positivity towards it. When faced with the awkward moment of having to actually explain it aloud to someone, however, the entire thing sounds really stupid to you. Is this something all writers have to deal with?

"So," smiles Daniel, "what's this idea you wanted to talk to me about?"

"OK," you begin, hoping your articulation skills don't fail you, "it's a musical about show business. But not like *A Chorus Line*, *Applause*, *[title of show]*, *The Producers*, *Follies*, *42nd Street*, *Curtains*, *Kiss Me, Kate*—"

"Got it."

"Ha!" you laugh. "I…Uhhhh… So, it's about show business…"

You're finding it difficult to put into words, and by the look on Daniel's face, there's a chance you might be losing him.

"Like," you continue, "ok. A while back I was watching them load *Amazing Grace* out of the Nederlander, and I was thinking, 'How much would it cost to rent a Broadway theater anyway? If I were a billionaire one-percenter-hedgefunder—where a couple million bucks was like NBD—I could produce a show myself with all of my friends in it, and keep it running like the revival of *On the Town*.'"

"Uh-huh," nods Daniel.

"So," you say, "the other day I was on the elliptical listening to some random music—not sure what song, but that detail doesn't matter—and I started thinking about my career, and my Broadway debut, and how I felt when I finally got the call, and it hit me: A musical about a bunch of friends from college making their Broadway debut!"

"OK, but what's the hook?"

"They're all making their debut because one of the character's billionaire dad buys it!"

Daniel leans forward. "I don't follow."

"Picture a rich girl who's always gotten everything she's ever wanted. She's not based on me, or anyone we know. She's more of a plot device we can center our own stories around."

"OK?"

"So, this rich girl can't catch a break after she moves to the city—and neither can any of her close friends from college. After a few months or so of this, she asks her dad if he can produce a Broadway show himself, using all of her friends. She brings in her composer friend—he can be based on you…and her best friend who is really amazing—that can be me…and a couple of other people we can figure out later. Then they put on a show in a barn like Mickey and Judy. Except instead of a barn, it's the Belasco, or something."

Daniel pauses for a moment. He's interested. "So, what is the musical we're writing?"

"The musical itself is the final dress rehearsal before the gypsy run of the musical they're doing—in real time."

"Got it," nods Daniel.

"It can be fraught with all of this drama and shit," you continue, really trying to sell it now. "I have an idea about the rich girl's mom being white-wine-drunk in the front row and interjecting all of the time."

"Wasn't that just the tech process for *Scandalous*?"

"Maybe the girl could freak out and refuse to finish the show, causing the mom to get up and wail the eleven o'clock number."

"This is so NYMF," laughs Daniel.

"I know, right? Wait—what?"

Daniel adjusts his glasses. "I get the framing device, but what's the musical *saying*?"

"Our stories!" you exclaim. "It's about the joy an actor feels when they first make their debut. I want to call it *Pieces of Me*."

"Shouldn't it be called *Broadway Debut*?"

"I like *Pieces of Me*."

"I think *A Chorus Line* more or less covers this kind of idealistic take on working in show business," advises Daniel.

"But nobody gives those cut dancers a track just for showing up," you clarify. "In *Pieces of Me*, all of the actors fail to make their debut, so someone has to buy it for them. It's so Millennial, and that's topical!"

"The satire interests me," states Daniel. "I could explore this."

"Great!" you smile with satisfaction at this validation. "So, I'll do book and lyrics, and you'll do—

"Music *and* lyrics."

"I…" you stop.

This could be a deal breaker, and you need to think it over. You know Daniel is more skilled at playing the piano than you, but the only familiarity you have with his writing is the dull shit he posts online. How can you be certain he'll be any good at crafting lyrics? Furthermore, if your show moves to a commercial run, he'll get two thirds of the royalties designated to the writing team. Is it fair for Daniel to be making more money off of *your* concept? That being said, you could truly suck at writing lyrics, and after experiencing that run-in with self-doubt while trying to pitch your idea to

Daniel, it might be better if you limited your responsibilities. Do you...

Let Daniel write the lyrics....? (page 87)

Demand that you write the lyrics...? (page 439)

This is it. This is the moment. With the confidence of a key change in a Wildhorn ballad, you open your laptop, cut and paste the revealing essay to your blog, hit publish, and tweet it out into the universe. Now, it's time to sit back and wait for the likes to roll in.

Beat.

Beat.

Beat.

"Cool," replies one of your followers.

"Huh?" replies another.

And then, as if all of Broadway Internet bands together at once with a collected, "new phone, who dis?" Irritating Performer Pal's identity becomes common knowledge; as ordinary and basic as when that one singer girl at the ECC wears the most expensive pair of La Duca's.

The "bang" you expected to go out on, lands flatter than most stunt casting. It's not that people aren't initially intrigued by you, it's that the attention fizzles faster than a casting office's interest in a recent conservatory graduate (which usually expires fifteen days before their twenty-third birthday.)

If only you had developed some sort of a plan of what to do with your life after IPP. Instead, you just threw yourself out there, and expected someone to hire you because you know how work a *Jurassic World* reference into a *Dames at Sea* tweet. I'm all for you taking this risk, but you should have given yourself a road map. There are so many questions that it would have behooved you to answer before taking this step. What kind of writer do you want to be? What other ideas do you have? What do you want to be when you grow up? STOP ASKING ME. I DON'T KNOW.

With no prospects or vision for the future, I have nothing else to tell you. Do I think that revealing your identity was something that eventually needed to happen? Yes. Do I think you chose the right time? Not really. Do I know when *would* have been the right time? HELL NO. Sorry I'm not much help right now. This was just a really hard decision to make, and I literally didn't know how to guide you.

So, I guess this is over now. Good thing you never quit that job at Fusion.

THE END.

*

All right season three! All the good shit happens in a show's third season. They've worked through the freshman year's growing pains, and the sophomore slump, clearing the path for some truly innovative material that comes easier because of the writers' true understanding of their characters. It's also when the Red Wedding happened, so this could all fall apart, too. Let's see!

As you enter your third year reinventing new ways to waste time in between sessions at Fusion, you're sort of at a loss for what to do next. You managed to draw your last book out for over a year, and fall back on drinking games for live events and topical tweets, but how long can you survive doing that? To make matters worse, it's January, and you'll need something to direct your focus or you'll kill yourself before you freeze to death just trying to exist. I hate to say this to you, but I think you might need to write something else. I realize that writing is a bitch. It's like banging your head against a wall; it feels so good when it stops. Writing is so hard that I had to steal that last sentence from an old Jack Lemmon movie my mom showed me when I was a kid (circa 2009) and hope you didn't notice. Even when you carve out a six-hour block to write, the time is usually divided up the following ways:

15% - Tweeting.
25% - Refreshing Twitter/waiting for notifications.
10% - Texting.
7% - Staring at your computer screen.
3% - Eating.
20% - Thinking about eating.
10% - Facebook, Tumblr, Instagram, other social media sites.
5% - Falling asleep.

4% - Having a nervous breakdown.
1% - Writing.

      In your first book, you mentioned that you might entertain the thought of writing a second book. It feels like that time is rapidly approaching. However, I can't stress enough how crazy a thing that is to consider for someone who flirts daily with ADD. Please keep in mind that the idea of writing another book (with all the stress that comes with desperately trying to recreate the original in a sequel), is so hashtag-horrifying, that if it were in a game of "Would You Rather" opposite waiting outside for an EPA in the freezing cold at 6:00 a.m., only to find out after you finally get let in hours later that your Equity card is one day past its expiration date, and you have no money left in your bank account, causing you to have to agree to taking a party pumping gig that night where you have to dance in a horrible costume at Brooke Shield's birthday party, surrounded by a group of your peers who don't recognize you from that one show you did six years ago at TUTS… you'd have to ask for a minute to decide which you'd rather, because writing is literally that hard.

      Even though you've come up with a "create your own show business destiny" concept for your second book in the time it took you to read that last paragraph, is it a fun enough idea for you to commit to? I guess it's up to you to decide. Would you rather…

Write a second book….? (page 198)

Hell no! (page 233)

*

"This is the right Starbucks," you think confidently to yourself, as you sit at the bar by the window and stare out at the traffic on Broadway. "*Metamorphosis: the Hilary Duff Musical* will be born here, in this very room."

Millennial culture is something you take very seriously, and you found a bottle of Adderall under your bed left over from a sublet, so writing this musical proves to be pretty easy. While blasting "Come Clean" on a loop, you're able to complete a first draft in three weeks—which is an entire week faster than it took to write *Wonderful Town*, and one week slower than *Motown*.

Being this productive in such a short amount of time makes you happy you chose the Starbucks you did. Can you imagine if you picked the other one? Who knows if you'd even have a single line written? Now, you have a very solid first draft that is ready to be *read*. So, which one of your friends should you send it to? Remember: You have to be very careful with who you send this script to. People have been clamoring for you to write something ever since you started posting moderately entertaining shit online. There will be a lot of interest in your debut musical, and while you want constructive criticism, you don't want too much advice thrust in your face, because that is when a product becomes deluded. It's best to pick one friend who shares your sensibility to help you make the best possible version of *Metamorphosis: the Hilary Duff Musical*.

There are three core friends of yours that are the go-to people for texting screen caps of unacceptable shit: Corey, Paige, and David. Any one of them is sure to deliver praises within twenty-four hours—but whatever notes they provide will directly affect your second draft, and, ultimately, your Tony chances. Deciding which friend to send your script to is going to come down to your gut. Do you...

Send your script to Corey...? (page 155)

Send your script to Paige...? (page 69)

Send your script to David...? (page 371)

*

Woohoo! A second book! You can do this! In just three short months of work, winter will be over, and you'll be well on your way to niche fame and tens of dollars. That's only ninety days of nose-to-the-grindstone focus and hey, did you see that thing online? Go look at it! Well, shit, now it's April, and you were supposed to be done by March.

Procrastination is a mean bitch. It seduces you with iPhones and happy hours. It tells you, "Everything is going to work its way out," before stealing six months of your life in exchange for Facebook likes you don't even remember. Most bad procrastination habits stem from a lack of vision for the desired objective. If you don't have a fuck of a clue how to get where you're going, the chances are greater that you'll be stuck refreshing sixteen social media feeds in the middle of the day when nobody is being active. Perhaps the even scarier truth is that even when you do have a plan, you'll still find ways to sabotage yourself, because Netflix. Procrastination is your nemesis. It's the Karen to your Ivy. The Ivy to your Karen. The Rebecca Duvall to your Ivy *and* Karen. The Karen *and* Ivy to your Rebecca Duvall. The ratings to your *Smash*. You can't win.

Your idea to write a create your own show business destiny book where you could be stuck having to construct hundreds of different outcomes is the definition of insanity and I saw [INSERT CURRENT BROADWAY DISASTER BECAUSE I THINK I'VE NAMED THEM ALL]. This is definitely a time where your confidence outweighs your ability, and not in one of those good ways that explains why that horribly untalented friend of yours manages to never be out of a job. You literally have no clue what you are doing or where to begin, so you just open your laptop and start making shit up. Outlines are overrated. Be organic! Be raw! Let the moment capture you and take you on a journey that—OK, that was fun for twenty thousand words, but seriously, you might want to start an outline.

After finishing a detailed and inspired outline, and by finishing a detailed and inspired outline, I mean finishing all available episodes of *Silicon Valley*, you sit down and get to work. Your create your own show business destiny book has four trajectory jumping off points. Once you've decided what the main focus for each story will be, you sketch out rough ideas of where they ultimately lead. Since you've decided to venture into some different territory, you're going to have to again do interviews with friends more experienced than you, which means a lot of extra hours hanging out at Panera.

They say, "write what you know," but it's surprising how little you know about life and shit, so it's getting difficult filling out some of these stories. The only thing you have a moderate understanding of is your personal origin story. People love an origin story! There have been three separate actors cast as *Spider-Man* in our lifetime (one hundred and sixty-eight if you include the musical), because we still want to learn how Peter Parker got all that power and responsibility. Maybe you could find a way to shoehorn your IPP origin story and its journey into your second book, and hide it amongst thousands of mini-plots. The facts don't have to be completely true either. You can tell the social media version of the story—the one where you curate which details need to be told? It could be a fun and not-in-the-least-bit-masturbatory endeavor. However, you're going to need to be careful. You'll have to change all the names to protect the innocent, and you can't call it Irritating Performer Pal, if Irritating Performer Pal is writing the book—that'll just get confusing. Maybe you could rename it Exasperating Entertainer Buddy, and pretend that in the universe of your sequel, Irritating Performer Pal doesn't exist. Also, you don't want to get sued by Fusion Health & Racquet, so you should probably rename it something safe like Shmequinox.

This all seems like an exciting idea, but what if it completely bombs? What if people don't give a shit? What if it's *boring*? These are all valid concerns, but you should weigh them against how much you love talking about yourself. Do you...

Write your origin story….? (page 204)

Nix the origin story….? (page 231)

"All right, Ashlee," you whisper to yourself, "this better be more inspiring than when you did *Chicago*."

It is. The moment the iconic acoustic guitar vamp of "Pieces of Me" begins, the thrilling throwback Thursday vocal stylings of Ashlee Simpson prove to be lubrication to your ears – penetrating the proverbial ball of writer's block wax obstructing the creative spirit inside your brain. As Ashlee's voice serenades your soul, it occurs to you how much her lyrics relate to your life in the American Theatre…

On a Monday, I am waiting… She's talking about having a final callback on a Friday, and then having to endure the anxiety of waiting through the weekend to hear if she booked!

Tuesday, I am fading… She didn't hear anything yet, but maybe Monday was Columbus Day, and agents have that holiday off?

And by Wednesday, I can't sleep… This isn't looking good. Give it a week, Ashlee. You gotta give them a week!

Then the phone rings, I hear you… This has to be it! Only agents and Time Warner Cable still use phones!

And the darkness is a clear view… Obviously she was hidden under the covers with a sleeve of Thin Mints when the phone rang.

Cuz you've come to rescue me… She booked!

Fall... With you, I fall so fast. I can hardly catch my breath, I hope it lasts… You totally relate! Nobody wants the euphoric feeling of booking to end. It's like eating pizza during an orgasm!

You are so overcome with how much this song speaks to you, that by the time you reach the chorus, you're belting at the top of your lungs on the elliptical—

"*Ohhhhh!*" You don't give a shit who hears! *"It seems like I can finally rest my head on something real! I like the way that feels!"*

YOU ARE LIVING! A rush of hope overcomes you. This is how live theatre is supposed to make people feel! It's in this moment that you become inspired to write a musical based on your life in the business, and it is going to heal the world.

The music swells and you sing even louder!

"Ohhhhh! It's as if you know me better than I ever knew myself! I love how you can tell! All the pieces, pieces, pieces of me!"

THAT'S IT! You'll call your musical *Pieces of Me*!

Whoa. That was invigorating. The crazy thing about creativity is that you never know when it's going to strike. There are millions of ways a brilliant idea can come to a writer, and right now you're very content in knowing you can be productive while working out, and not have to get blitzed, like me and Ernest Hemingway.

You've been told in the past that all of the greats use substances when they write. Even Stephen Sondheim said on that HBO documentary that he's never written a lyric without some alcohol. You understand that and all, but HAS HE EVER LISTENED TO ASHLEE SIMPSON? Because *shit*! You've got the entire first act structured out in your head and the song isn't even over yet!

Leaping off the elliptical, you rush home and start outlining the story. You've never written a musical before, but you've been in a lot of them, and you saw how they did it on *Smash*, so you got this.

Writing the libretto shouldn't be a problem. Years of experience texting, tweeting, and Facebooking have given you the assurance that you know how to construct sentences, so putting them into story format should be real easy. Lyrics won't be much of a hurdle either, because there's probably an app for rhyming. The issue right now is the music.

You took a year of piano keyboarding in college, and are fairly comfortable playing chords, but whether or not you're able to progress them together into a song is unknown. Perhaps it might behoove you to bring a composer on board to ensure you don't write a steamy pile of poop emoji.

There's a friend you know from college named Daniel who was a theatre major in your class, but he transitioned into music directing after graduation. He's the guy you go to when you want someone more capable to play through your audition material. You heard he was working on some original music, so maybe he'd be a good person to pitch your idea to. Or, you could take a stab at writing the musical loosely based on your early experiences in show business yourself. I mean nobody knows your pain as well as you. Do you...

Pitch the idea to Daniel...? (page 188)

Write the musical yourself...? (page 137)

*

Well, this is a fairly self-aggrandizing choice, don't you think? I mean like, whatever, live your life. But do we all have to read about it? I feel even worse for @Gratefulterns, who is going to have to edit this section and pretend to like it. You, by definition, are literally "the worst." Still, I guess I'm obligated to tell you how it all pans out, huh?

I don't know. I honestly don't know. This entire thing makes me feel excited, well, excited *and* scared— except not excited at all, just mostly truly fearful of what the future will bring for you. You can't undo this choice. You can't un-publish a section of a book. This isn't a tweet you can delete and pray nobody saved the hyperlink. You're all in, and once this book is out there, it will be too late to rewrite this story.

Keeping that in mind, you wake up on the day of your book's release, crawl to the foot of your bed, where you rock back and forth in the fetal position, lit only by the dim glow of your smartphone, and speak softly to yourself:

> *How long can I stay lost without a way to rewrite?*
> *I wish I could rewrite this story.*
> *Change every word of every line.*
> *Write any story but mine.*
> *Someone tell me when I can start again,*
> *And rewrite this story.*
> *Yeah.*
> *Yeah.*

After three straight hours of repeating these *Hit List* lyrics on a loop, you realize that while writer Benj Pasek has a valid point about the urge to "fix shit you fuck up," it applies to someone else. These words do not define your story. This is a Karen and Jimmy song. Are you a Karen or a Jimmy? You only identify with Jimmy when you're hangry, and you're certainly not a Karen. Only a Karen would choose to focus on Karen Cartwright from *Smash* at a climactic moment such as right now.

During this time of anxiety (which has become so familiar to you lately, that you're actually not sure if you're dating, or married, or sleeping together with no kissing) I can offer the following words of encouragement: Who. Gives. A. Shit.

You built this entire social media distraction-from-real-life on the foundation of just having fun, and not giving a shit. Why start now? The moment you begin taking this seriously for a greater amount of time than you spend laughing about it means you've taken it too far. I don't think you've gotten to that point yet, but when you do, I suggest you stop. This isn't that moment. I hope it never comes to that. I hope you always accidentally stumble into a new element of this extremely elongated bit. I hope you keep writing horrible tweets that fail. I hope you revel in those failures and learn from them. I hope you do the exact opposite of everything you did when you were an actor.

If you stay anonymous, I hope you find happiness in that. If you choose to end that element of the story, I hope you find a way to reinvent the character. I hope you keep trying to move it forward. I hope people embrace the joke. I hope people like you, but I also hope you piss some people off, too, because that means you're not boring. I hope you remember that, in the end, you're just playing around and none of this matters—and I hope you remember it also does matter. I hope you walk that line without falling to either side. I hope good (but mostly, lucrative) things come to you. I hope this entire thing was not for naught.

You're looking at me like I have all the answers for what will come next because I've been guiding you for what feels like decades now. But still, all I can say is: "I don't know" and "I hope."

EPILOGUE (page 465)

The clean Hail to the Kale feels so good going down your throat, and fills you with such unparalleled energy, you decide to grab another one right before your audition. This seems like a good idea in theory, but the influx of that leafy-green-goodness into your system causes some problematic intestinal issues as you make your way to your appointment. Normally you can control your gas, but as you stand in the center of the studio, swiftly approaching your money note, you're confronted with the Patti LuPone of farts—this flatulence will not be contained!

As you breathe deep and belt with the best of them, you're upstaged by the double dose of Hail to the Kale making its way back into the world. There's no delicate way to put this… You shit yourself. You shit yourself at Pearl Studios. You literally shit yourself at Pearl Studios *and* don't book.

THE END.

*

In the mood for some risotto balls and attention, you head to Glass House Tavern, because that's where it's at. It's not so much that Glass House Tavern is *new*, it's that it's *now*. It's a place to go with friends where you can also network, and, unlike Bar Centrale, it's much more accessible (i.e. cheaper).

Post-show hour at Glass House is a Broadway fuck-fest potpourri. Someone from everything is there. It's like God told Stephen Sondheim to construct an arc in the middle of the theatre district where two actors from every Broadway show would flock nightly to evade the flood of Times Square tourists and mass audience exodus. It truly is a location built for the heavenly divine.

While you've decided to venture to Glass House alone, you're confident it won't be long before you run into someone you know vaguely enough to engage in a conversation where you can casually drop your recent crowning achievement of booking a new Broadway workshop. Your real friends don't want to know about things like that. Accomplishments are for acquaintances.

After a few minutes of networking and social netwerking (i.e. talking to one of the Platt brothers and then taking a picture with them and posting it on Instagram), you slide up to the bar and order a vodka soda.

While you wait for your drink, you see that the majority of the crowd has cleared out to go to either Broadway Bowling or Anthony Rapp's poker game, so you strike up a conversation with the person next to you, who is nursing what looks like a whiskey sour. After a few minutes chatting with this person (who is clearly in the business, because they're at Glass House), you realize by their disposition that they must be a Broadway Senior.

You've encountered these rare creatures at auditions, but never in the wild. Broadway Seniors seldom find themselves alone in open venues where they can be exposed to a highly concentrated amount of schmooze. While this Broadway Senior is certainly a downer, you're fascinated as to why they are here—and since there's not an average-prospective-theatre-major's-chance of getting into CMU that they'll be asking you what you're working on, you decide to flip the script and ask *them*.

To your surprise (and delight), you discover they recently booked the exact same job as you!

"I'm doing that workshop, too!" you scream with the glee of the general public during season one of *Glee*.

"That's great," they sigh, with the glee of the general public during seasons three through six of *Glee*, "but it's not a workshop; it's a Lab."

"Yeah, same thing."

"No. *They aren't*," they snap with cold eyes. "You know *A Chorus Line*?"

"Yeah," you nod, "I saw the revival with Mario Lopez."

"OK, we'll get back to that, because I have stories… but, *A Chorus Line* is where all this shit started."

Your new friend proceeds to finish their whiskey sour and order a double Johnnie Walker Blue, neat. They must be on one of those government job production contracts.

"In the '70s," they continue, "Michael Bennett rounded up a bunch of his dancer friends after a class and they all sat around talking about the business and their experiences within it. He recorded their stories and then persuaded Joseph Papp to fund a 'workshop' at The Public where he could develop a musical about Broadway dancers based off of those recorded tapes.

This wasn't going to be a normal musical-making procedure; *A Chorus Line* would need a rather unique rehearsal process, with a group of dancers collaborating closely with Bennett to create it. Papp agreed to produce the workshop, and the rest is history."

You roll your eyes. "Anyone who's ever owned a starter pair of Capezios knows this."

"Yeah," they nod, "and if you've ever had your foot traced by Phil LaDuca, you know that because of their contribution, Bennett worked out an agreement with Equity for any of the performers involved—with either the taped recordings or the original workshop—to receive one-half of the one-percent of the weekly box office gross receipts designated for the author. Why? Because not only were the dancers co-creating the show, they were also getting paid a fairly shitty weekly wage in exchange for their heavy collaboration."

For the most part, this is a lot of information you already know, so you're thinking, "Ugh, I got stuck with a drunk talker." I'm sorry.

"This is really fascinating and all," you smile falsely, "but I just saw my friend walk in. She's really mad I haven't retweeted her in a while, so I should probably go do damage control—

Your subtle excuse goes ignored.

"So then sometime around *Ballroom*—I think maybe 1977? I don't know, text Jen Tepper—Bennett refined the agreement with Equity so that actors who take part in an original workshop of a production share a separate percent—or 'point'—of the box office instead of the writer's, and that more-or-less became the standard contract used until recently."

"OK, cool," you nod, "So, like, why are you yelling at me?"

"Because nobody produces under the Workshop Contract anymore!"

"Then what are *we* doing?"

"I told you, it's a Lab," they explain, "Nobody has used a real Workshop Contact since *The Book of Mormon*. After that, it mysteriously became a Lab, and yet you kids walk around town calling it a workshop instead of calling it what it actually is: a LAB—or, as I call it, 'Lazy Ass Broadway' because I swear it only exists because someone wasn't paying attention."

"A 'Workshop,'" they say, using air quotes, "Is now a word that has become branded in the lexicon like Kleenex; a tissue isn't always a Kleenex—sometimes a tissue is made by Puffs!"

Now you're confused. "Then, what's a Lab?"

"It's the exact same thing as a workshop, but without the good shit."

"Isn't the good shit just the joy and personal validation of being allowed in the room with the creative team to help craft a new work?" you ask.

"*No*. The good shit is the *dollars*," they say sternly, "not the immediate salary –which is somewhere between $630 and $750 a week—but the dollars that you earn if the show becomes a bigger deal.

"When a new work is presented under a standard Workshop Contract, the company involved splits around one-percent of the weekly gross box office receipts should the show transfer to a commercial run— no matter if you're in it or not. You also get first right of refusal. That means that if the show moves to Broadway, and the creative team is like, 'Oh, sorry, we forgot that you're short,' and decides to replace you with what I call a 'Tall Boring,' then they have to pay you no less than four weeks of production contract to compensate you for them wasting your time and killing your dreams."

Your eyes widen. "Whoa."

"Not bad, huh?" they smirk. "Guaranteed royalties *and* protection, in exchange for your contribution and time spent devoted to the original development? That's literally why the workshop contract was created—to give actors special benefits in lieu of full salaries during an extended creative process."

"But, wait," you urge, "Aren't we getting a thousand dollars a week for this Lab? That's more than you said we'd get paid under a Workshop Contract, so that's better, right?"

"You're part of the problem!" exclaims the fired up actor, throwing their arms up in the air. "Sure, a Lab is more money on the front end, but if it were a workshop that became a hit, we'd get to split a percent for every single commercial production."

You sort of see their point, but "One percent isn't a lot when split between twenty or thirty people."

Frustrated by your constant combating, the self-proclaimed Leader of the Anti-Lab Movement orders another scotch and proceeds to break down the math for you.

"Say there end up being four productions—Broadway, First National, West End, Second National—and each one grosses half a million dollars a week… If you split that between thirty cast members, your share comes to over twenty-five hundred dollars a month."

"You know a lot about this," you admit, surprised by how easily this person is able to do math while completely blasted.

"It haunts me every day," they say, polishing off their second scotch and ordering a third. Woof. You'd be on the floor by now.

"I guess it makes sense that producers wouldn't want to lose that money over time," you say, "No wonder the Workshop Contract is gone."

"It's not!" they scream, slapping the bar, "Just like the Full Production Touring Contract, the Workshop Contract still exists, but people don't use it anymore because there are other options *and I'm trying to find out what the eff happened.*"

It's at this point that you start to side with your new cast mate. Sure, they are bordering on belligerent, and the addition of the third scotch they just ordered is only going to get them more fired up, but—

"We saw how the tiered touring thing happened!" they continue on with no regard for cutting me off just now, "we watched those contracts devolve over time! In many ways we were able to understand the choices made by Equity because there was a greater fear we'd lose the jobs on the road to non-union actors if the salaries weren't cut. But like…Where the fuck did this Lab thing come from? AND WHY? Why did someone say 'yes' to this? Did a major producer walk into Equity one day and say, 'So, these Workshop Contracts…I want to do them and all? But like…without all the actors' rights,' and then did someone random just say, "YES! We can call them…Labs!" while looking at a picture of their Black Labrador on their desk!?

"What would have been the alternative if someone said 'NO?!' It's not like a producer is going to think they'll land investors from mounting a presentation of *Don't Tell Mom the Babysitter's Dead: the musical* without a boatload of Broadway talent to back it up. They have the option to go non-union with tours that are launched after Broadway, but it wasn't like they were going to do the same thing with shows *pre*-Broadway. This wasn't one of those situations where producers had another alternative, *and yet we gave them one.*"

"Huh." You're stumped.

"Literally: WHAT. THE. FUCK. HAPPENED."

"But, I mean, I get it… We don't write the shows," you offer, trying to think of a reason this happened, because everything happens for a reason. "We don't direct them, or choreograph them or—

"HAVE YOU EVER DONE PRE-PRODUCTION?"

"No."

"More like *Free-Production*," they scoff. "Look, I love my choreographers as much as anyone, and I want to continue to work for them, but, I've done a lot of unpaid work in an effort to help facilitate a vision that will be used in the actual rehearsal process—often one I'm not even going to be a part of. I'm not asking for much! People would be surprised what a gift card to Outback Steakhouse can get them!"

I'm going to have to butt in here and just say that if there is pre-production pay, it usually comes from out of the choreographer's pocket; this is an entirely different problem, so I wouldn't bother getting the Senior started on it because they can clearly lay into a subject when provoked.

"And don't get me started on this bastard hybrid of a Workshop and a 29-Hour Reading known as an 'Experimental Staged Something-or-Whatever' where in ten days you essentially block the entire show and learn fully choreographed numbers, but are required to hold your binders like it's effing Encores. I did one of those this year, and because we were all so damned stressed trying to get the thing together in that amount of time— and weren't protected by any kind of first right of refusal—we memorized the entire show in an attempt to impress the creative team so they would actually use us again. The presence of binders doesn't mean we aren't contributing to the final product.

"The moment you start to put a show on its feet, it changes. There's no way to deny the fact that when you move a piece of theatre off the page and hand it to a group of actors, their mark will be made on it in some way. It doesn't have to be as drastic of an impression as *A Chorus Line*; sometimes it's a funny bit a performer made up, or some staging that gets suggested, or a line that is rewritten because the actor found a way to make the structure of it flow better, or a special trick a specific dancer can do that the choreographer finds a way to showcase. Shit like that works its way into the original staging and, eventually, scripts licensed from MTI. However small they may seem, contributions from the actors in original workshops have helped people win Tony awards.

"Look, workshops, and labs—or whatever—die every day. I know the odds that our little show will even get to Broadway, let alone become *Hamilton*, are about as likely as anything beating *Hamilton*—but there's a chance. I'd forfeit the extra couple hundred dollars a week that the Lab provides, in exchange for what I could be rewarded, should what I'm contributing to become a hit. None of us walk into a project assuming it'll fail, and yet the only people who've seemed to grasp this fact are the producers—now that they've found a way to save money, should the project succeed. Props to them for doing their job! Seems like the only people not marking on Broadway these days are the producers.

"We've been fighting for years to get a percent of grosses split amongst an original Broadway cast, but how do we expect to do that now when we've lost it in the workshop? This is all just a further example of how actors are constantly looked at as expendable—just grateful to be there. The workshop contract was forged from a group of artists coming together to create a show out of love for what they do, and they were rewarded for it. The final ballad from the musical that started it all is literally called, 'What I Did For Love'—the sheer irony that *Hamilton* performed a tribute to *A Chorus Line* on its 40th Anniversary *at The Public* and none of those actors' contributions were protected under a true Workshop Contract is even more fucked up than when I didn't book *Hamilton*."

All of this interests you, but you can't let them go on without saying, "I see what you mean, but I feel like there's too much 'us' vs. 'them' when it comes to Equity. It's *our* union. If we want something in the future, we have to be active *now*. What good is venting over drinks instead of attending membership meetings or voting in any union elections? We don't have anyone to blame but ourselves."

And with that, the Broadway Senior slams back the rest of their third double Johnnie Walker Blue label and gazes at you hazily—their head barely able to sit upon its shoulders. You don't know what to say, except—

"So unless we're going to do something, we *should* be grateful. We get paid to sing, and dance, and live our dreams. Who cares about all the ugly crap? You must always be grateful."

Fearing they didn't hear you through their boozy-delusional-fog, you further press them with this important question:

"Why can't you just be grateful with what you have? I'm always grateful."

At the third uttering of the word "grateful," the Broadway Senior's eyes jump back into focus.

"You know what? You're right," they say, as they stand and come around to embrace you from the side.

It looks like you really got through to them. Perhaps you've managed to convert this Broadway Senior down a grade!

"I've been so foolish, ignorant, and hashtag-ungrateful," says your new friend, as you feel one hand upon your chin and the other on the back of your head.

(I guess you're dating now?) "You have led me to the light, and now I'd like to return the favor."

What the—are you guys going to make out?

SNAP! Your body falls awkwardly onto the floor.

"Did the chair *break a leg*?" you think as you hit the ground. (I guess even the furniture at Glass House has theatre in its blood!)

Fearful that someone important saw this incident transpire, you quickly pick yourself up like nothing happened. When your eyes adjust, you see what looks like the non-Eq, standby version of you passed out on the bar. Wait a minute. That *is* you.

In shock, you step quickly away from this disconcerting sight. What in *An Act of God*'s name is going on here? Are you so excited about your workshop/lab/whatever that you're having a literal out-of-body experience? Is this what Cloud Nine feels like? Or is it possible that…you're dead? You don't know! This could be anything, and since you never got papered into *Ghost*, you have no real understanding of what is happening right now.

"Neck break?" says a boyish voice behind you. "That's rough."

You turn and see a spritely little figure with Resting Angst Face.

"Am I dead?" you ask.

"Yeah," says the elf child, "sorry."

Whoa. Hold up. Being dead is going to be seriously inconvenient for you. There's no way you'll be able to do your "Lab" now. This sucks! It was a job you wanted more than anything in the world! More than greens, and fiddleferns, and lettuce—or a child. More than life. More than anything—and you were willing to die for it.

You stand there, staring at your peaceful body lying face down on the bar, bewildered by so many things in this new reality—primarily how ugly that top looks from the back.

"I see it all the time," says the boy, who looks about twenty-three, going on eleven. "Most of you don't linger this long after, though."

"Where am I?" you ask.

The boy cocks his head like you should know. "Why, you're in Broadway Purgatory, of course."

"Is there a Broadway Hell?"

He nods. "Sure. You just came from it."

"How do I get to Broadway Heaven?"

"It depends," he says. "The level of impact you made upon Broadway history will determine how quickly you float over to your orientation theatre. I wonder if you'll get into the Hellinger."

"The *Mark* Hellinger? Don't you mean the Times Square Church?"

"Only the live ones see it as a church," laughs the boy. "In Broadway Heaven, it's still the Hellinger. In fact, all of the theatres exist where you are now. You should see the Hippodrome."

Whoa. The Hippodrome was demolished during World War II. You remember this fact from your Musical Theatre History class in college. Harry Houdini used to do his disappearing acts there, and it was so big, they could sink an actual ship on stage. The closest thing to the Hippodrome now, is the Lyric—except instead of ships sinking, it's shows, and the only thing doing disappearing acts is investor money.

"What's the Hippodrome like?" you ask.

"I don't know. I haven't been summoned," sighs the boy. "That's why I said *you* should see it, at the very least. Most anyone who's been cast in a Lab gets into the

Hippodrome because it's the biggest. Apparently not big enough for me, though."

The kid continues to mope around as he talks to you—like he was just given a lot of homework on a weekend. There's something recognizable about his tormented aura, but you can't place it. He is familiar in his forgettableness.

"The Hellinger is the most elite," he continues, "but you might have a shot because they take a shine to the idealistic and blissfully unaware."

"How did you die?"

He shrugs. "Plot hole."

"Pothole?"

"No. *Plot* hole," he corrects you sternly. "Everyone thinks I was hit by a truck, street sweeper, or the Long Island Railroad – but actually, I was just dodging a Chinese food delivery bike and fell into a convoluted plot hole."

That sounds more tragic than anything, you think. "Why aren't you…um…in Broadway Heaven yet?"

"I haven't been invited in yet," he frowns. "They're taking their time with me. I only wrote the book to one Broadway show, and the entire thing got cut and restructured by someone else, but I still managed to win a Tony. They don't take kindly to stuff like that."

It finally dawns on you who this kid is. "Wait, are you –

"Yes. I am."

"But… how? You're not real. You're a TV chara –

Pissed off by this, the boy gets right up in your face. "Anything that has to do with Broadway that has died comes here. Fictional or not," he spouts. "Ethel Merman, Richard Rodgers, David Belasco, Bernardo, The Baker's Wife, Wendla's unborn fetus, half the characters in *'night Mother*, Bailey Hanks' career. They're all here."

Clearly you questioning his existence has struck a chord, so you decide to back off. "What do you do in... uh... Broadway Purgatory?"

"I mostly just lurk around Midtown and haunt shit," he explains, having now calmed down. "Like dressing rooms and Michael Riedel's bathroom. But I spend the majority of my time drifting around the Lily Hayes. I'm what they call, 'stuck.'"

"What if... I'm stuck, too?"

Loud laughing emanates from the behind you. You turn to see your killer gesturing to your body slumped over the bar.

"One too many vodka sodas," jokes the Broadway Senior to the bartender.

Twisting back around, you proceed to ask your ghostly friend about your fate again, but he has vanished.

"Curiouser and bi-curiouser," you think to yourself with regard to that peculiar fellow.

Alone for the first time, it occurs to you that everyone at Glass House was so engaged in networking, not a single person witnessed your murder. You can't tell if you're unfazed by this because you're dead, or because you empathize with them. Either way, there's not much time to dwell on it because you spot your killer draping your body's arm around their shoulder and *Weekend at Bernie's*-ing you out the front door.

Determined not to let your body go (because you had *just* done a juice cleanse), you race straight through the closed door (which is a pretty odd sensation, like that time you had to do a survival job) and follow your killer across the street, as they continue to make like they're dragging an inebriated friend back home.

The three of you come to a stop at a dimly lit section of 47th Street, and when nobody in the vicinity appears to be looking, you see your body get hoisted up and thrown inside the dumpster outside Buffalo Wild Wings.

"No!" you scream. "Anywhere but there!"

The killer doesn't hear you as you continue to scream in guttural anger at the idea of your body being put to rest in the garbage of a Times Square tourist trap. Dropping to the street, you clutch the apparition that is your face with your ghost hands. This new reality is harder to bear than when a play is advertised as 90 minutes with no intermission and is actually 110 minutes. You're so overcome by this fresh horror that you don't see your killer escape into the night. You've never felt more lost than you do at this moment, and that includes the time you second acted *If/Then*.

When you finally work up the courage to stand and face this new reality, you find that you're no longer on 47th Street, but a few blocks north, standing in front of *the* Mark Hellinger theatre. This is really it. *The* Mark Hellinger. No sign reads "Times Square Church." 51st Street is blank. Blinding, bright white light envelops you from both sides of the street. The doors swing open and beaming light shoots out onto the sidewalk, giving you a fierce silhouette.

You turn to me, as I am now present for this crossover. "Are you coming?" you ask.

"I can't," I say, as I peek past you and see the shadow of George M. Cohan beckoning you from a balcony in the lobby. "You're on your own now."

You smile, and take note of how you feel. "It's amazing Molly," you tell me. "The grateful inside, you take it with you."

Wait go back. "I'm sorry, did you just ask me to do Molly?" I ask.

Alas, it is too late. You have already turned, and walked through the doors and into the great beyond. Shit, I missed it.

THE END.

*

"I'd like to keep the title *Pieces of Me*," you insist, "but if there's anything else you think I should change, let me know; I'm open to listening."

"Well," Daniel mutters nervously, "there are a few things I was thinking about bringing up…"

Daniel delves into his notes and concerns about elements of *Pieces of Me*—notes that primarily have to do with your book, but, whatever, you said that you were open to listening. Being the trooper you are, you agree to implement all of Daniel's suggestions (including the axing of two main characters he deemed "superfluous") and in exchange for your sacrifice, Daniel consents to cutting an entire verse out of a song in act two. Writing partnerships are all about compromise.

Excited by the new changes (and the cast you assembled through bribery), you quickly draft a press release stating that a "private industry reading" of your new musical *Pieces of Me* will be held this week starring, "a cast of Broadway favorites that include: Corey Michael Cooper, Ashley Marie Smith, James Tyler Doyle, Brittany Beth Adams, Holden MacGroyne, and Ellyn Marie Marsh." You then toss in a few buzzwords like, "a creative team has not yet been announced" and "Broadway-bound," before firing it off to your friends who work at Playbill and Broadway World with the subject line, "Should Be Fun."

Within a few hours, the press hits the interwebs, and you start getting "Congrats!" texts from "friends" you haven't spoken to since the first time Karen Olivo left the business. People are really coming out of the woodwork due to your perceived success. There's even a small thread starting on the Broadway World message board—and those always end positively. You can't wait to not read that shit!

When the day of your Broadway-bound-informal-industry-read-thru-in-your- shoebox-apartment-with-a-case-of-cheap-wine finally arrives, you are *psyched*. Unable to control your enthusiasm, you decide to open up the message board thread on Broadway World and WHAT ARE YOU DOING DON'T DO THAT STOP!

The first couple of posts are fairly harmless, and even optimistic! There's the typical back and forth about which theater *Pieces of Me* will take, a few casual comments about the relatively unknown cast involved (which some are excited about, some imagine will change, and some are like, "but will they sell tickets?") and then user "Quarter2_9" drops a surprising endorsement…

> "**Quarter2_9:** Happy news! And great news! *Pieces of Me* appears to have all the makings of a truly innovative piece of musical theatre. With a young creative team at the helm (and a title that suggests a raw and authentic look into the complicated psyche of the Millennial generation) we are bound to be in for a real treat. There needs to be more fresh ideas from unknown writers developed for Broadway. I'm tired of these pretentious pop composers and Europeans commanding all the attention of producers and critics with their drivel dredged from the sewer. I trust it won't be long before several investors latch onto this project that will no doubt be hip and buzzy when it debuts on Broadway—where it will hopefully take the place of another boring revival. Am I wrong in believing that this inspired piece of art will prove to be terrific?

You know the answer.

We all do.

Great, great news!"

The posts written after Quarter2_9's follow suit in tone and overall awesomeness. It's crazy how positivity is occasionally contagious when people try. It's also a really good omen for a show to receive solid reviews before the first read. You're confident that once your work is read aloud, the buzz will be so great, it'll only be a matter of time before *Pieces of Me* is in the hands of hopefully anyone but the Weisslers.

***

You awake the morning after the industry-only reading of *Pieces of Me*, plagued with a Charles Shaw Chardonnay hangover that's only slightly coloring your memory of the success of the previous evening. From what you remember, the intimate presentation of your debut musical was very well received by your peers, and not just because you pumped them full of free food and booze. Your friends aren't going to blow smoke up your ass just because they're under the influence of alcohol. In fact, it's more likely that in those circumstances, they'd tell you if your show sucked.

Daniel and you celebrate the euphoric bliss of hearing your work read aloud by congratulating each other over text. After no less than an hour of gushing, the two of you come to an agreement that before you can proceed in the process of finding a commercial producer (or whatever comes next) it's a good idea to request individual feedback from your friends. Even though you know everyone loved *Pieces of Me*, there are always things to improve upon, and you're both prepared to implement suggestions that best help facilitate the vision of the story you're trying to tell.

"It all seems pretty positive" you remark to Daniel at your next work session. "The feedback... It's more or less what we expected."

"Yeah," sighs Daniel, "I want to sit on it a bit more, and see what we think after being away from it for a while."

A piece of the usual spark in Daniel's voice is missing. He doesn't seem as inspired as he was a week ago, before the reading. It's not that he received any negative feedback from the cast; he actually came away from the entire thing unscathed. You, on the other hand, have quite a few adjustments to make—and you're happy to do them. Daniel, however, did not obtain any negative critiques, or comments in general—good or otherwise.

"Oh," you think to yourself. You now understand the problem.

Daniel has often lamented to you that it is a "crime to be boring," and now you're wondering if the tepid response to his music and lyrics are leading him to believe he's fallen victim to his greatest fear.

"We can take a break," you suggest to Daniel. "It'll give the piece room to breathe, and then we can come back to the table in a few weeks and have a better idea of what we need to fix."

"Yeah," nods Daniel, "that sounds like a good idea."

The two of you agree to stay in close contact, but not discuss *Pieces of Me*. This plan seems to work, and is aided by you suggesting to focus on something else in the meantime.

You remember reading somewhere that Robert Lopez and Jeff Marx got their start writing *Ferdinand the Bull* for Theatreworks/USA. Jeff Marx would go on to earn millions on *Avenue Q*, and Robert Lopez would do equally well on *Avenue Q*, *The Book of Mormon*, and *Frozen*—so maybe the two of you could make money following the same trajectory. This compels Daniel and you to write a treatment and a few songs for a musical of a popular children's book series.

An already established franchise that's easily adaptable is a great thing to further cut your newly-minted librettist teeth on. *Pieces of Me* was your first time out the gate, and you now know so much more about how you and Daniel work together. Developing a side project will make you better writing partners going forward, and a stronger team when it comes to returning to your first project to fix the shitty parts.

"Just three or so songs," you suggest over coffee, "and I'll write a complete outline that we can present in an effort to get the rights to the book."

You and Daniel decide on musicalizing Tim Federle's *Better Nate Than Ever*, which is the story of a thirteen-year-old boy from a small town in Pennsylvania who runs away to New York City to audition for *E.T.: The Musical*. You remember liking the book because it has a lot of insidery jokes about Broadway—and you can never get enough of those in any book, no matter how contrived or insufferably niche they are.

"And then," you continue, "If Tim likes the idea, we can go from there."

"Do you even know him?" questions Daniel.

"No," you shrug, "but he liked one of my tweets once, so we're probably OK."

During the weeks following the reading of *Pieces of Me*, Daniel bangs out two solid songs to accompany your extensive treatment of *Better Nate Than Ever: The Musical*.

"I'm really proud of these songs," he says to you the next time you meet up. "They came easier for me than what I wrote for *Pieces of Me*, and I think they're better."

You agree, but don't articulate that. Daniel has proven to be a tremendous talent, with strong confidence, but rather thin skin. You've taken the time away from *Pieces of Me* to reflect a lot on your contribution, but also that of Daniel's. You're grateful to be working with him, but there is something missing from his debut score that you (and everyone in the reading, apparently) can't pinpoint.

Daniel fidgets contemplatively with his coffee cup. "It makes me want to go back and rewrite the score of *Pieces of Me*."

"The *entire* thing?" you question.

"I feel like I'm getting better," he says. "These last few songs are proving that. I think I need to keep working on myself."

Resisting an eye roll grander than any you've executed since they called that character on *Smash* a "dramaturg" instead of a "show doctor," you nod, and politely smile at Daniel.

"I agree," you lie, "I feel like I'm finding myself as a writer, too."

The truth is, you don't think you're half bad at the moment. Sure, you definitely need a lot of work, but you're not about to throw away an entire draft and start over before finding out if there's at least a passing bit of interest in what you've already written. I can relate to that. For example, I let my social media posts linger online for at least twenty minutes, and if they haven't received the requisite amount of attention, I delete them and cry for an hour. You need to give this draft the time to fail before trashing the entire thing—and it doesn't look like Daniel has the confidence to do that.

When it comes to project #2, you want no less than three songs finished before you attempt to acquire the rights to *Better Nate Than Ever*. Your treatment is completed, but Daniel has only written two numbers, so the ball is in his court.

While Daniel works on the last song, you decide to apply the adjustments to *Pieces of Me* that were suggested by the cast at the reading. Once you've concluded what turned out to be a rather large overhaul to the script, you get back in touch with Daniel to see where he's at in his process.

"Things have been crazy lately," laments Daniel, the next time you talk.

And by "crazy," what he really means is he got a kickass "music person gig" that pays him a boatload of cash and he hasn't had any time to focus on your shows—or what has increasingly begun to appear to you like inconveniences to him.

Unfortunately, after a significant number of attempts to get Daniel focused on the next steps, it becomes apparent that his attention has drifted to a place from which you can never recover him. No matter how hard you strive to get him motivated, he always seems to have an excuse to explain his way out of it. After consistently trying, you realize you're beating a dead horse. Daniel's heart is no longer in the work, and you can't seem to figure out what went wrong.

Was it you? Were you too passionate about working on so many things at once that Daniel got burnt out? Was it him? Was he suffering the self-loathing of his work in silence and you didn't notice? Or, did he just stop loving it? Daniel is a complex individual who hides his emotions well. You wear your emotions proudly on social media because you are an artist. You'll never know why Daniel grew so reticent about your work, and to make matters worse, you can't pursue these projects with another writing partner because Daniel's contributions make up half of what's on the page. In some cases, you can't remember where your contributions leave off and his begin.

None of this matters to you anyway because *Pieces of Me* is so tainted now that even if you could develop it from scratch with another writer, you're not so certain you won't be let down again. The show was called *Pieces of <u>Me</u>*, not *Pieces of <u>We</u>*—and sadly, it turns out it was something only you could have trusted yourself to complete. Sometimes you can make all the right choices, and ultimately find yourself at the whim of someone else's insecurities.

THE END.

You win! Choosing not to write about yourself in an extended second person narrative for far too long was the best and easiest decision you've ever made, and you literally didn't have to do anything. Not only did you save the hours of turmoil it would take to try and explain yourself from the perspective of the reader, you also spared people the boredom of having to read it. Your second book is now better than the first solely because of this non-decision. Better yet, it's more successful to boot.

It's crazy how fast you're trending up. You're rich and famous now. Everyone on Twitter follows you *and* you're verified. CAA signs you. Joe Machota is your agent, and you're the only one he lets talk to him about his *Mamma Mia!* days. Everyone wants you, and even time itself has agreed to work around your schedule so you can have the opportunity to take breaks and travel first class to everywhere without losing progress on any of your high profile projects. You've been asked to write a play for Roundabout, take over as showrunner for the Hulu reboot of *Smash*, and even work for BuzzFeed. You have an indefinite, free open table and tab at Bar Centrale. Calories don't count anymore. Winter in New York doesn't apply to you. You beat Lin-Manuel Miranda to an EGOT. Tina Fey texts you in emojis. Literally, everything in life is now possible.

This isn't the end. It's the beginning.

EPILOGUE (page 465)

*

"Um, duh!" exclaims Paige when you randomly run into her at a gypsy run for something. "Send me your script like yesterday!"

A week following yesterday, it becomes clear that Paige was not leaping to read *Metamorphosis: the Hilary Duff Musical* in quite the way she implied.

"I am literally the worst," she explains. "I've been doing this Broadway.com vlog, and it's taking up *all of my time*. It's like… I can't even—whatever."

OK, looks like Paige is out. Your next option is to send it to Corey.

Corey doesn't read it either.

Now the only choice is to go to the B List: your friends Ashley or Ellyn. Ashley is sensitive and Ellyn is brash. Both will offer solid critiques, it just depends what tone you want to color your feedback. Do you…

Send your script to Ashley…? (page 336)

Send your script to Ellyn…? (page 343)

*

    Um. I don't know what to say. I'm going to ask the guys from [*title of show*] how to handle this decision.

    THE END.

Oh, I see. You chose the cookies. Cool. First you skipped the gym, now you're making it a fat day. That's fine. No judgment here. It's not like you're popping into a bodega to shovel a package of Neapolitan wafers down your throat; this is freaking Schmackary's, where the calories don't count because they're made with non-Equity blood and Broadway-debut tears.

Schmackary's burst onto the Broadway scene in 2012, around the same time as Corey Cott, and has been equally successful ever since. They built an audience by seducing casts with cookies during rehearsals for anything from Broadway shows to workshops, readings, tours, benefits, and Feinstein's/54 Below concerts that featured a minimum of three Newsies. Free Schmackary's became a status symbol that represented a major accomplishment. If a tray of Maple Bacon cookies appeared on a table in your studio, you knew you had arrived.

Being unemployed makes this occasional salty-sweet treat seem bittersweet—like you're eating your feelings, instead of indulging in the success that usually accompanies a Schmacker-doodle. Luckily, you're not the only one. Chances are good that at any given moment at Schmackary's, there's another customer experiencing the same tragic trajectory as you.

As per usual, the tiny store is crammed tighter than the pants on an aging *Chicago* dancer who's dangerously close to being put on weight probation. It doesn't matter what time of day it is, Schmackary's will feel like two chorus calls let out into a subway car that smells like gluten-free oats—and in the midst of all that crazy, there's always some random asshole trying to write the next Great American Novel while seated on one of the only bar stools, like this is some kind of

Starbucks. Next time that happens, you need to tell me to get an office.

While standing in line, you're able to ignore all of the people that you don't want to speak to by scrolling through social media on your phone and reading their posts on your feed. I love New York City in the Don't Look at Me/Please Look at Me age. My old annoying actor friend always talks about how much better Times Square was when it wasn't strange to see a hooker doing an eight ball with a Cosette around the corner from the stage door. That sounds like it was great and all, but what good is anything if I can't Instagram it?

When you reach the front of the line to order your usual standby (Funfetti), you notice there is a special cookie of the day that you've never tried before: Chocolate Telsey + Co-coa Cream. Oh, the dilemma! Do you…

Play it safe with Funfetti…? (page 449)

Take a walk on the wild side with Chocolate Telsey + Co-coa Cream…? (page 179)

*

BAHAHAHAHAHA. Yeah, right. You're a fame whore who loves attention. I don't believe this choice for a moment. Try again.

BACK. (page 110)

*

Taking chances and trying new things is hard, so you should stick to what you know. Better to continue the blog, and engage the audience you have, than risk losing them by disappearing into the Fusion lounge for three months to write some book, only to return lacking relevance.

Determined to strike while the iron is hot, you keep blogging for free, while simultaneously ignoring your real life job obligations (like getting more clients and keeping the ones you have). After three months of pouring your heart into sassy blogs about BFA programs and Funemployment, you find that you can't pay your rent because you've devoted all of your time to sassy blogs about BFA programs and Funemployment. Furthermore, to add insult to injury, Stuart (remember him?) calls you into his office:

"You're disengaged in your sessions and your clients have sent me a few disheartening emails about your overall behavior," he bemoans.

"I'm having money issues."

"I'm sorry about your financial problems, I really am, but they are *your* problems, not your clients'."

"I'm stressed."

"This is Fusion. We don't do 'stress" here. We're about fitness gains, mental health management, and cucumber water. If any of those words sound stressful to you, maybe this is no longer a good fit."

"Are you firing me?"

"If you can commit to putting the time back into your business, your job is secure here."

With that, you cease blogging, and return to pounding the pavement at Fusion in an effort to rebuild your business. By the time you are financially stable again, IPP has fallen into Internet obscurity and is all but a distant melody.

Broken, you turn on your DVR, flip to *Peter Pan Live!*, and sing silently to yourself in the cold darkness of your studio apartment:

Once upon a time and long ago,
I was someone tweeting
You'd follow.
Now that I have quit
Because of greed
I recall the tweets you used to read.
"So blessed, so very blessed,
Retweet these please, lest I be stressed.
Mean Girls ref'rence, Smash,
Hamilton joke."
Long ago these tweets were writ by me,
Now they're just a distant melody.
Social media fame I used to know,
Once upon a time
And long ago...

THE END.

*

Deciding *Pieces of Me* is too personal for mainstream (and that it's probably a better idea to keep the Facebook status it was adapted from far out of view of the public), you give your baby one last cathartic read, before shelving it forever.

Whether or not you realized it while it was transpiring, the entire endeavor has changed you. Making yourself remember the very real pain the business has caused you in the past has added a subtle layer of negativity to your usually positive disposition. Actors are complex characters, and you're finding that with this change, comes great consequences. You're no longer the person who loved Broadway, but pretended to be indifferent to it; your journey into the dark truth that lies buried deep within the underbelly of the business has altered your perspective of it, and you can no longer continue on pursuing it in the same way.

While fully embracing this change, you're prepared to embark on whatever quest the business brings next in the darkness of this new dawn…

Journey on… (page 458)

When taking to social media, it's always best to master one platform before trying to immediately become proficient in everything. The Internet is just too much information at once, like a BFA program. Hashtags and Vines are flung at you with the same reckless abandon as ballet terms, music theory, and Sondheim flops. If you don't properly place your focus on excelling at one thing first, you will burn out. Successful multitasking is only attainable if you wrote *Hamilton*, and if you didn't, I suggest building a solid bridge from one project to another, *before* you try to cross over—because you will fall and drown. And die.

I suppose this advice is a little moot, considering you've already chosen to create an IPP Instagram before developing a solid brand on Twitter, so I guess we're just going to have to see what you do with it.

Considering you're still anonymous, you can't really post pics of yourself. You could pull creative content off of Tumblr and such, like The Fat Jew, and get famous by posting other people's work, but you already decided against Tumblr, and also, you're not a fucking monster. The option you settle on is the posting of screen caps of irritating social media statements with the offender's name blurred out, accompanied with satirical commentary. This puts the entertainment in what you write, and not in the blatant poaching of someone else's genius. *You're* the genius. Remember that!

Except, you're so not the genius, because just like *Bring Back Birdie*, this idea is uniquely flawed. I'm speaking from experience, because when I was in high school, I contacted Tams-Witmark and requested a perusal copy of *Bring Back Birdie* to find out WTF that was about, so I know flawed shit when I see it. It's not that what you're writing on Instagram isn't rich with wit and cynicism; it's actually pretty good. The problem is you've gone back on the rules you've previously established: to not directly troll another actor. You've now confused your audience. It's like at the end of *Bring Back Birdie*, where you find out that Albert's mom was Spanish the entire time. Like, that completely fucks up a third of *Bye Bye Birdie,* and now, thanks to me, you'll never un-know that fact, and *Bye Bye Birdie* will be forever ruined for you in ways you never imagined—which is really saying something after that Roundabout revival.

So... I guess that's it for IPP? Want to go to Blockheads and talk about it?

THE END.

Opening up your Facebook app, you quickly fire off one of the many versions of callback posts you have saved in the drafts folder you had surgically implanted in your brain during the first weekend you auditioned for NETCs. There are several kinds of "positive vibes" requests you've done in the past, but because this one is extra special (a job you'd die for, truly) you make sure to include a lyric from *Into the Woods*; that means you really want this.

After making certain your vibes request has been funneled through all of your social media outlets, you spend the remaining hours before your callback poring over the new material you just received from your agent. There's a healthy amount of extra sides to learn now (like, a Telsey amount) which is somewhat uncharacteristic of Tara Rubin's office in comparison to others. Whatever! You've got time to burn, and you're riding epic endorphins from all the positive vibes coming in.

By the time you arrive at your callback, you are so high on the love and life of friends, that you actually morph into the last three minutes of the *Smash* pilot… sans Ellis. *That's* how powerful you are at this very moment. From the getting ready, to the performance in the room, everything about the rest of your day goes perfectly.

Normally, when auditions and callbacks are executed with this level of flawlessness, it means anything but a booking. However, in this case, there's simply no way the power of positive vibes can possibly fail you. You will receive a call, oh yes, you will receive a call.

***

You received a call.

Now, here's where things get conflicted: You neglected to note during this process that the big, new Broadway show you were auditioning for is just a workshop right now, meaning you're a few pretty big hurdles away from opening night Instagram likes. You'll first have to do the workshop, then get asked back for the out-of-town tryout (should there be one), and then get asked back for the Broadway transfer (should there be one, and, if there's another tryout, you'll have to get asked back for *that one*, and if there's nothing else after all of that, then you're probably me).

None of this seems to really bother you, because you're still reeling from the combination of "booking excitement" and positive vibes that continue to flow in, even though it's the day after the callback (because anything you post online fails to fall below three hundred likes, causing it to remain at the top of newsfeeds for weeks.) All of this exhilaration refuses to mask the painful realization that you won't be allowed to post about this workshop until well after these heightened emotions have died down and you're over it—Broadway is hard. Still, you tell yourself that Not Broadway is harder, while trying to find a place to go tonight to unofficially celebrate your recent accomplishment.

The obvious choice is Glass House Tavern, because you're bound to run into someone who will ask you what you've been up to. However, you could try, for once, to keep it chill and visit your roommate Carol at the bar where she works—and have a casual cocktail because it'll be free.

Should you see what's up at Glass House, in the hopes that people will want to see what's up with you? Or, should you visit Carol for free drinks and friendly conversation with someone who actually gives a shit about you, even though she's currently not theatrically employed? Do you...

Visit Carol…? (page 28)

Go to Glass House…? (page 208)

Kickstarter it is! It's time to gather appropriate funding in order to move forward with production.

First, you must create a Kickstarter page. This requires pretty much every miniscule detail imaginable, along with a blood test and urine sample. In fact, if you're able to successfully publish this Kickstarter page without flinging yourself in front of a cab, then the city should back you with a $500 pledge simply for not blocking traffic.

Once you've completed the painstaking process of filling out the extensive profile for *Pieces of Me*, you proudly make it live for the entire world to see…

PIECES OF ME

About this project:

Pieces of Me is a piece of art packed with passion. For anyone who has ever dared to dream the American Theatre dream, this musical is not only for you, it's about you. It. Is. EVERYTHING. It's *A Star is Born*, *Hamlet*, *Romeo and Juliet*, Gaga, JT LeRoy, and also none of those things. It's utterly unique, yet insanely relatable. It's a new direction for musical theatre.

Risks and challenges:

People might not like it! EEEK!

Rewards:

Pledge $5 or more: A HUGE thank you and shout out on my Facebook page!
Pledge $10 or more: A HUGE thank you and shout out on my Twitter!
Pledge $20 or more: I'll follow you on Twitter for at least a month!

Pledge $25 or more: I'll pretend I remember your name when I see you around town!

Pledge $50 or more: I'll HANDWRITE you a THANK YOU letter!

Pledge $100 or more: We should talk! Like, on the phone! THANK YOU!

Pledge $500 or more: An autographed copy of the *Pieces of Me* script.

Pledge $1,000 or more: I'll bring you backstage at my Broadway show.

Pledge $2,500 or more: Are you serious??? Let's get drinks at Lillie's!

Pledge $5,000 or more: I'll follow you on Twitter forever.

Pledge $10,000 or more: I'll follow you on Twitter forever *and* not mute you.

Pledge $15,000 or more: I'll retweet you.

For the next thirty days, your social media presence becomes a balls-out-crowdfunding-craptavaganza. You really go for it. Nobody is safe from your self-promotion. You don't give a shit! This is about *art*! While your friends might be put off in the present, you're positive that sometime in the near future they'll forget it ever happened—and your family won't be annoyed with you because blood is thicker than water and resentment. This is your time to shine.

Unfortunately, in the over-saturated market of crowdfunding, you simply cannot compete with your peers' projects. There are just too many albums being made for anyone to pay attention to your show. This causes your Kickstarter to go over like a negative tweet during *The Wiz Live!*.

Without substantial backing, you're unable to reach your goal, and have to withdraw from NYMF.

Ashamed by this failure, you lose all motivation to further pursue a commercial run for *Pieces of Me*. Failing to receive the financial support from friends and family is a major personal blow to your ego. You may never recover. In fact, you don't.

THE END.

*

In a sensible display of restraint that could benefit all of those people who post on Broadway message boards, you close your laptop and decide not to make any more bold moves for the remainder of the evening. Instead, you open up your Seamless app and channel all your bad decisions into Chinese delivery. After a post-Broadway-Bares-style binge on a bowl of Mai Fun noodles (I feel like not having a theatre-inspired Chinese food restaurant that serves dishes like Singapore Mai Fun Home and Spring Awakening Rolls is an opportunity missed) you retreat to your bedroom and pass out, alone.

While you're asleep, you have back-to-back anxiety dreams—one of which involves you being in a dinner theatre production of *Pirates of Penzance,* and if that weren't horrifying enough, the set transitions into an actual pirate ship that sinks in the middle of the ocean, and while you're struggling not to drown, all you can think of is that your iPhone is still in your pocket and the thought of your child dying before you is too much to bear. This very true fear thrusts you awake in a cold sweat. You swiftly reach over to where your iPhone is charging, and find it safe and dry. Whoa. That was close. You breathe out a refreshing sigh of relief.

Your iPhone might be safe, but you know what isn't? Your ego. There still isn't any action on your new parody Twitter account. There's a part of you that figured it would have blown up on its own. Good work should be naturally recognized without any effort, right? I mean that's not quite the kind of thinking that got you here. Perhaps cautiously training clients with injuries has softened your ability to be an insufferable go-getter.

You don't remember exactly why you chose not to do anything last night to progress the success of your Twitter account. All you remember now is carbs and regret—but in a rare bout of irony, your regret, for once, does not stem from dietary choices, but from the complete bombing of a project you were once excited by. If you count your personal account, this is the third Twitter handle you've created that has failed. It appears your social media presence is being embraced like a James Barbour casting announcement.

For whatever reason, the spark of creation that was flickering within you is out and you don't have any drive to light it again. Why should you? You're a personal trainer and should really be focusing on furthering that career and becoming a smarter asset to your clients. Stop trying to be something you're not, you stupid, untalented, wannabe. You were never going to make it on Twitter. You didn't come up with anything groundbreaking. I feel like it's been done before anyway, tbh. You tell yourself all of these horrible things as you quietly delete Twitter from your phone and go back to your everyday life, where you continue to coast by without any enthusiasm.

It's funny, you know? With that much self-doubt, you probably *could* have been a writer.

THE END.

*

The prospect of producing a funny cabaret is intimidating to you, because you're not entirely certain if you have any comedic timing. I urge you to relax, and take heart in knowing that the New York Times said, "He has a sly sense of humor," in reference to Aaron Tveit's concert at the formerly-titled 54 Below—so you're probably going to be hilarious.

Now that you have decided upon a tone for your cabaret, it's time to find your team. While you will be the creator of your own material and the master of your own fate, you'll need a solid group of people surrounding you to help shape your show and take care of all the incidental crap that you cannot be bothered with. These are the positions you'll need to fill:

Producer: In charge of press, marketing, filming, photography, comp tickets, editing promotional YouTube videos, making the PowerPoint, dealing with the rehearsal studios, dealing with the venue, dealing with your crazy, and handing out drink tickets.

Music Director (MD): Your right hand man and main collaborator. They will be in charge of structuring all of the ideas you sleep-text to them at three in the morning.

Director: Tells you when something sucks. At least from my experience—I think that's pretty much all he did.

Deciding whom to recruit is a no-brainer because you only keep around people who share your sensibility. For producer, you recruit your friend Katie because she's got a dry sense of humor about her, knows how to use Final Cut Pro, and once wrote a press release.

Your MD will be your friend Andy, whom you met while doing *54 Below Sings A*Teens* where you connected halfway through sound check when you both said out loud, "literally what the fuck is going on." Finally, you make your girlfriend (a girl who is also a friend) Joey (like *Dawson's Creek*) direct your show. Joey is cool to bounce ideas off of, and while she may not be reliable, you're positive it will all pay off in the end.

Now that your squad is complete, it's time to pick a venue for your concert. This is going to be a very difficult and important decision: Feinstein's/54 Below, Joe's Pub, or Birdland?

If you choose Feinstein's/54 Below, you're guaranteed to get a lot of traction on Director of Programming Jennifer Ashley Tepper's social media. An average Tepper status garners roughly 300 likes, so that could be good for ticket sales. Birdland has a classic big band vibe to it, and Jim Caruso is really cool and produces a great concert series. Joe's Pub has the "edgy downtown" thing going for it—and *Hamilton* played in the same building, so there's gotta be something in that. Do you choose…

Feinstein's/54 Below…? (page 306)

Birdland…? (page 292)

Joe's Pub…? (page 120)

*

Ideas are overrated. It's probably best you didn't act on the one you just had. Instead, you delete your Twitter app and never visit its world again. After nixing Twitter, you let go of all social media platforms, because you think it will bring you closer to people – and for a while it does! You start walking around outside with your head up, instead of stuck in your device. Did you know New York City has buildings? This is so refreshing! There is a brief amount of time where you feel calm and open to the world, content that you aren't obligated to live tweet, or learn which acronyms come into vogue after smh, irl, af, and tbh. It's a refreshing feeling, and you start to sense yourself becoming a new person.

However, that time quickly dwindles. It's like Shakespeare, Sondheim, or Lin-Manuel Miranda said: "I tweet, therefore I am. If thou does not tweet, ye doth disappear." Truer words were never spoke.

Without the constant knowledge of what is trending, your body begins to become transparent. Look down at your hand. You know that part in *Back to the Future: the musical* where Marty's hand starts to disappear? Without social media, you are suffering the same fate. Without an online presence, you're being erased from existence.

Before you know it, your body dwindles away like the soul of an actor who pours their heart into a Lab, but gets replaced by Broadway. You fall into obscurity, and nobody ever hears from you again.

THE END.

Snagging a spot dead center in Bryant Park, you take off as many clothes as is legal in the state of New York, and use them as a blanket to lie upon and let the sunshine in. You are living your best funemployment life right now, and are not in the least bit concerned that your last unemployment check is a mere three weeks away, because you know you're going to book this shit later in the afternoon. Sometimes you sense the Universe telling you "yes" and you just know.

Feeling especially Zen right now, you pull out your iPhone and put in your ear buds in an attempt to further drown out the negativity of New York City. You will be having none of that today. It's only feel good music from now until your audition at 3 p.m.

After a few minutes of shuffling through your songs, you feel like none of them seem to hit the right tone you're looking for, so you switch over to your podcasts and select the episode of The Ensemblist that you were a guest on. Ahhhh... Nothing is more soothing than the sound of your own voice.

Lying back and closing your eyes, you think about how marvelous it is that you live in a world where technology makes it is so easy for people to create their own thing, and then you get to be part of that thing without having to do any work. Between web series', podcasts, and retweets, you've gotten your name out there on the backs of friends—and isn't that the American Dream?"

These thoughts float freely through your brain as you are rocked sweetly by The Ensemblist's transitional music until you drift off to sleep.

***

When you wake up, The Ensemblist podcast has come to an end (but how long ago, you don't know) and a wave of fear overcomes you (but not the usual uneasiness you're confronted with when you remember that Nikka Graff Lanzarone and Mo Brady have the audacity to produce an entire podcast devoted to the career of a Broadway ensemble member without using a Kickstarter). The fear in the pit of your stomach stems from post sleep disorientation that is making you question what time it is.

Quickly, you reach for your phone, and holy ball sack, it's an entire hour past your appointment time. HOW DID THIS HAPPEN. Everything was going so well! You had an amazing workout! You chose not to be a hussy with Ashton Reed! You knew your sides! You were just taking a sensible hour of "me time" and it completely screwed you! DAMN YOU ENSEMBLIST AND YOUR CALM, COZY, COFFEE SHOP ACOUSTIC GUITAR INCIDENTAL MUSIC!

In an effort not to embarrass yourself, you fire off a quick email to your agent explaining that you missed your audition because you got horrible food poisoning from the Sardi's Actor Menu that kept you glued to the toilet for most of the afternoon until the stomach pains got so great, you passed out on your bathroom floor. It's not that you have anything against Sardi's, it's just that something had to be thrown under the bus and it certainly wasn't going to be Schmackary's.

This really is unfortunate, isn't it? There will be other auditions of course, but this show had your name written all over it, and there may not be an opportunity as equal in its greatness to come to your aid before your unemployment insurance runs out. And the worst part about falling asleep in Bryant Park and missing what could have been a life changing show for you? The sun was in a shitty position the entire time… THE END.

*

"Um, duh!" exclaims Paige when you randomly run into her in Midtown. "Send me your script like yesterday!"

A week following yesterday, it becomes clear that Paige was not leaping to read *Metamorphosis: the Hilary Duff Musical* in quite the way she implied.

"I am literally the worst," she explains. "I've been doing a lot of pre-pro for this thing, and it's taking up *all of my time*. This choreographer is like… I can't even—whatever."

OK, looks like Paige is out. Your next option is to send it to David.

David doesn't read it either.

Now the only choice is to go to the B List: your friends Ashley and Ellyn. Ashley is sensitive and Ellyn is brash. Both will offer solid critiques, it just depends what tone you want to color your feedback. Do you…

Send your script to Ashley…? (page 336)

Send your script to Ellyn…? (page 343)

*

"I think I'll pass," you tell Stuart. "Things might get awkward, considering I used to audition for him."

"I understand," Stuart sighs, and you walk out of the office.

Feeling the need to do some soul searching, you decide to take a contemplative walk around the Upper West Side. Before you leave the club, you set your Pandora station to *Spring Awakening, American Idiot,* and/or Augustana, and prepare yourself for a sensible stroll of self-discovery while scrolling to angsty white boy music.

As you exit out of the revolving doors, you stop and wonder if maybe you made the wrong decision. Maybe landing that casting director as a client would have jump-started your confidence. Maybe you'd get inspired and become a personal trainer to the stars. Maybe far away, or maybe real nearby, you could have become the best personal trainer since...since...Forever. Maybe—

CRASH!

The deafening sound of a window smashing rings above you. You look up. Veiled within the shards of glass, you see a large black object sailing down directly toward you. You realize it's a kettlebell that some careless member must have let slip during their swings, and it's hurdling at you faster than the shade you threw at that bitch online who knows what he did. This is really unfortunate, tbqh. You don't have enough time to get out of the way before the kettlebell crushes your skull— and that's exactly what it does. It crushes your skull like I crushed my callback last week. And now you're dead. Because you didn't take the opportunity that was handed to you.

THE END.

You have an Instagram account. You have a phone. So, you have experience with which filters work for your selfies, and that means you can probably use those filters on other people's selfies. You have all the tools necessary to become a professional headshot photographer. Feeling confident that this is the correct career into which you should transition, you give your show the appropriate notice, and begin to mentally prepare yourself for this new life.

After years of being sent requests on social media to sift through acquaintances' headshots and vote on which ones you like the best (because people still do that, even though it's 2017), you've noticed a lot of terrible photography. Most everyone's headshots are terrible! Even your own headshot is terrible! Why? Because when your headshot session was mostly good, your agent inevitably picked the worst ones to showcase. Judging by what you've seen in the wild (on the Internet) you're clearly not the only casualty of poor agent choices, and it's time for you to change this epidemic destroying most of the New York acting community by becoming the one photographer who doesn't take a single bad headshot.

To figure out how to become the best photographer in town, you must first analyze what it is about people's headshots that you don't think works, and that starts with the pictures the agent picks. When you were an actor, you would try to bypass an agent's poor decision-making skills by eliminating as many horrible shots from the session before letting the office look at them. However, in an effort to make it not seem like you filtered through the session first, you would throw in two shitty shots just to show that you did take a couple duds, and that would skew the eye to your prize pics. Unfortunately, this plan never worked. No matter how many times you tried it, the agent would, without a doubt, choose the two worst pictures. You know, the ones where you're dead in the eyes, or looking slightly off-camera? It never mattered how bad the shot was. Each time, your agents would be like, "*That one*," and it'd be the only shot taken during the six seconds when your face turned into the witch from *Snow White*.

The more you think about it, the more fired up you get about this subject. For example, a recent trend in headshots that makes you glad you aren't an actor anymore (but could prove lucrative in the coming months as a photographer) is that because of Actors Access, some agents are getting comp card happy like it's 1987. Comp cards means several looks, which means several opportunities to gouge a client for dollars. At the rates they are now, if this trend continues, Peter Hurley and Dirty Sugar will be able to make down payments on apartments every time someone books them (more on that later).

Digital submissions have been around forever, and I guess now when an agent takes on a new client (and sometimes with older ones as well), they want multiple looks, and by "multiple looks," they mean *one thousand* looks. Since it only costs around ten bucks to have a photo album of headshots available for submissions on Actors Access, some agents are getting *really specific*. They don't just want a few standards. Unless the actor is Sutton Foster, that headshot from the La Jolla Playhouse tryout of *Thoroughly Modern Millie* is not going to cut it anymore. Agents want a Girl Next Door Look, a Newsie Look, a Sexy *and* Slutty Look (there is a difference), Teacher, Doctor, Druggy, Hipster in Summer, Hipster in Winter, Hipster Regular, Kinky Boots, Lion King, etc. Once the actor has completed the vast ranges of shots required to fill out their online comp card, the agent will undoubtedly pick the worst of each one.

Even though nobody knows an actor better than himself or herself, agents insist they have the strongest concept of how to best represent their clients. What agents fail to understand is that when a headshot is terrible, the creative team is never going to blame anyone but the actor. They aren't going to think, "Oh, why did the photographer pair a bowtie with a polo shirt?" or "Why did their agent have them dress like a lion?" They're going to think, "Why would this actor choose to present themselves this way?" When it comes to headshots, the actor will always be forced to suffer the consequences for the bad choices made by the agent.

What many forget is that while agents can be super awesome, they are only working for 10% of commission. When you were on Broadway, the chunk they took from your check seemed huge to you, but probably only covered office supplies at most. While a lot of those Production Contract commissions can add up, agents are making the majority of their salary off of their big guns. So, the actor must remember that they are their own business and should be pulling up the other 90%—especially in this digital world where a careless mistake could lead to a Cinderella Look being submitted for an audition when it should have been the Fosca Look.

Even though you've only been out of the business for five minutes, multiple expensive headshots are just one of the many concerning challenges facing actors in the world of digital submissions. I know you're supposed to be diving into a photography career right now, but I have to take the time to indulge this rant spiral. When you were deciding whether or not to transition into another career, I refrained from mentioning that digital submissions was one of the key reasons you had been feeling so helpless and jaded as an actor.

There was a time when you believed yourself to have tremendous control over your place within the business, and most of that perceived power came from having a password to Breakdown Express. The day you first gained access was more special than your Broadway debut, because of the power it gave you. You were able to log in and see what roles you weren't being submitted for, and knew when it was appropriate to bug your agent. Then, one unseasonably hot day at the beginning of autumn, everyone's secret passwords were changed. In that moment, you felt a great disturbance in the Broadway community, as if millions of actors suddenly cried out in terror, and were suddenly silenced.

The password was never recovered. No matter how many people you reached out to, you always came up empty. There was even a moment when you and a few friends wanted to find and pay a hacker after you spent a weekend binge-watching season one of *Mr. Robot*—and you didn't care if this hacker wiped out your student loan debt, because all you wanted was a Breakdown Express password.

For months, you felt like a homeless renegade. People would post about having an audition for something and you couldn't log in to Breakdown Express to see what it was for. This was a very trying time that ultimately led to your own personal disillusionment with the industry. An actor has such little control to begin with, so when someone takes away their small amount of power, they become emotionally invisible.

Now that you've sufficiently reconciled the truth that the digital submission process brought upon the end of your acting career, you're finally free from that empty feeling of helplessness and are ready to begin your headshot business.

Since every third friend of yours is also a headshot photographer, you decide to contact the least offensive one of the bunch (Marie) to pick her brain about how she got her start, and what steps to take after getting the ball rolling. Of course, you take careful precaution to make sure you do not lead her into believing you're stealing all of her best ideas. It's not difficult to do this because if you give Marie a few drinks, she'll have no problem talking about herself for an hour or two—after all, like you, she was once an actor.

"I got a grant from Career Transition for Dancers," says Marie, sipping on her happy hour rosé at the pseudo-theatre-scene place where she agreed to meet you (probably Hourglass) because she hates Midtown, but you're newly graduated and don't yet know much about life outside the bubble.

"Career Transition for Dancers just bought you a camera?" you ask.

"It was a little bit more of a process than applying for a yoga certification, because it's essentially a business grant, but yeah. Career Transition for Dancers is the shit!"

Marie proceeds to fill you in on her style of shooting. Up until now, you were really only familiar with the techniques of Peter Hurley and Dirty Sugar. They are the Bandwagon Headshot Photographers of New York City. Everyone uses them because they think they're supposed to. When you were first new to the city, you *had* to shoot with Peter Hurley because his iconic white background graced all of the senior showcases that came before you, and probably still do to this day. When you got a little older, you switched to Dirty Sugar— which is Peter Hurley with color. Both provide a great service and are in such high demand that some people might need a Kickstarter to do a session with them. This level of esteem has led many actors to believe they have to pay a lot of money to obtain headshots that will bring them work. You've seen a stigma form where people think it is someone else's brand that will get them called in for auditions, and not their own. No shade thrown at these wonderful photographers (specifically Dirty Sugar, because they're 100% the reason I still attend the Broadway Prom); if their product is in demand, there's absolutely no reason they shouldn't charge what they do.

You start to think a lot about this as Marie explains cameras to you. Maybe there's a way for you to undercut the average cost of a headshots in the city (you've seen some really shitty ones for around $600). After adding up some of the higher costing photographers (on the side of $2,000+), it's possible that actors could buy the equipment themselves.

While you realize people are also paying for the art of the photographer, does the average actor really need to spend all that money to get an audition? A good picture is a good picture, no matter how much it costs. It's not like it's going to come across a casting director's desk and they'll think, "Ooooh. She spent two thousand dollars on these." No. They're going to say, "She's blonde and they want a brunette."

All of these things continue to marinate in your head as Marie switches from discussing camera equipment to how to make a website on Squarespace. You'll have to research all this on your own because your eyes glazed over a while back when you started thinking in dollar signs. You're pondering the idea of gaining the monopoly on a high quality, low cost product. You figure that if you can master the ability, perhaps you could be the people's photographer and only charge $350. Surely, you'll blow the eff up, right?

"Then there's the crazy clients," sighs Marie.

You cease your daydreaming. "Wait, what?" While you loved a good crazy Broadway fan, you never had to spend hours looking at their face through a lens or on your computer.

"They're mostly harmless when you shoot them," she says. "They don't rear their ugly head until Photoshop, when they want you to retouch to the point they don't look like them anymore."

Marie goes on to explain an average exchange she's had with a client who doesn't think she captured the essence of his face:

"He was like, 'My eyebrow looks funny,' and I was like, 'What part?' He couldn't answer me. He just kept going on and on about how I needed to fix his eyebrow and I was like, 'That's what you look like,' and then he was all, 'Change my face,' and started requesting that I airbrush him beyond recognition. Look, I'm not going to turn a fifty year-old man into Ariana Grande. When you smile, you get lines under your eyes, people. Everyone gets lines. Even the Matildas get lines when they smile. Seriously, it's –

As Marie continues her tirade about neurotic actors nitpicking their appearance, a pang of nostalgia hits you in the gut. WOOSH! You suddenly cycle back to a time you had thought was long gone. A time where you took joy in gazing at the various facets of your face for hours on end, giddy with all the possibilities that the perfectly chosen photograph would bring you. This pang, this nostalgia, is not what *Mad Men* literally told you means, "the pain from an old wound," because there's nothing painful about your face. The ache of sadness that usually accompanies your longing for another time (like when it was socially acceptable to hate-tweet a live NBC musical event) is gone, because you know it's not too late to go back to before.

The carousel has turned around again, and now you don't want to leave the business. You don't want to have to deal with anxious actors who analyze every detail of their headshots and make you reverse all of their Gollum-like features. You want to *be* that actor again. The childlike idealism about Broadway has found a way to creep its way back into your bloodstream, and all it took was remembering that what you loved most about acting, was you.

While you don't feel you have completely transitioned back to Broadway Freshman territory, you're definitely feeling like the first day the Internet listened to the *Hamilton* cast recording on NPR, with undertones of hating everyone for not shutting up about listening to the *Hamilton* cast recording on NPR.

Congratulations,
you have officially become a— (page 454)

Joe's Pub it is!

Shit. Joe's Pub is also booked for the dates you want.

Do you…

Pray that
Feinstein's/54 Below is available…? (page 306)

Quit. (page 4)

*

"Holy fuck," you stammer, foreseeing the grave danger that lies in your future if you don't get the hell out of Times Square right now.

"Get 'em!" shrieks a little girl dressed as Susan Stroman.

Choosing "flight," you place your lips to the microphone and shrilly belt out the masturbatory descant from the middle of Craig Carnelia's "Flight." This blows the speakers, causing everyone to scream and clutch their ears in pain. The short diversion gives you just enough time to leap off the stage and race out of harm's way without anyone seeing you. That was close.

While heading East of Broadway where you won't be recognized, you call your agent.

"I'm done," you state into the phone. "This city. This business. I can't. Nope."

Your agent tries to console you, but it's too late. Your mind has been made up. For far too long have you pretended to love what you do, and this is how the fans repay you? Absolutely not. You need to get out of this town. Winter is coming. It's time to go some place warmer, where the people will embrace you with honest love and support, and that place is Los Angeles. Pilot Season is coming up. Let's go west.

Having slogged through New York City pilot season in winters past, you're more than happy to spend late January through mid March someplace sunny, where you don't have to brave blizzards in order to make it to six different auditions while trying to protect your sexy look from getting pummeled by the elements.

In California, you'll be able to warmly commute to your screen tests within the safety of your car without arriving like a snow-blown mess. It's going to be awesome. You won't have to deal with the MTA, running into people on the street that you hate, frigid cold weather, or the obligation of attending shows that you don't want to see. Instead, you'll get to go to the beach whenever you want, and be minutes away from glorious and infamous cuisine such as: In-N-Out Burgers, Pink's Hot Dogs, Rubio's Roberto's, Alberto's, Filbertos, Sombrero's, Los Panchos, Las Parillas, and Del Taco. You're so excited to get to Hollywood.

After talking it out with your agent, it is agreed upon that you will move to LA on January first, and remain there until you book a series. The two or three months preceding pilot season are dead, so you decide not to leave your apartment to a random from Gypsy Housing until after the New Year. Perhaps being in the city during the holidays will warm your cold dead heart, and give you fond memories you'll want to come back to.

It doesn't.

When the Rockefeller Christmas Tree fails to elicit even the slightest bit of joy, it's time to leave New York City. You can't wait to wing your way west.

As moving day swiftly approaches, you weigh your options of where to stay in LA. A friend of yours booked something that shoots in Toronto for the winter, and offered you his room in Studio City. The only catch is, you'll have a roommate whom you know nothing about. It's really a shame that you aren't a kid, because then your parents could pay for you to join the Child Actor Program at the Oakwood Toluca Hills. Then you'd be in a place of your own, right by all of the studios—and you'd also not have to pay rent. Damn your parents, and damn you for being old.

The other alternative is a long-term sublet for a one bedroom in Van Nuys that you found on Airbnb. This apartment and the one with the roommate in Studio City are your best options because everything else has already been taken by the onslaught of hopeful New

York actors who've covered one lead on Broadway and co-starred on an episode of *Law & Order: SVU* that are about to descend upon LA in the vain attempt to book a pilot.

The Studio City location is probably closer to everything, but you don't know if you want to have to deal with a roommate. The Van Nuys apartment will give you more privacy to run lines and cry, but you're not entirely sure if the location is perfect. To be quite honest, all you really know about LA you learned from *Clueless*, so you're going to have to go with your gut on this one. Do you…

Move to Studio City…? (page 123)

Move to Van Nuys…? (page 151)

Committing to stopping is one thing; how you do it is another.

Uh-oh. It looks like you're in a parenthetical decision making situation right now. Do you stop the accompanist and blame the tempo on yourself? Or, do you make it look like it's their fault? In college, you were always taught to take ownership of the mistake in circumstances like these. However, you don't want to be looked at as weak. Only the strong survive in war and musical theatre. Do you…

Blame the tempo on the accompanist…? (page 23)

Blame the tempo on you….? (page 54)

*

I respect you for trying to stick it out. Broadway is like a marriage. When it's great it's *great*, and when it's shitty, hold onto your fucking hat. If you're going to stay, you and Broadway should probably go into couples therapy—but you can't do that, because Broadway is not a person. The next best option is to try and figure out what it is about you that needs to be fixed in order to make this relationship work. You shouldn't have to adapt who you are to fit the needs of the opposite party, but since Broadway is not going to change, because it is a literal street (unless de Blasio's idea to remove the Times Square Pedestrian Mall becomes a reality #notMYmayor), you're kind of obligated to fix the problem yourself.

Of course, Broadway is a lot more than a thing cars drive on. It's a history. A way of life. A religion. That doesn't mean it can't engage in emotional domestic violence. There was a time when the two of you loved each other deeply. It was magical. You were the third act of a Nora Ephron film. The parts you don't make fun of in *Love Actually*. Julia Roberts in the Nineties. Now you're a community theatre Tennessee Williams with heavy Edward Albee influences, set to Sara Bareilles ballads. What can you do to change this?

Perhaps you're just in the wrong show. Why don't you try finding another one? You could get lucky and land in an environment where the cast and creatives click, and the project is actually good. That's basically the unicorn of Broadway, but those experiences do exist, and it could make you two fall in love all over again. However, you might end up in a flop, and unemployed. Maybe you should stay and find a way to use your time as a swing more efficiently. You're basically getting paid for office hours. You could do anything with 24 hours a week to yourself.

Do you…

Find a new show…? (page 272)

Use your show as office hours…? (page 322)

I appreciate your determination to book another show while you're currently employed. No need to spread those jobs around when you're part of the 1% of Actor's Equity. That would be unconstitutional. One would think that it's not that easy to find a Developmental Lab to get into, but Labs come and go so quickly around here; there's plenty to go around for any working actor eager to pull double duty.

If wide-eyed, recently-graduated college seniors are the crabgrass of Broadway, Broadway-bound Developmental Labs are the bed bugs. You can't see them, but there are thousands hidden deep within the crevices of the theatrical industry, waiting to bite you by either grabbing a theatre before your Lab gets an out-of-town tryout, or by your own Lab replacing you before the commercial run, without so much as a high five or a buyout. You don't feel the bite of a bed bug, but rather experience the painful symptoms long after the attack—and like bed bugs, the damage done to you by Labs happens when the Powers That Be make creative decisions you don't find out about until it's too late.

Not all Labs are like bed bugs, but ever since the death of the Workshop contract circa "After *Book of Mormon*" (ABM: because the new Lab contract is Literally a Bowel Movement compared to what it used to be), you never feel fully safe developing a new show until you've made it to opening night on Broadway, because of the lack of protection provided to you by the Lab contract. You don't really want to think about it right now, or you'll start talking like that old annoying actor friend you have, and that's a dangerous slope to slip down when you're trying to get jazzed about finding a new show to be in. You might want to lock that shit up for now.

Inspired by your forced positivity, you head to the front of the theater where you work, and flawlessly execute three counter-clockwise Julie-Andrews-mountain-spins while whispering to yourself, "Dear Universe, send me a Lab, so I can scr012 far, far, far away from here."

Almost immediately, you feel a strange vibration emanating from where you keep your phone. It's safe to say that you're not at all ashamed of your ability to decipher the difference between the vibrations that accompany texts, Facebook messages, emails, etc., but the unfamiliar extended vibration of an actual phone ringing has grown foreign to you. When you pull your baby out to see why it's crying, the word "Broadway" illuminates across the screen. Your agent is calling. You've managed to log all of the various 212 numbers in your phone as "Broadway," a feat that was difficult to fix after a dark period in 2011 when your inability to get noticed by Broadway urged you to change all of your agent's numbers to "Shitty Regional Theatre."

It's crazy how the Universe works. Not seconds ago, you were asking it for help, and now you're on the phone with your agent, who is delivering the marvelous news that you've got an appointment for the Developmental Lab of *The House Bunny: the musical*. This is fantastic! And just what you asked for. The only catch is, this Lab is being cast by Tara Rubin and *not* Telsey.

You're more of a Telsey Cast person than a Tara Rubin Cast person. When someone Instagrams a Lab program, you can usually tell who cast it based off the names in the ensemble. The only two people to successfully span all casting offices are Aaron Albano and Cameron Adams—and you're nervous you can't live up to that level of prestige since you've somewhat neglected nurturing your auditioning skills due to the fact you've

273

been sitting pretty in your long-running show for some time.

Sure, you've attended the occasional TV or film appointment, but when it comes to singing or dancing while acting in an audition setting, you're a bit out of practice. Add to that, you also have a scratchy throat. Not so much a "sick" throat; more like the kind of tickle that would make you engage in "down the octave Sunday," on a Tuesday. It's probably all in your head, or extreme nerves. Either way, you don't want to blow your audition because of it. It might just be something that popping a simple Ricola before can fix. However, it could be a psychosomatic symptom born from extreme anxiety caused by sitting pretty too long when you should have been working on your craft, instead of werking on your Kraft—Macaroni & Cheese. The only way I know how to block out that kind of anxiety is via an audition Xanax or a shot of vodka – sometimes both. Do you...

Take a Ricola…? (page 275)

Take a Xanax…? (page 280)

Take a Shot…? (page 290)

There's no career-debilitating cough or illness that a Ricola can't cure. Unless your vocal affliction has progressed to steroid use, popping this simple lozenge is bound to do the trick. Usually, if I bomb 25% of my notes, it's because I should have had a Ricola, and not because there are like a million notes in a score and you're bound to miss some.

Confidently, you place a Ricola inside the pearly gates to your vocal temple, and wait patiently for the actor ahead of you to finish their —

The door to the audition room opens suddenly, and a young, sad actress rushes out, pretending like she didn't just completely suck in there. You know she sucked because you only heard her sing, thus proving she wasn't asked to read her sides. What a loser!

Tara Rubin herself pokes her head out and calls your name. You're not at all surprised that Tara Rubin is monitoring this audition, and not some intern, because Tara Rubin is effing classy like that. Tara Rubin gets shit done herself.

"Come on in!" Tara Rubin smiles.

You stand and walk inside. As the door shuts, a horrific realization overcomes you: the Ricola inside your mouth hasn't had time to dissolve. In an effort to not have your mouth full during this audition (like *some* of those people who work all the time) you decide to frantically chew the Ricola while you smile at the creative team.

The House Bunny: the musical has been in development hell for years and you don't know why, because it's such a great idea. However, you've read that there have been a lot of creative team issues. They seem nice as you continue to smile, trying to swallow this bitch of a Ricola, but you don't recognize any of the writers.

"Hello," the librettist says with a British accent. You know he's the librettist because he's stuck all the way at the end of the table.

Even though the Brits loved *Legally Blonde* more than a tween during the housing crisis, it's surprising that a bunch of English lads would want to musicalize *The House Bunny*. I mean this seems right in Nell & Larry's wheelhouse, or at least a Pasek & Paul. However, if the guy who created *Downton Abbey* can adapt Jack Black to the stage, Anna Faris shouldn't be a problem.

As you move to dry-swallow this Ricola that won't quit, you wonder which Broadway favorite will land the lead role. Who would you dream cast as Anna Faris in *The House Bunny: the musical*? Let's ask Broadway Internet:

Playbill: Lists Ten Blonde Actresses, Starting with Annaleigh Ashford.
Broadway World Message Boards: Laura Osnes.
All That Chat: Patti LuPone.
Broadway.com: Aaron Tveit.
Broadway Fan Twitter: Tags Lesli Margherita.
Broadway Actor Twitter: STOP DOING THIS.

Perhaps the vomit-inducing thought of dream casting was not the best thing to enter your brain as you tried to swallow something. Luckily, you manage to get the rest of the Ricola down, but not without the slight regurgitation reflex that naturally accompanies the mere reference of anyone being dream cast in anything.

One of the Powers That Be behind the table politely asks you to sing, "Whatever you feel most comfortable with!"

Taking their request, you imagine that *The House Bunny: the musical* can't be very ballad heavy, so you decide to bust out your best and "yelliest" up-tempo.

Everything goes fairly slick for you as you delve into your song—this is to be expected; by this time in your career, you're a well-oiled machine that never makes mistakes.

As you approach the screlty sequence of the song, you take an epic inhale, dig deep, and prepare to let your gift hit the back wall, but holy shit it doesn't. CODE RED! You were positive you had it and now it's like you're Idina Menzel singing "Let it Go," live on the anything (we should really let Idina jokes go, so please stop getting yourself into situations where I have to make them.)

You're in complete shock. You took a Ricola. *You had this*. Unfortunately, the speed of mastication that was required to eliminate the Ricola as quickly as possible, caused an unnatural digestion process during which shards of the cough drop became lodged secretly in areas of your throat, only to be kicked back up when forged ahead into fortissimo. Needless to say, you bombed this audition. No, you choked. Literally.

The entire production team looks horrified (except Tara Rubin, because I told you: she's an effing class act). In the most considerate manner possible, they ask you to leave. You didn't even get to read your sides out of courtesy. What a loser!

Ashamed that you didn't book, you head to the spot you used to frequent after bad auditions in your youth: Wendy's. As you binge on a few of your favorite meals, a notification pops up on your twitter. Broadway Spotted has tagged you in a tweet, mentioning your regretful status at Wendy's. Your life is over.

THE END.

*

As the class begins, you quickly hop into the open space in front of Ashton Reed before some bitch you hate takes it. Wow. That move was so smooth, I'm giving you a "double werk" and a "YAAAAAASSSSSSS" with *six* A's, instead of the usual five.

The instructor today (Tiffany Amber) is wasted on coffee/MFF Kool-Aid, and you can't wait to drink up and show Ashton Reed how to drive through those heels and squeeze your glutes. Kettlebell swinging is a delicate and nuanced exercise that involves careful contraction of the kegel muscle—the one that was made for people to squeeze in a poop or their lady parts, and who doesn't love to watch that?

Since the theme of the day is "literal ninjas," Tiffany Amber has compiled a playlist of inspiring songs that make her feel like she can Ninjitsu the shit out of life's great burdens. It's truly an amazing mix, you think, as you spend the class sweating and thriving to techno mixes of "Electricity" from *Billy Elliot* and "Role of a Lifetime" from *bare*. The invigorating class is only further fueled by the knowledge that Ashton Reed has seen you kegel.

The exhausting workout finally comes to an end when the fitness glory gets so great, Tiffany Amber turns into a tiny bottle of fuchsia-colored Puffy Paint and rolls across the room, at which point, Hotness Expert/Life Coach/Manimal, Brian Patrick Murphy, picks her up and places her on a shelf next to a pile of Beanie Babies that you assume are teaching the afternoon classes.

As you dry off with an MFF towel, you turn around and catch Ashton Reed eyeing you.

"Hey!" you smile, knowing exactly what you're doing.

"Hello," says Ashton Reed.

Door. Open.

"Rough class!"

Ashton Reed nods. "Sure was."

Making certain that your hand is dry and ready to be shaken firmly with direct eye contact, you introduce yourself.

Ashton Reed takes your hand. "I'm Ashton."

"You're not part of my primary group, are you?" you ask, keeping it chill.

"No, but I like this time better," grins Ashton Reed.

"We're a pretty good group of ninjas," you nod. "A little incomplete without Jen Cody in this round, but maybe not so much anymore—if we have you nailing it from behind. I mean… like… you were behind me, nailing it. I mean you nailed it."

Ashton Reed laughs. "Want to get a protein shake?"

"Yeah," you agree, "we should get a protein shake now, shouldn't we?"

"We're *supposed* to have a protein shake."

"Mark *wants* us to get protein shakes."

"Then we should go. Get a protein shake."

OK, this is the worst meet cute since you met that military soldier in the middle of Washington Square Park while listening to a random white guy play acoustic guitar. Are you going to go get a protein shake with Ashton Reed or not? This is what you wanted, isn't it? To get "in" with a hot director/choreographer? Well, here's your chance. Do you think you can handle the responsibility of what might come after? Also, shouldn't you be preparing for your big audition later? Do you…

Get a protein shake with Ashton Reed…? (page 293)
Not get a protein shake with Ashton Reed…? (page 121)

*

An Audition Xanax should be taken at least thirty minutes before going into the room, but I recommend forty-five minutes to an hour. Also, an Audition Xanax is a smaller dosage than a regular Can't-Deal-with-My-Life Xanax. So, for you, it might be a quarter of one pill, and for me, it might be four. You want to make sure you have just enough to eliminate the racing heart and high anxiety, but not land you completely on the floor. Auditions set your emotions high, and Xanax levels you out—but the anxiety is still there, even though you don't feel it. That means when the natural nerve crash that accompanies the completion of an audition comes, you want to be certain you didn't take too much Xanax beforehand, because you'll turn into something that would happen if Judy Garland smoked a blunt lined with Alice Ripley's Tony acceptance speech (it might be better just to take beta blockers).

Having taken your Audition Xanax at the appropriate time before your arrival at one of the Pearl Studios, you sit calmly in the hallway waiting for your appointment time. The slow release of alprazolam makes the actors around you, as well as the business in the room, seem to disappear.

After a euphoric collection of minutes, Tara Rubin herself calls your name, pulling you back into focus—a silky, smooth, focus. You're not at all surprised that Tara Rubin is monitoring this audition, and not some intern; Tara Rubin is a delightful flower in a sea of concrete on the first day of spring in New York—when the daffodils and crocuses appear as if from nowhere.

"Yeah…" you exhale deeply. Xanax is awesome.

"We're ready for you!" Tara Rubin smiles.

You stand and walk inside. As the door shuts behind you, the simple truth of the room reveals itself to you: "This audition is for *The House Bunny...the musical*," you think to yourself. "It's been in the works for like, for forever. Clearly, they don't know what they want."

It's true. Judging by the completely male creative team (save Tara Rubin), there's a good chance these fellas might not have a solid grasp on how to construct a musical about girl power at a sorority house. I'll bet The Interval is pissed. In fact, you're pissed, too, but the Xanax is masking your rage and putting you in a relaxing state that allows you to execute your audition with full confidence and control.

The Powers That Be request you to sing a song of your choice, and after you calmly nail that, you move on to the music from the show (which is more "needs two workshops and a tryout" than it is "direct transfer"). To no surprise, you're then asked to do the sides with the reader who will be playing the role of "Anna Faris' Part"—but there's a twist... For reasons unbeknownst to *anyone*, the reader for "Anna Faris' Part" (a 6'2" male) is told to stand next to you so you can really, "live in the scene."

OK, LIKE WHAT? Readers are supposed to stay seated! You can make believe this dude is Anna Faris when he's in his chair, but not when he's towering over you. You're not *that* good of an actor. The only actor I know who can handle this kind of curveball is *maybe* Alex Sharp, but hasn't he been through enough?

Somehow, you manage not to get thrown by any of this (because Xanax) and have what feels to have been a fairly strong audition. You're not like, "Oh, that was so hashtag-booked-it," but you're also not like, "I totally bombed it—and am also fat. I should just quit, you fat, fat, fatty." Instead, you're essentially feeling on the positive side of neutral, which is a good place to be about it all. It could be the Xanax talking, but since you didn't face plant after the post-audition endorphin crash, there's a solid chance you took the right dosage and your optimistic view of the last eight minutes is both objective and realistic.

Finding out if you book a job can sometimes take forever, but this is not one of those times. At least it doesn't feel like a long time, because deep down, you still don't give a shit about this business and promptly forget about your audition upon exiting one of the Pearl Studios. Your self-proclaimed reticence about Broadway is odd because you gave enough of a shit to need to take a Xanax before your audition, but I'm not going to question the emotional stability of an actor because then I'd have to look in the mirror and face my truth. This is all too horrible. Why did you make me think about myself like that? I need to take a minute to Instagram a scantily clad pic of me with the hashtags: #hot #body #broadwaybody #gymlife #motivation #abs #eatsmyfeelings #hasnofeelings #eatstheabsenceoffeelings #sociopath.

OK, cool. I'm better now. While I was gone, you were offered and accepted the Lab of *The House Bunny: the musical*. In honor of this accomplishment, you think it might be fun to celebrate this triumph by not posting about it online, but by getting blasted after your show instead. It's not like you need a reason to go out and drink with your friends, but you always feel a little less guilty if the occasion isn't "work is done."

Should you go the Glass House, or somewhere less "sceney?" In your non-Broadway Senior days, you'd jump at the chance to accidentally drop word of your recent booking to an acquaintance you randomly see at Glass House. Now, you're feeling a bit reflective for the old days when you went to Chelsea Grill ironically with your Broadway upperclassmen friends because they talked about a bartender there who used to work at Marlowe. Those friends have since graduated Broadway, and as of a few days ago, you were well on your way. This new Lab could change things, but you're wondering if it'll all been in vain.

The true Broadway Senior would probably embrace their status quo and go to Chelsea Grill. A Broadway Senior trying to drop back a few classes, to feel fresh and new, would totally go to Glass House. Should you remain true to who you are, or try to be something you're not?

Go to Chelsea Grill... (page 310)

Go to Glass House... (page 313)

"This is the right Starbucks," you think
confidently to yourself, as you sit at the bar by the
window and stare out at the traffic on Broadway.
"*Metamorphosis: the Hilary Duff Musical* will be born here,
in this very room."

Millennial culture is something you take very
seriously, and you found a bottle of Adderall under your
bed left over from a sublet, so writing this musical proves
to be pretty easy. While blasting "Come Clean" on a
loop, you're able to complete a first draft in three
weeks—which is an entire week faster than it took to
write *Wonderful Town*, and one week slower than *Motown*.

Being this productive in such a short amount of
time makes you happy you chose the Starbucks you did.
Can you imagine if you picked the other one? Who
knows if you'd even have a single line written? Now, you
have a very solid first draft that is ready to be *read*. So,
which one of your friends should you send it to?
Remember: You have to be very careful with who you
send this script to. People have been clamoring for you
to write something ever since you started posting
moderately entertaining shit online. There will be a lot of
interest in your debut musical, and while you want
constructive criticism, you don't want too much advice
thrust in your face, because that is when a product
becomes deluded. It's best to pick one friend who shares
your sensibility to help you make the best possible
version of *Metamorphosis: the Hilary Duff Musical*.

There are three core friends of yours that are the
go-to people for texting screen caps of unacceptable shit:
Corey, Paige, and David. Any one of them is sure to
deliver praises within twenty-four hours—but whatever
notes they provide will directly affect your second draft,
and, ultimately, your Tony chances. Deciding which

friend to send your script to is going to come down to your gut. Do you...

Send your script to Corey...? (page 155)

Send your script to Paige...? (page 69)

Send your script to David...? (page 371)

Feeling adventurous, you hop on the C train at 42nd Street and travel all the way north of 59th, to the stop at 72nd. Once above ground, you find yourself in front of The Dakota, where you pause to reflect on John Lennon and Julia Murney, before sauntering into Central Park's Sheep Meadow.

When you descend upon the open grass area that plays home to many an amateur Frisbee game and gymnastics meet, you spot several collections of people you know: You got your *Kinky Boots* peeps doing Dubsmashes on the south side, *Matilda*s flipping in the north, the *Phantom* and *Jersey Boys* families are with their children over by the rocks, and in the middle is an empty space that used to be home to the folks from *Mamma Mia!*. Basically, all the greatest and worst hits are here, and you are able to quickly find neutral ground with a group of friends who share your funemployment status.

For the next hour you partake in standard Sheep Meadow activities like doing an extended handstand, and then doing it again so one of your friends can snap a pic for you to post on Instagram. Since it's a weekday, none of the non-theatrical folk are around to drain the LTE in the area, so uploading is not an issue, and this provides you with such elation that you're not even remotely upset at all of the effing idiots who've tagged the area as "Sheep's" Meadow so many times that Instagram has made that the official title when you check-in.

I envy you for having such a sunny disposition about this truly tragic problem facing New Yorkers today. It's not hard, people. Say it with me, "Sheep. Meadow." Again, it's not "Sheep's" Meadow. The sheep never had possession of the meadow. It's a meadow where sheep used to be. You haven't called it the Empire "State's" Building since your freshman year of college, so how come people continue to refuse to apply the same laws of grammar to Sheep Meadow?! AGH. Every time I look at people in Sheep Meadow, I'm like, "I know you're the douche-bag tagging it with an apostrophe." I'll bet it's the Murray Hill crowd.

Anyway, after you've received an appropriate amount of likes on your post, you politely bid goodbye to your friends and casually drop that you're on your way to an appointment for a big, new Broadway show. You try to make it sound like it's no big deal, because you don't want them to think it's something important that they are missing out on.

With a much-needed Vitamin D high, you race back to your apartment to get ready, hoping the recent rays will radiate your aura in the audition room. Once you pull together an outfit that you're certain the Powers That Be picture all of the characters in the show wearing, you have just enough time to grab your book and give yourself a look before jetting down to one of the Pearl Studios for your appointment.

Breezing through the hallway, confident as ever, you approach the studio just in time to hear your name called. Once inside the room, all bets are off. This creative team doesn't know what the fuck is coming at them. You are riding high on workout endorphins and vitamin D, coupled with an already natural belief that you kick fucking ass. Nothing can stop you now.

Except for this bullshit accompanist.

As you stand in the middle of the room, smiling at the lovely group of gentlemen and lady behind the table, you're aghast as to what the actual fuck kind of music this guy is playing. It's certainly not the tempo you told him ten seconds ago. You're positive you were clear. You even did the typical shit pianists like you to do when notating proper tempo. Still, this guy is playing your up-tempo like a Sam Smith song overdosing on Vicodin.

Seriously, he needs to pick it up, or you're going to be here all day. More importantly, he is *murdering* your chances right now. You've got to do something.

As you move through your song slower than *The Visit*, you consider your options: You could stop your audition and give the accompanist the tempo again. However, you can't be certain he'll play it right the second time around. Furthermore, you don't know this creative team, and they may think you're a self-righteous douche. Do you...

Ask for a new tempo...? (page 269)

Keep going...? (page 17)

*

"I love your shit!" cheers Corey over text. "Of course I'll read your script!"

With great expediency and enthusiasm, you send a PDF of *Metamorphosis: the Hilary Duff Musical* to Corey, and eagerly await his response.

A day passes.

Two.

Three.

"Hey, you get a chance to read yet?" you inquire in an email to Corey.

Another day passes.

Two.

Three.

You'd assume Corey was dead, but he's been active on Twitter, and you're pretty sure you can't tweet without a pulse (however much it seems some still do.)

After another brief bout of silence, Corey explains that something crazy came up at his show and it set him back a bit, but he hopes to get to it soon. I guess it's onto David.

David doesn't read it either.

OK, this is going about as smoothly as a post-opening night booze poop. Although they might not be your first choices, your friends Ashley and Ellyn are always good for a laugh. Maybe one of them will be willing to read your script. Do you…

Send your script to Ashley…? (page 336)

Send your script to Ellyn…? (page 343)

*

When drinking before an audition, it's important to take your shot fifteen to twenty minutes ahead of time, for the alcohol to properly settle. This means you'll have to drink at the location of the appointment, so it's best to stick to vodka that is concealed in something like a small Poland Springs water bottle. Try not to worry about the alcohol absorbing the plastic and killing you. This toxic-horror-threatening-to-eat-you-from-the –inside-out is nothing compared to your general self-loathing.

You keep all of this in mind as you arrive at your audition at New Pearl (probably good you didn't drink yet, because you often go to Old Pearl by mistake). You take a shot from your secret booze bottle while you wait, making sure to chase the vodka with sixteen altoids and a pack of sugar-free wintergreen gum. Clearly you've done this before.

As you look over your material, you feel the alcohol hit you a little quicker and stronger than usual. Apparently you forgot to eat again today, making it easier for the vodka to missile straight to your bloodstream and now you're rocking a pretty solid buzz. Like, third-hour-of-a-live-NBC-televised-musical kind of buzz. You're so distracted by this dangerous feeling of awesome that you don't even hear Tara Rubin call your name to come in.

"WHOA!" you think to yourself. "TARA. FUCKING. RUBIN. *Of course* she's running this audition and not some assistant. Mother Fucking Tara Rubin is *boss.*"

"You're up!" smiles Tara Rubin.

You stand and say, "Great!" but you think, "Fuck yeah! Tara Rubin rocks!" You might be drunk.

When you walk into the room, it immediately understands that you own the shit out of it. This room is happy to submit to you, but not in a lazy Christian Grey

290

kind of way. I'm talking like in all the twisted ways we've imagined for the Sondheim Sex Dungeon that doesn't exist. Essentially, this room is ball-gagged and ready for you to give it what it wants: fierce singing and strong acting choices.

To no surprise, you realize that the vodka continued its rapid release into your body pretty aggressively in the time it took for you to enter the room, so you don't really remember much about this audition except that at one point you yelled, "Yeah! *House Bunny: the musical?* Flipping awesome!" in a voice that was frat-boy-level intense. Sometimes when you drink, you sound like every male contestant doing a confessional on *Big Brother*.

Feeling fairly certain that you hashtag-nailed-it at your audition, you head back to take a nap before your show. When you awake three hours later, there is a voicemail from your agent with an offer for the Lab of *The House Bunny: the musical*. This is exciting because you've done a few auditions blasted and always failed to book. Either this creative team dug your college vibe and thought it worked for this show, or maybe (and this is a big maybe), the stars and planets aligned for you this time in a way they never seem to do for me.

Now that you have successfully landed a Lab that works conveniently around your Broadway show schedule, you should probably acknowledge it with a celebration, because you're happy about all this, right? This is exactly what you wanted! A new project to help make you love performing again! That's how this works, so go out, party, and write an ambiguous Facebook status about booking this job, or else it didn't happen.

Where should you go tonight for drinks? Some place new or some place nostalgic?

Nostalgic... (page 310)   *New...* (page 313)

*

Birdland it is!

Just kidding, Birdland is booked for the dates you want.

Do you…

Choose Feinstein's/54 Below…? (page 306)

Choose Joe's Pub…? (page 265)

"Cool!" you say, throwing the rest of your day under the bus. "Protein shakes it is!"

SMASH CUT TO:

Queen's "Under Pressure" blasts from your iPhone alarm, waking you abruptly from your sweet slumber on this sunny Sunday morning in June. It's Tonys day, and you can't believe how quickly it came. The last nine months are a complete blur, but you're ever so grateful looking back on that important day at Mark Fisher Fitness, where you met Ashton Reed—the only visionary who would truly come to appreciate your ability to werk, slay, thrive, and YAAAAASSSSSSS, ultimately forging a relationship with you (that may or may not be romantic) which led to a track developed specifically for you in their new hit show. You can't believe how lucky you are to be originating the role of Random Person Who Carries Luggage in the Background and Moves Some Sets. You're doing important work in the original cast of a Broadway show, and now you get to perform on the Tonys *and* be nominee Ashton Reed's date. It's like Queen said, "These are the days—it never rains, but it pours."

Taking in a deep breath, you open the window as "Under Pressure" continues to blare in the background. Looking down at all of the people on streets, you can't help but marvel at the amazingness that is your very existence. The air is clean and the sky is bright, inspiring you to reflect upon how a chance meeting changed your life.

It's crazy to think how much of your future hinged on the intricacies of a handful of tiny decisions on a random day. What if you didn't get a protein shake with Ashton Reed? What if you had left before class began because you literally couldn't even? Heck, there was even a moment when you considered not going to MFF at all that day. Can you imagine if you'd done anything different? You could be dead!

In fact, you barely remember the audition you had later that day (the one that meant so much to you when you woke up that morning). You didn't end up booking it because you were so distracted from the high you were riding after hanging out with the renowned director/choreographer (Which was actually pretty tame. Ashton Reed got a berry smoothie, and you got the Laura Osnes Special – two scoops of vanilla protein powder dropped into a cup of liquefied fairy dust. After that, you followed each other on Twitter and met up a couple more times, and then whatever else happened subsequent to that led to where you are now.)

Looking back on it all, you're thrilled you didn't book that random show, because it turns out, it was just some busted workshop that didn't lead to anything, anyway. Now, you're sitting comfortably in a hit, and are about to perform live on television for tens of thousands of people.

"The last few months have been crazy," is what you've been telling all of the friends you haven't seen because you've been married to your show since the first table read in January. Between teching in the dead of winter and being thrust into hundreds of early morning press events throughout the spring, your cast has been battling a cold for nearly six months, making it impossible for you to carve out some much needed social time. A company-wide cough sounds too "Basic Broadway" for some, but you don't give a shit. You're like, "pour me a Venti Pumpkin Spice Soy-Blessed Latte, because I'm proud to be a Basic Broadway Bitch."

Despite all the craziness, your recent success has come with many privileges such as: more followers, not having to stand by random stage doors with a messenger bag to get someone to tell you "good job," and the luxury of leaving your old roommate Carol in the dust in favor of a sexier studio that's even closer to your theatre (*and* has southern exposure).

As you hang your head out the window and bask in your light, "Under Pressure" eventually comes to an end, which means your morning reflectional "me time" must also cease so you can prepare for this day that will be 100% devoted to Broadway.

Tonys day is exhausting, and not just because most of the Internet still spells it "Tony's." No... the day of the Tonys is a sunup to sunup again Kristin-Chenoweth-bathing-Jonathan-Groff-in-the-ink-of-Lin-Manuel-Miranda wet dream set inside a Chita Rivera hallucination you had once—with lots of Instagram, occasional catered sandwiches, and Audra. It's a fun day because you're actually encouraged to let your Self-Promoting/Arguably Non-Forced Love of Theatre Flag fly with reckless abandon, and few can judge you for it because in someway they're doing the exact same thing.

You *love* the Tonys. You love the Tonys so much that when you're not on them or at them, you keep yourself connected by tweeting about your friends who are involved that year from the moment you wake up, to the red carpet coverage on NY1, and straight through the telecast. The Tonys are a very important moment for Broadway Internet. It's a chance for members of the community to show their support by striving to write the next best "Ring of Keys" tweet and land themselves on a Playbill article dedicated to top tweets from the telecast. This is where the real gold is at. The winners aren't those who take home some award. Pfffsh. No! The *true* champions of the evening are revealed in the retweets.

Unfortunately, this year you will not be provided much of an opportunity to be social medially active during the show, because you are both performing *and* sitting next to Ashton Reed during the best director category (Ashton Reed wasn't nominated for best choreography this year because Joshua Bergasse did all of the other shows). Being mostly absent from the interwebs won't be that big of a loss for one year when you exchange it for the reward of looking like a big fucking deal on TV, so all of those douches who bullied you in elementary school can suck it JOEY BRUNTON.

The random memory of some bully who may not have actually been yours breaks your daze and sends you speedily into the shower and then to your closet where you get ready for the events of the day in Quick Change Booth time. You're now ready to go. It's time to head to your theatre for one of the most thrilling and memorable days of your life!

SMASH CUT AGAIN TO:

Queen's "Under Pressure" blasts from your iPhone alarm, waking you abruptly from your blacked-out slumber on this sunny Monday afternoon in June. It's Day After Tonys day, and you can't believe how quickly it came. Even though the day was long af, it went by faster than the shelf life of a Matilda. You were so high on celebrating American Theatre that you don't remember a lot of the details from the past thirty or so hours. Fortunately, you were one of the rare MacArthur Genius Grant winners who was able to live tweet the entirety of the Tonys *while living* the Tonys.

Let's look over your tweets from the day so you can relive the magic—and to be helpful, I'll provide you with some commentary…

Your #Tonys Day Tweets

Getting ready at the theatre! It's SO EARLY! #Tonys

You got to your theatre at a ridiculous time – like 8:00 a.m. – but it didn't seem too crazy because it was kind of around the same hour of the morning as the Broadway Bares dress rehearsal (which you're going to be doing in a few weeks anyway and you've been preparing for early Sunday call times in June by replacing sleep with hunger).

Already in full makeup & hair for dress rehearsal. Here's a pic of me & bff cast mate Corey Michael Cooper making duck faces! #Tonys

Once you arrived at the theatre, you got into full show beat AS QUICKLY AS YOU COULD—and then waited for the bus to where the Tonys were held this year (and you still aren't sure what theatre it was at because it all happened so fast, and the location of the Tony Awards changes with the frequency of the general public's warmth towards Neil Patrick Harris).

HURRYING TO THE BUS—But here's a fun pic of us pretending to hail a cab! #Tonys

The day was framed by a lot of HURRY UP AND WAIT.

Look I'm on a bus with a cast and it's not a bloody mary Monday because I'm on broadway and not on tour! #Tonys

Your cast piled onto the bus and then waited for a long period of time, after which, you drove approximately ten blocks, when it would have probably been much quicker to just walk.

Hanging in the audience with all the other shows while we wait to do the full dress! I love our competition. They're like family! #Tonys

There was a fun "street clothes" camera rehearsal on Thursday, but at the full dress, you got to hangout in costume at the venue with all of the other casts spaced out in the house in their individual groups. While you aren't close friends with anyone in the competing new musicals, you had fun seeing the awesome folks from the revivals: Deaf West's *Hairspray*, both *Gypsy*s, and John Doyle's five-person-and-a-tuba production of *Wicked* that got so much acclaim at Menier Chocolate Factory, it moved to Broadway, even though the original *Wicked* is still playing – because a cat taking a nap on a piano could move to Broadway if it played at the Menier Chocolate Factory first.

THIS IS THE BEST HOSTING TEAM EVER. #bae #Tonys

You ran through the entire show, and enjoyed watching the hosts (Laura Benanti and Jennifer Lawrence—both nominated for best actress in a musical) play around, banter, and work on funny bits that you knew at least one guy at everyone's Tonys party would probably *hate* (and I can attest that the one at mine did, and we kicked him out).

This is the last time we'll run this number before tonight! #Tonys

HURRY UP TO YOUR PLACES!

I mean at this theater. We still have a matinee. #Tonys

DO YOUR NUMBER!

Heading back to do our matinee! What a day! #coffee #caffeine #Tonys #dreamz

After the run-thru, you bussed back to your theater to DO A MATINEE WTF IT'S TONYS DAY WHY WEREN'T YOU BUSSED TO A SPA (you soon remembered that you were going to make an additional week's salary performing on the Tonys, and were able to calm down in time for lunch.)

HURRY UP TO LUNCH!

You ate lunch. But didn't share that on social media.

HURRY UP TO YOUR MATINEE!

Can't believe the next time we do this number it'll be preserved in history. #wow #whoa #whatismylyfe #Tonys

Once the show was over, you transitioned from "stage" hair and makeup to "camera ready" hair and makeup. That meant gluing down the lace on your wig, contouring your cheekbones with that high definition white shit, and getting complete facial reconstructive surgery.
You then ate dinner and neglected to tweet about that, too. But I saw. I always see.

EEEK! It's HAPPPEENNNNING!!!! #Tonys

At the start of the Tonys telecast, you sat in your theater with your cast watching and cheering along.

This Benanti/J Law duo better SLAY! Jennifer Lawrence is the new Chelsea Nachman! #Tonys

Cool, I'm going to skip your live tweeting because it didn't offer anything constructive to the proceedings.

As the telecast continued, you anxiously awaited your call time to the bus. The Tonys have their shit down to the minute. This isn't the effing Oscars. Hell no. If you're performing at 10:18 p.m., you're performing at *10:18 p.m.* Luckily for your nerves, your show was featured on the earlier side (9:01 p.m.) giving you plenty of time to quick change into more Broadway Style Guide approved attire for when you sat next to Ashton Reed in the audience.

HURRY UP TO THE BUS!

Back on the bus! #Tonys

You're bussed to the venue.

Backstage!!! #Tonys

You hung backstage with your cast for about fifteen minutes.

Going on stage!!! #Tonys #Tonys #Tonys

You went onstage.

And you guys killed it. Seriously. It was the moment of the night. There were instant YouTube videos, Tumblr GIFs for days, and memories forever.

WORDS CANNOT EXPRESS THE THRILL OF DOING LIVE TELECAST THEATRE! #Tonys

Your blinding excitement caused you to plow over a presenter (Dame Helen Mirren, you think) on your way to making a quick change into your formal wear. Everyone else had to bus back to the theater for the rest of the show. Amateurs!

Commercial break selfie with TONY NOMINEE Ashton Reed! #Tonys

Sitting in the audience in the "recognizable talent" section was pretty exciting, and you didn't waste a moment of gratefulness. The best director category was given more attention this year because there were celebrity people nominated – so you got a lot of facetime on camera when the nominees were read.

ASHTON REED WINS! #proud #Tonys

A passing jolt of excitement overcame you when Ashton Reed's name was called, but it soon turned to fear. You were now in deep with a successful Tony Award winner. You understood immediately that your chances of being taken care of in this business were in reach, but could also be ripped away from you should you be cast aside for something shinier. You pondered this central conflict as the evening approached the show's biggest prize: Best Musical.

For some reason, it was a big season for sequels, and your show was the only one that did not fall victim to that trend. The other nominees (*Caroline or Change… Again!, Mean Girls 2: the second meansical,* and *The Open to the Public Between Six A.M. and Eleven P.M. Garden*) were mostly there to fill out the category, leaving your show in a dead heat with *Thoroughly Millennial Millie*.

Just when you thought there wasn't enough dying to be literally had left in the world, the presenter for best musical took the stage...

OMG. DAME JULIE ANDREWS. QUEEN. In the same room as ME. Dead. Dying. DEADER. #allthehashtags #Tonys

Now, despite the fact that Mary-mother-effing-Poppins herself was there to blow your mind, you did not rule out the possibility that she was chosen to present the award to *Thoroughly Millenial Millie*—the meta-modern musical sequel to her 1967 film—because why would they make Dame Julie Andrews truck her ass to the Tonys to give the award to—

WE WON!

Since your entire cast was back at the theater, you didn't get to bum rush the stage. It didn't matter anyway because twenty seconds into your lead producer's speech, a mega-mix anniversary tribute to *The Phantom of the Opera* barged in to close out the show.

At the Copa! Copacabana! The winners are here in Havanna! #tonysafterparty

Huh... Looks like there was a giant gap in your social media activity from between when your show won the Tony, to when you ended up at the company after party on the roof of the Copacabana in Midtown. This was your last tweet of the night, so there are no further clues here for me to decipher.

What I don't understand is why you didn't go with Ashton Reed to the fancy, important people party at The Plaza. What happened?

***

Confused – and clearly heavily hung-over from the boatload of booze you must have drunk at the after party to black out anything from the remainder of the evening—you scroll through your texts.

There are about a billion "congrats!" messages from friends, with variations on celebration emojis, and one from Ashton Reed:

"I guess that's that."

Holy shit. Did you break-up?

It dawns on you…When Ashton Reed was led to the pressroom after the show, you decided to join your cast (your *family*) at the Copacabana, instead of selling out and going to The Plaza party with all the glitz, glamour, and *celebrities*. UGH. You aren't supposed to make decisions like that without consulting me first! You could have snagged a selfie with Katniss Everdeen! Who cares about celebrating with the original Broadway company you share a best musical Tony award with! Integrity is overrated!

Things are never the same between you and Ashton Reed. You go about your business in your show, occasionally trying to mend broken fences with the Tony award winner, but Ashton Reed completely freezes you out. Apparently showing up to The Plaza with a Tony award, but no date, was exceptionally embarrassing.

After a year in the show, you start to put your feelers out for other employment opportunities. Being in a hit is great and all, but your resume is starting to look dated, and you think it's time to add a new credit. The only problem is you can't seem to make it anywhere at

303

your auditions. You're nailing ninety percent of your appointments, but they're failing to yield a single callback. It couldn't be that Ashton Reed has blackballed you, could it?

By the end of your second year, you're finding it increasingly difficult to keep your performance as Random Person Who Carries Luggage in the Background and Moves Some Sets fresh. You're dying to find a way disrupt the status quo, and since they won't bump you up to any of the roles you understudy, and you're failing to find another job, you develop a plan to be moved into a swing position the moment one becomes available.

Being a swing in your show is pretty cushy. Your friend Corey Michael Cooper has been one since the beginning, and he barely ever has to go on, but when he does, it's often a different track than the last time. Not only would becoming a swing aid in fixing the monotony you've fallen victim to, it would also prove more lucrative, and provide you with much needed reflectional "me time."

When the swing who covers you finally gives their notice, you approach company management and say, "I want to be a swing now," and then they are all like, "No." A day goes by and you ask again, but are turned down once more. Finally, after holding auditions and not finding the perfect replacement, you bang down the door and demand the job. Company management finally agrees to present the idea to your lead producers who like to weigh in on everything because dollars, and after that, you're finally granted your request.

Being a swing in year three seems great on paper, but proves to make you grow more and more jaded with every eight-show week. To add insult to injury, you haven't received so much as an appointment from the casting office of your show, because as a swing that covers principals, you've grown too valuable to replace. Looks like you shot yourself in the foot with this lateral move.

Gazing into your dressing room mirror, you don't see the young, idealistic youth who so long ago stressed over whether to go to the gym or have coffee with their college voice teacher. That person is gone. It's been three years since you attended a college reunion and shared your successes with your fellow alums. You don't even know the last time you had a Schmackary's cookie, or tweeted something about your job. The person you once were has disappeared like a Snapchat #SIP—and also, the general relevance of #SIPs after 2013.

As you reflect upon your reflection, it occurs to you that you are no longer the optimistic Broadway Freshman you once were, but something far more evolved—and you're ready to embrace this new chapter in your life with care and understanding. You don't regret the choices you made that brought you to this place, even though they made you into an actor who is content in their own indifference towards an industry that gave them so much. So what? The choice may have been mistaken, the choosing was not. You have to…

Move on… (page 6)

*

Feinstein's/54 Below it is! You're about to grace the same stage as Patti LuPone, Laura Benanti, and those guys who make people eat hot peppers before singing. The acts at Feinstein's/54 Below redefine "not giving a shit." The randomness is truly inspiring. They'll follow Christine Ebersole with a concert adapted from a parody Twitter account. They will literally let anything on that stage. I'm not entirely certain if *Broadway Eats Chipotle* was a joke, or if it actually happened. All of this makes Feinstein's/54 Below the perfect place to embrace your potpourri of crazy.

When conceiving and creating your show, collaboration is going to be key. You've been asked to perform as a guest in plenty of concerts, but those were short appearances that required little planning. This will be much different. You're going to have to come up with seventy minutes of material without boring all of your friends to death. You'll need to rely heavily on the trust, advice, and direction of your team.

In an effort to stay closely connected to your collaborators at all times, Joey suggests starting a group Voxer together. Voxer is not an app you're used to, but it's the shit in circumstances such as this. It's like a group text, but with voice messages (yes, you realize this is also like "voice text" on the iPhone, but I promise you, that function sucks). Voxer allows you to word vomit all of your ideas and ramble on ad nauseam. It's a collaborator's dream. You wonder how the fuck they wrote *Guys & Dolls* without it.

"We need a title," you state on your first vox to the group.

"What kind of show do you want to do?" asks Joey.

306

You know the answer immediately. "One that's fun, where I can say and sing inappropriate stuff. Maybe we can call it 'Tasteless?'"

"Or 'Unsuitable,'" suggests Andy.

"'Wrong?'" says Katie.

"'Unacceptable' would be a good title for a show with inappropriate material," continues Andy.

"Why don't you just call it 'Inappropriate'?" asks Joey.

"I like 'Unacceptable,'" you say. "I'm kind of known for saying that word a lot."

"Love it," agrees Andy. "We can do a bunch of Unacceptable medleys."

"So many medleys," you say. "I want to do a medley of unacceptable auditions I've had for shit I didn't book, *The Bridges of Madison County* in five minutes, a medley of every Wildhorn chorus played over the same four bars, a medley of shit that's too high, maybe a lightning round with someone funny (or a kid), a section where I sing a high-stakes cover of 'Barbie Girl,' and then I will be closing with that rap version of 'Meadowlark,' because they have a tally at Feinstein's/54 Below for every time someone sings that song."

You're not sure where all of these ideas came from. It's as if you've had them inside you you're entire life and they were waiting for just the right moment to break free of you.

"This is great," says Joey.

"Yep," agrees Katie.

"Maybe," offers Andy, "we should bring it down for a segment because you don't want the entire thing to be at a ten."

"OK," you say, "We'll do some ballad mashup with an acoustic guitar."

"Great," says the team.

"And Katie," you continue, "There's going to be a lot of PowerPoint, photo shoots, YouTube teasers, and a fuck-ton of photoshopping of posters and flyers. Is that going to be easy to do?"

"It shouldn't be a problem," assures Katie.

Andy goes on to offer a few additional brilliant ideas to fill out your show that will undoubtedly push you over the allotted time limit.

"What do you think, Joey?" you ask.

"This is great," says Joey. "Except, we can't do that deconstruction of Katy Perry lyrics idea, because they did it on *Unbreakable Kimmy Schmidt.*"

You groan and then vox back: "This is why we have you Joey."

With only two short months before show time, it's time to get cracking. Between the intricate medleys you're forcing Andy to assemble, and the transitional banter (or patter, as we call it in the cabaret scene), you've got a lot of material to learn and rehearse in a fairly short amount of time. In addition to all of this, you need to develop a solid marketing plan.

Social media is going to be your answer when it comes to getting word out about your solo concert, *Feinstein's/54 Below is Unacceptable.* Unless you're Dan Smith Will Teach You Guitar, nobody finds success flyering the city the old fashioned way. A strong social media strategy is sure to yield ticket sales.

How do you want to go about handling the marketing of your show in this world of new media? You're pretty capable yourself (your follower count has reached its fair share of cookie cakes), but you might want to toss this responsibility to someone who could be more skilled, like Katie or Joey. Smart delegation is the mark of a good leader. However, relinquishing control could completely backfire.

What do you think you should do?

Ask someone else
to design the marketing plan... (page 445)

I got this... (page 161)

Feeling nostalgic, you head to Chelsea Grill on Ninth Avenue, with a few friends from your cast. After a couple rounds of drinks, they bail on you to go meet more important people at Glass House. After they leave, you turn to the younger, more impressionable person sitting next to you at the bar.

"Broadway Sophomores," you say, rolling your eyes. "I hate those guys."

"My friends left too," says the kid. "I'm leaving for tour tomorrow and was throwing a balls-out-celebratory-going-away-bash. We started at Hourglass, but I couldn't get anyone to bar hop beyond here."

"What tour are you going out on?" you ask.

"That Short Engagement Touring Agreement. The category six one."

"Oh, shit," you blurt out, "Don't get me started on tiered tours—OK, I will."

Happy to rant about something, you order another round of drinks for you and your new friend.

Clutching the kid's shoulder in one hand and four-fingers of Jack Daniels in the other, you begin:

"In the past, when you were no more than a babe, I earned an enviable living out on the open road…"

You proceed to delve into a drunk-matic tale, chronicling the fall of the first national touring contract, complete with all of the necessary theatrics needed to justify your opinion. No… Not opinion… FACT. You know *all* of the facts. When it comes to knowledge regarding how actors managed to get screwed out of making money on tour, you're like Wikipedia—in more ways than one (meaning that you also have a lot of self-edit).

This kid doesn't even know what's happening because you're pulling out details from last century. I mean, you take it back to the non-Equity *The Music Man* tour that happened in the 1930's. From there, you cover everything from *42ⁿᵈ Street* to a *Hello, Dolly* tour you had a few friends on in 2013. Even though you told your agent, "I don't tour anymore" years ago, when it comes to the ability to deconstruct the devolving of dollars earned on the road, nobody knows more than you, because nobody really has that kind of time to be that bitter about something they don't do anymore.

Just as you're about to delve further into a diatribe about the tiered *Kinky Boots* and *Newsies* tours, you realize your fourth drink has hit you hard and you completely blackout.

When you wake the next afternoon in a state of disarray, you try to trace your steps from the previous evening to figure out how you even got home. The last thing you remember is shouting, "Does anyone still wear a show jacket?!" You've no recollection of what happened after that.

What you do remember about the evening is that it ended with you forcing some kid to listen to you bitch about a business that once brought you such happiness. As you lie there naked, with one sock on, and your phone on 1%, it dawns on you that your current state is a metaphor for how you view Broadway. No amount of trying is going to change how you feel. The animosity you have toward tiered touring agreements is nothing compared to how you feel about Lab contracts. Starting work on one in an effort fix what's broken inside of you is a futile Hail Mary. All signs on this road point to inevitable eternal bitterness. It's in this moment when you realize it's time for you to graduate. It's time for you to move on.

Your Broadway legacy will be remembered fondly because of your self-awareness. You didn't just quit when it got hard. You tried to make it work.

Coming to the realization that this career is no longer for you is not easy, and sometimes it takes pulling out all the stops and failing, to learn that you succeeded. As you prepare to take the appropriate steps to leave the business, you can do so confidently, knowing you did it when it was right.

EPILOGUE (page 465)

*

It's not so much that Glass House Tavern is *new*, it's that it's *now*. It's a place to go with friends where you can also network, and unlike Bar Centrale, is much more accessible (i.e. cheaper).

When you arrive at Glass House with a few of your friends from the show, you're instantly enveloped by the onslaught of people you know, and even more people you don't, but are still friends with on Facebook. It's like the Broadway Hunger Games, where every show sends two tributes to fight for oxygen and career longevity by having to network in a sardine can. Thank goodness Nikka Graff Lanzarone and Mo Brady of The Ensemblist are there to be the common connection between everyone and everyone else. They haven't asked you to do their podcast yet, which is probably a good thing, because you're in such a bitter place about the state of Broadway right now, you probably shouldn't have a microphone anywhere near you.

Your friends in the show are pretty great individually, but when you let them loose in a room of people from the biz, they're like dropping a bag of marbles. So, naturally, you lose them pretty quickly upon entering Glass House. Whatever. Sometimes, you have to cut Broadway Sophomores some slack.

Instead of getting sour about the absence of your friends, you slide into a bar seat and order a Whiskey Sour, because apparently you hate bartenders. Next round, I suggest getting whiskey neat, because I'm not even sure if a class joint like Glass House is going to put up with making a real Whiskey Sour.

As you sit at the bar with a glass of whiskey that's topped off with a soda gun shot of sour mix (because I was right), you strike up a conversation with a kid who is clearly a Broadway Freshman. Turns out, this kid is also going to be in the Lab of *The House Bunny: the*

313

musical with you. Wonderful… Regretfully, but expectedly, this kid is a little too eager to be developing their first new musical. All they can talk about is how cool the process is going to be, how amazing it'll be to contribute to a new work, how exciting it'll be if it turns into a hit, and how the two of you were there at the beginning. Ugh. This kid. Please. Someone stick 'em in *Wicked* for a week just to level them out a bit.

After a few minutes of this, you can't take it anymore. It's time to set this kid straight. You slam back the rest of your "Whiskey Sour," order a double Johnnie Walker Blue (because years of production contract) and proceed to lay into why the Lab contract sucks in comparison to what a real workshop used to be.

Due to the high concentration of alcohol running through your body at this moment, most of what you say to this kid is somewhat foggy. You definitely give the Lab contract a piece of your mind, but whether or not you're being coherent is something that will have to be debated later – should you even remember anything about this evening tomorrow morning. In fact, as you sit here, getting progressively shit-faced, your consciousness begins to fade away. Things turn to black, and the details of what happen next neglect to place them into your memory. This almost cinematic transition to the next day comes to you smoothly, as you wake to find yourself in a state of disarray in your bed.

It's one in the afternoon. You've no recollection of how you got home, or what you did after Glass House, nor do you have any idea why you are completely naked. Oh God. Hopefully you didn't bring that Broadway Freshman home with you.

As you stumble around your room, assembling an ensemble, you can't find a single article of clothing you wore last night. Weird. Once dressed, you grab your phone (which you managed to charge last night) and look for any clues in your texts as to your whereabouts. Nothing. You next open Twitter to see if you drunk tweeted at Daryl Roth again. The good news is no, you didn't. The bad news is that Twitter (and not just Broadway Twitter) is blowing up over a body found late last night in the Theatre District. The body of the kid you were drinking with at Glass House was apparently discovered around three in the morning, murdered by way of a clean break to the neck.

Double-Ewe. Tee. Eff. This must have happened right after your rant about Labs. In shock, you race to the bathroom to throw water on your face, in an effort to wake your hung-over ass up. Upon entering the bathroom, you find your clothes from last night hanging up on the shower line. Why would you wash your clothes last night?

A memory flashes through your head. "You must always be grateful," says a voice. The face of the kid appears, smiling at you, dimly lit by the glow of the Great White Way.

"Why can't you just be grateful with what you have?" the kid asks, "I'm always grateful."

The memory refuses to expand further as you stare at your nearly dry clothes hanging hauntingly over your shower curtain—like a dismembered scarecrow. All you're able to deduce from this is that you were at Glass House with that kid and something led to you needing to scrub your clothes clean. Why would you do that? This is strange drunk behavior, even for you. You only clean things that immediately when you're trying to forget a one night stand or—

Three loud knocks reverberate from your apartment door. A man's voice you don't recognize calls your name. You stay quiet. The knocks continue –

"This is Detective Zach Feldman from the NYPD," the man says.

"And Detective Dick Barkowitz," adds another, dumber sounding man.

Quietly, you approach the door and look through the peephole. You're able to do this without making a sound or upsetting the floorboards because of everything you learned from *Cats*.

Peering through the peephole, you see the two men: one tall and younger, who continues to bang on the door. He must be Feldman. The other, Barkowitz, older and stouter, looks on, confused.

"We just have a few questions for you," says Detective Feldman.

It all begins to come together in your head. They're here because you must have been the last one seen with that kid alive. Add to it all the systematically cleaned clothes in your bathroom and your general blacking out of the entire event; it's pretty clear to you now, that you potentially murdered this kid. Whether they have the evidence to convict or acquit you is inconsequential at this moment. Right now, you know that you're about to become their prime suspect.

Unfortunately, I'm not so confident you aren't guilty. It's complicated. Your behavior was suspicious last night, but your motive is pretty shitty. Why would you want to kill someone for being grateful? It's possible you spilled something messy on yourself and wanted to make sure it didn't stain your clothes. However, it's pretty convenient that you managed to blackout the majority of what happened after you were at Glass House. Whatever the case, you might be screwed, because there's enough shadiness here to lay the ground for a solid case against you.

Regretfully, when it comes to who killed that kid in the dark shadows of Midtown, we probably won't ever know if it was you or not—and no amount of speculation, blogs, or podcasts are ever going to give anyone a satisfying conclusion to any of this. So, I guess we'll just stop right now. But, keep in mind as you go forth to court, trial, jail, or whatever, this happened because you stayed in the world of Broadway when you should have graduated. Forcing yourself back into a career that you've fallen out of love with can only lead to murder and death.

THE END.

*

Tentatively, you make direct eye contact with Roxie.

"Chicago on *Broadway*?" She asks.

"Um…" You fumble, unable to form an appropriate response.

"It's Broadway's smash hit musical! Whoopee!" She exclaims and pushes the outstretched flyer closer to your face.

"Yeah. I've heard of it," You say.

"Skidoo!" She giggles.

Roxie proceeds to do a little bump-and-grind around you. She struts. She turns. She pops her head. She puts her hands behind her back and does that swivel-Fosse-walk thing where it looks like her arms are underwater. You know what I'm talking about. That thing. I think it's called a Fosse Walk? I've auditioned for *Chicago* once, and I know you're supposed to keep your shoulders down when you do it, but it looks like Roxie Red Tights has chosen to avoid that direction.

Roxie continues her routine for about thirty seconds. She throws in a few kicks to ninety degrees for a finale and then ends in a deep lunge with her hands to the side in a classic Fosse pose.

"That jazz!" She whispers.

Her dance was performed in silence, with no vocals, so I guess ending with just those two words was a fun choice. I don't know if you like this girl, but I think she's fucking awesome.

Technique aside, you're actually sort of impressed with how uniquely she moves. You've been suffering through over-trained dancers since *So You Think You Can Dance* and it's inspiring to see someone dance in a way that is unexpected. I mean it's terrible, but it's interesting. Without even considering an alternative, you accept Roxie's flyer.

"If my friends could see me now!" She squeals, and then jazz runs straight up Broadway, disappearing behind smoke emanating from a cart of steamy hot dogs.

You pause for a moment. Did she just quote *Sweet Charity*? She's fuddled her Fosse cannon. How funny would it be if she's never even seen *Chicago*? You ponder this idea for a minute and then finally make your way into H&M.

The Times Square H&M is straight out of Caesars Palace in Las Vegas. It's ostentatious, and, depending on the season, the mannequins hang from the ceiling by their necks. H&M is really nailing that metaphor of show business.

It might be the middle of the day, but it's still Times Square, and the place is slammed with more teenage girls than the number who clicked on the *Newsies* ALS Ice Bucket Challenge video. Thank goodness you know all of your sizes, because you're able to throw a few tops and bottoms (slightly less than the number that were present in the *Newsies* ALS Ice Bucket Challenge video) into your basket and jet to the cashier faster than a Fansie can write a disconcerting fan fiction about what happened *after* they filmed the *Newsies* ALS Ice Bucket Challenge video.

Once you reach the front of the line, you ask the cashier, "Do you still have a student discount?" and then hand her your ID from Broadway Dance Center.

The bored attendant (Her name is Hannah— you checked her nametag because I can't keep referring to people as "you" or "her.") takes a long look at your ID.

"This is a dance card," mutters Hannah.

"Correct. I am a student of the dance."

"We only do student discounts during spring break."

"You never get a break from Broadway."

319

Hannah hints at a smile, and applies a ten-percent discount to your purchase. She may have been humoring you, or even patronizing you, but you're not sure because things always seem to get handed to you and you don't know the difference.

After politely thanking your retail angel, you stroll back outside. Taking in a deep breath (Ahhh – you love the smell of unnecessary impromptu retail therapy) it hits you that you never checked that email your agent said they'd send you regarding your callback.

Upon opening the email you find an additional fourteen megabytes of sides on a .PDF you've never seen before. Unable to handle too much stress, your heart leaps out of your chest and nerve-taps up to George M. Cohan's statue, where it promptly explodes all over the face of a non-Equity kid who's on his way to the Equity building to see if they are honoring the unofficial list. No big loss. You have enough heart left over to brighten the darkest dressing rooms at *Wicked*, or even the progressively growing-jaded halls of *The Book of Mormon*.

Once you've taken a moment to catch your breath and allow your heart to rejuvenate, you try to construct a plan to tackle all of this new material, and still have enough time to get hair and makeup ready so you resemble something like what you think the Powers That Be are looking for. Checking the clock on your phone, it becomes hauntingly clear that there is not enough time to do both with full commitment.

Do you work on your sides or werk on your look? You could quickly throw yourself together and pour over your sides until it is time, but what if you choose the wrong shirt, or the wrong shoes, or the wrong *face*? There's a solid chance that casting may only ask to see a few pages of your choice, and you could defer to the material you're most comfortable with. This would allow for time to appropriately prepare your hotness.

You always feel more confident after spending hours painstakingly putting yourself together. If you look good, then everything should come together. And surely they'll understand that you *just got* the material a few short hours beforehand. Right? Do you…

Work on your sides…? (page 402)

Werk on your look…? (page 440)

*

You're a swing, and that's nothing to be ashamed of. I'm not going to treat you like garbage the way *Smash* did. Many swings have the most difficult job in the show. Depending on the cast, you might never have a performance off, and more often than not, get thrown into split tracks with little to no notice. It can be dangerous work. I think the swings in *Legally Blonde* and the *West Side Story* revival actually died. You, on the other hand, have been parked comfortably in a government job of a production contract for three years, where you maybe perform once a month. You don't have any injuries. Your voice is always on point. Debt is a foreign concept. Your only life conflict is "boredom." I'd punch you in the throat if I didn't sometimes relate. All you want at the moment is something thrilling to focus on and fill your time.

Unfortunately, at the moment, you are stuck sitting in the balcony of your theatre. Outside it is Thursday afternoon, but in here it is Saturday Night on Broadway—for some. This is your one hundred and fiftieth understudy rehearsal and you are over it, but the figure on stage belting her eleven o'clock number is *living*. She is Bernadette P. Peters, a perennial understudy who stands by for the lead and refused to change her name when she joined Equity, choosing instead to add her middle initial. She's a lot.

As Bernadette approaches her money note, she stops abruptly. "Mark? I'm going to mark this."

Mark, your tired production stage manager seated in the orchestra, rolls his eyes in the darkness.

Bernadette continues on, "It's the mold in the theatre, you know? I want to save the gift in case I have to go on tomorrow."

Mark sighs. He's been dealing with Bernadette's bullshit for far too long.

"You haven't gone on in two years. And that was only because there was a hurricane," he groans. Most PSMs use understudy rehearsal as an opportunity to unleash their inner director. It sucks. They need to stop doing that. You're thankful that Mark is not one of those PSMs who's going to try and give you an intricate back-story for that role you've been covering for three years.

Bernadette doesn't get it. "Remember how they loved me?"

Mark remains disengaged. "I remember how half the audience exchanged their tickets when they heard the star was out."

This continues on for a few minutes. You're used to it. Bernadette's psyche lives permanently in the land of self-delusion, and she pulls this crap whenever handed the opportunity. She might have a fierce E, but no amount of enviable screlting is worth being subjected to this much crazy at any given moment.

"There's always an understudy who needs to bring their art to it," mutters the familiar voice next to you.

Corey Michael Cooper is your best swing friend and kindred spirit. The two of you are like the Anne and Diana of Shubert Alley. Never have you ever found another performer more in synch with your sensibility and utter lack of giving a shit.

You turn to Corey, annoyed. "Our job is to relax until someone rolls an ankle or gets too wasted at brunch."

"We literally get paid to do nothing."

"It's the Holy Grail of Broadway," you say proudly.

Corey folds his arms in disgust. "She's missing the point."

"I guess boredom gets to people in different ways."

Corey yawns dramatically. "I'm so bored I could die."

Bernadette keels over and breaks into an hysterical coughing fit. "Mark, I'm dying. I need a Ricola," she manages to say through manic gasps.

Mark doesn't even look up from his phone. "They're backstage."

Bernadette continues to cough. "Just the Honey Herb kind... I can't have those... Calories..." She is nearly throwing up. Mark is unfazed. "I need the Sugar Free Menthol Fresh... In my dressing room."

Mark lets out a loud exhale. "Should we take a ten?"

Corey stands. "I'll get them." He turns to you and speaks quietly in a sing-songy voice, "Anything to get me out of here."

Bernadette falls onto her knees and gasps, "What if I get nodes!?"

You leap to your feet. "Take me with you."

You follow Corey to the dressing rooms. Bernadette is half the reason you've wanted to quit the business. The idea of turning into some form of her one-day has kept you up at night. You don't normally seek out drama, but you must always have something to give you anxiety when you're trying to sleep. Since you haven't had to worry about student loans in a while, and actually have a 401k now, the subject of your night terrors is focused primarily on the fear of becoming Bernadette.

"She's a mess," Corey says, for the fourth time today.

You pause in front of Bernadette's dressing room and glare at the name written outside the door. "Last week she spent eight minutes telling me that she was actually the *first* Bernadette Peters, even though the dates don't even remotely sync up," you sigh in a monotone voice.

"She's a mess," Corey says, for the fifth time today.

"I'm going to need her to not, real soon," you grumble. "It's the same bullshit with her and this show every day. I wish something exciting would happen for once."

Corey swings open the door and lets out a blood-curdling scream. Lying in the middle of the floor is the body of a man in his fifties dressed in 1920's underwear, black socks, garters, and a tank top. A single bullet wound pierces his forehead.

You stare catatonically. "OK, Universe? That wasn't a challenge."

***

As you, Corey, and Bernadette sit nervously outside Mark's office, you try to play back the last hour in your head, but it's all a blur… A body in a Broadway theatre. Like literally, WTF? The closest you've ever come to seeing a dead body was when you performed in Thursday matinees at Paper Mill Playhouse because the audience. This is a lot for you to process right now.

You remember running to get Mark, and Corey calling the cops. You remember the detectives arriving. There were two of them: a short, chubby man, and a younger woman in a suit, who you think is his superior. They asked you to wait in your dressing room and then started casing the scene of the crime. You could hear them talking quietly through the door, but couldn't make out any words. After a few minutes, a third voice appeared. He sounded angry. The altercation went on for a while and then the lady left. Now, you're waiting for Mark to finish getting interviewed, still wondering what the eff is going on.

Bernadette has been quiet for longer than she's ever been in the entire span of time you've known her: twelve minutes. Her eyes have been fixated on the callboard with wonder and confusion, like she's trying to figure out why someone would pull focus from her by showing up dead in her dressing room.

She finally speaks. "Was it a suicide?"

"I saw a bullet hole in his head," says Corey.

Bernadette's eyes widen. "Who would shoot themselves in our theatre?"

You turn your head to Bernadette. "Have you seen our show?"

The door to the stage management office opens and Mark walks out. He shrugs to the three of you as the short, chubby detective pokes his head around the doorframe and calls your name. With all the nerves of every single callback you've ever had combined, you enter the office and the door shuts behind you.

The non-Broadway-Body detective makes his way behind the desk where another younger detective, who must be the one who was yelling earlier, is seated. He's handsome, but seems like one of those young hot-shot-detectives who got a little older (like 30) but is still not old enough for people to take him seriously.

"You can sit down," he says indifferently. You sit. "I'm Detective Zach Feldman, and this is Dick Barkowitz."

"*Detective* Dick Barkowitz," the fat one corrects. You're getting a real C-movie buddy cop vibe from these guys.

Barkowitz thumbs through one of your playbills. "It says here you're *swing*?"

"Yeah," you reply.

"What's a swing?" Feldman asks breezily. He hides his confusion well.

You still haven't gotten your parents to understand what a swing means, so this is going to be rough, but you'll try:

"When someone in the cast can't perform, we go on. It'd be like if one of your detectives was sick, or died, or something, and someone else had to do the job."

Feldman looks at you pointedly. "We're investigating the murder of my partner."

"Oh. Awkward," you respond, trying to stay cool. No wonder he sounded pissed off earlier.

Zach continues. "So, your job is to be backstage, and yet none of you were backstage when a man's body showed up?"

"We were in rehearsal." You hate explaining Broadway to non-theatrical folk.

Barkowitz continues looking dumb. "Why? This show's been running forever?"

You ignore his question like when you ignore people who ask you shit they could have googled. "We were in the balcony. I didn't hear anything. I didn't see anything. We came down to the dressing room and there he was. I'm sorry. I wish there was more I could tell you."

Realizing how little help you are to the case, Barkowitz leads you out of the room and brings Corey in.

Being a good friend, you decide to sit outside the stage door and wait for Corey. Being a good social media contributor, you spend about fifteen minutes trying to come up with a funny tweet about how sometimes Broadway is murder—like literally—before deciding to shelve it in your draft folder because there's a chance it might be in bad taste. After this, Corey finally exits the theatre, looking really upset.

You stand. "Well, that was the closest I've ever come to booking an episode of *Law & Order: SVU*," you say jokingly, but also seriously, because you've been forced to watch all of your friends on that show without a residual check to show for it.

"I can't believe he ignored me," says Corey.

"Who?" You ask.

"Zach."

"The detective? What, did you try to ask him out?"

"He's my brother," Corey reveals out of nowhere and then storms off, with all the flair and dramatics you've come to expect from him.

In three years of being nearly inseparable from each other, Corey has never once mentioned a brother. He's never even mentioned his family. You thought maybe he didn't want to talk about them on the off-chance they dumped all his student loans on him when he was living off a credit card after just moving to the city—you know, like your family.

You catch up to Corey. "You didn't tell me you had a brother. His last name is Feldman. Why is yours –

"Stage name," Corey says as he slows his walking pace to a Moderate Aaron Sorkin. "We haven't spoken in five years. He doesn't want anything to do with me."

"Why..."

Corey's pace picks up. "I got a Broadway show."

"Worse things have happened." You may hate your job, but at least you're self-aware.

"It was my debut. Zach made detective the week we opened. He was Chicago P.D. at the time. He wanted our parents to go to his ceremony, but I insisted they come here. I didn't even go on," explains Corey.

You're perplexed. "Kind of a lame reason to hate you."

"He was pretty mad. And that was before my dad hit black ice in Stamford, and flipped the car into oncoming traffic."

"Corey…" You have no words. Except for the one you just said.

"They had to use forensics, or whatever, to identify the bodies."

Corey's been hiding some deep shit—definitely not on brand for your friendship. "Why haven't we talked about this?"

"I don't talk about it to anyone, and he won't talk to me. He thinks what happened to our parents is my fault."

"You didn't do anything."

Corey gazes pensively down Shubert Alley. "Didn't I, though?"

You've never seen Corey so distraught, and that includes the time not two hours ago when you were both staring at a dead body. He needs a distraction. You have some time before half hour. Do you ask him if he wants to get an early dinner somewhere, or do you just say, "fuck it" and drag him to happy hour? Getting wasted is frowned upon before going to work on Broadway, but Corey just unloaded an avalanche of shit, and clearly needs a release. You're just trying to be a good friend. Do you…

Grab an early dinner…? (page 338)

Go to happy hour…? (page 436)

I can't recount the DM conversation between you and Jordan Roth in real time, because the moment it happened, you were too busy screen-capping it and sending it to your close friends to show your status. I get that you're on Cloud 9 and all, but I suggest looking over the messages again, because they aren't *that* big of a deal...

> Hi, Jordan! Thanks for the follow! LOVE #MakingMondays. I have a wonderful idea for a new musical using the songs of a generation defining voice in the music industry. I am interested in bringing it to the next level and would love to pick your brain on what steps to take next. Thank you for your insight!

Hello! The next time you put on a reading, send the information through Jujamcyn and we'll see if someone can make it. Thanks for watching #MakingMondays! Jordan

I know you're excited, but that wasn't a definite confirmation that Jordan Roth is coming to your reading of *Metamorphosis: the Hilary Duff Musical.* Furthermore, you're not actually putting on a reading of *Metamorphosis: the Hilary Duff Musical,* which means that for you to get your show in front of someone from Jujamcyn, you're going to have to produce a staging of it.

This could be a good thing, though. If you have the weight of a producer (and possibly even an open theater!) it should be fairly easy to get the Hilary Duff estate to grant you the rights to the *Metamorphosis* album. Things are looking up! Time to cash in your chips, because you're about to ask all of your friends (and any famous people you know) for a bunch of favors.

You're not entirely certain if Actors' Equity Association will allow a bunch of union members to perform in an informal reading under the mutual understanding that nobody is getting paid. Wait, what am I saying? That's called a 29 Hour Reading. Surely you can find enough nickels in your couch (or leftover from your last Kickstarter) to fund the one-hundred dollar stipend each Equity actor is required to receive upon completion of 29 hours of participation in a new work that will never see the light of day again. Or, you could just do it rogue and hope nobody gives a shit. It's for the art, after all.

Lucky for you, *Metamorphosis: the Hilary Duff Musical* only has a handful of parts, so you won't have to bend over backwards (or forwards!) too many times in an attempt to complete the cast. The most important role to fill is the leading one, because she'll be the one making the main "metamorphosis," which the audience will also be experiencing. It is imperative that you find a star, otherwise nobody will care. Once you've done that, all of the other roles will fall into place. Once a star name is attached, you could sell your show to anyone no matter how good or bad it is. You once agreed to do a reading just because John Stamos was in it.

Given all of the creative ventures your friends have embarked on in the past, it was only a matter of time before they were subjected to yours. You've always been more than happy to donate to a project, cameo in a web series, sing backup in a concert, attend a live album recording, retweet a link, like a Facebook status, pretend to care—all because you knew that one day you'd be able to use all of these pleasantries in your favor.

The first order of business is to think of the most famous actress you know (who is mildly appropriate for the part) and tell her that the most famous actor you know (who is mildly appropriate for the part) is already attached and *really* wants her to do the reading. The next step is to apply the exact same method in reverse. Once the two actors hear of the other's involvement, they'll sign onto the project because someone else they respect has already vetted it. This plan works smoothly, and you weren't even the least bit worried it would backfire because both of them owed you, and you know how to work a guilt trip.

Now that you have a buzzy leading lady (whom you'll probably replace with Jessie Mueller or Jenn Damiano for Broadway) and a notable supporting male, it becomes a real cinch rounding out a company with attractive credits, as well as a capable director and music director (the ones from the last Feinstein's/54 Below concert you did). *Metamorphosis: the Hilary Duff Musical* is going to slay.

Since everyone agreed to forego their hundred-dollar stipend in the name of art, the only dough you have to front is for rehearsal space. One residual check from six lines on an episode of *Elementary* ought to cover that (a small expense for the reward of sharing your work with the world).

The rehearsal period for the reading is short, but magical. The cast clicks, the words resonate, the music soars. *Metamorphosis: the Hilary Duff Musical* is sure to be one for the ages. You can hardly wait for the day of the show, when you can incorrectly quote *Waiting for Guffman* on Twitter.

A week before the presentation, you make sure to send a very official-looking press release to all of the theatre news sites so that the folks at Jujamcyn will know you aren't fucking around. When the story of *Metamorphosis: the Hilary Duff Musical* hits the interwebs, it receives immediate and positive response online (like

Gilmore Girls reboot level response). What can you say? Hilary Duff resonates with men and women ages 18-34. Your show is going to have an epic student rush line.

Since the buzz is as good as you hoped it would be, you feel confident drafting a letter to Jujamcyn, inviting them to the reading (and making sure to drop Jordan Roth's name in the process). You receive confirmation that someone will be representing the company at the presentation (eek!) so it is in your best interest to have your cast pack that audience with as many blindly enthusiastic friends as possible. You want this shit to be like being at a live taping of *Saturday Night Live*, where the audience in the studio is so effing excited to be there, they actually sit all the way through a "Californians" sketch.

The presentation goes off without a hitch, and you couldn't feel more proud, grateful, and humble about the experience of witnessing live theatre that you created. Something special happened in that room today. You made a new kind of theatre. All other musical endeavors that have come before *Metamorphosis: the Hilary Duff Musical* are now passé. This medium-sized stuffy studio at Pearl where the windows refused to open (providing an interesting smell for act two) is the *real* room where it happened.

"We'll be in touch," smiles the representative from Jujamcyn as she shakes your hand.

"Wonderful!" you squeal.

Feeling the need to celebrate, you invite the company out to anywhere but Glass House.

While enjoying a sensible vodka with diet soda water, you take in the great unexpected fortune you've stumbled upon. Not long ago, you were just a successful actor without a purpose. Now, you're surrounded by warmth, friendship, and the strong prospect of single-handedly changing the landscape of Broadway, and becoming part of American Theatre history with one solitary piece of art.

"We got a problem," says Ashley (your friend who originally neglected to read your script but had no trouble jumping on board the project when stars were attached.)

"Ugh," you think. You're riding on too much ego to be bothered right now.

"What is it?" you ask.

Ashley looks down at her phone. "So, like," she says with trepidation. "I just got a text from my friend Ryan... He came to the reading today, and is friends with some guy who is dating a guy who was on the second, or fifth, national tour of *Hairspray* with Haylie Duff."

"Haylie was here!?"

"No," she continues, "Apparently, it got back to Haylie, or someone, what the show was like... and then they talked to Hilary Duff's people... and I guess they're going to contact you to shut this down?"

OH FUCK.

"Such bull," laughs Ashley. "I mean, surely you got the rights for her music before –

LITERALLY FUCK.

Scared shitless, you hastily begin refreshing your phone to see if there are any emails, texts, or whatever, suggesting that *Metamorphosis: the Hilary Duff Musical* is on a fast track to getting the *Rebecca* treatment.

The familiar ding of an email rings out from your hand computer, and it is indeed a very thoughtful cease and desist letter from Hilary Duff's people.

Well shit.

THE END.

Feeling bold and brave, you slip into a black outfit that makes your body tight. With a swagger in your soul, and in your step, you strut down to one of the Pearl Studios for your final callback with the creative team. You're confident that there's no possible way you won't land this job given the amount of preparation you have devoted to both the callback material and to your appearance. Time. To. Book.

You totally don't book.

Looking back on what happened, you can't think of anything that went wrong in the room. By all intents and purposes, you nailed every aspect of that callback. Each choice you made was the right choice. You wouldn't change a thing about your performance— which is rare in cases like these where you can always think of some way that you sucked.

The only decision to question is your outfit choice. Maybe it was too dark and sinister for this show. Perhaps it set the wrong tone for the direction you went with the material. The fear that you didn't look your best is lingering in the pit of your stomach as you ponder how things would have turned out had you chosen to wear your fun colored top. I guess you'll never know, but will forever believe that the outcome would have been different had you picked the other outfit. Remember this as you go forth unto your next audition.

THE END.

*

Ashley is your fourth effort to get someone to read your script. This is a shame because you figured that by the third attempt, someone would have at least glanced at it. All good things come in threes: three dollar bills are gay, your mom taught you to always decorate in threes, and *Smash* managed to make a charming chamber musical out of a horrifying World War II superstition where the third soldier to light their cigarette off of a single match was the next one to die (*Three on a Match*.)

It's growing increasingly tedious to stay motivated when none of your friends seem to realize that you are the star of their life story. Hopefully, Ashley will!

Ashley doesn't read it either.

You know what? Fuck your friends. Yeah, I said it. All they care about are their web series' and their families. It's so dumb. What good can any of them offer you, anyway? A couple of notes? They aren't going to get your show *produced*. *Metamorphosis: the Hilary Duff Musical* demands to be seen, and the only way to make that happen is to shoot for the moon, and land among the investors. You don't play just to finish. You play to *win*. It's time to get your script in front of the people who matter.

There's only one hurdle you need to tackle before you can send your script to someone who might be interested in producing *Metamorphosis: the Hilary Duff Musical* and that's finding someone who might be interested in producing *Metamorphosis: the Hilary Duff Musical*. The only person you know who could potentially help out is Jordan Roth, president of Jujamcyn Theaters. He's a fairly established individual, and he follows you on Twitter because one time you tweeted about the #MakingMondays show he does on Periscope. Maybe you could send him a DM and see if

336

he'd be interested in producing *Metamorphosis: the Hilary Duff Musical* on Broadway.

This is a pretty ballsy idea… What if Jordan Roth doesn't respond, or worse, unfollows you? You can't afford to lose someone who has a verified account. Do you…

DM Jordan Roth…? (page 330)

Don't DM Jordan Roth…? (page 358)

*

Feeling oddly responsible for once in your life, you decide to walk Corey to Just Salad for dinner, instead of Just Alcohol, the name of a bar you wish existed. You pick up your usual salad and Corey asks if you can find a place to sit outside. You oblige, and let him lead you to a desirable location where the two of you can talk in peace. This will be the last time you allow Corey to pick anywhere to hang outside, because he leads you to the effing Times Square Pedestrian Mall and sits down at an open table.

You are bewildered by this choice. "Um. I know you're down and all? And I'm your friend? But... here?"

Corey smiles with wonder at a pair of children playing with a busted Bootleg Elmo. "Look at them. Remember when Broadway was exciting?"

Your glance shifts to a fat tourist shoving a costumed Spider-Man. "I relate a bit more to them."

The fat tourist throws a punch at the Spider-Man. They fall to the ground and start wrestling in a violent, yet comically awkward fashion.

"Yeah," you sigh. "I'd say my relationship with Broadway is exactly like that."

Two policemen race over and break up the brawl. One of the policemen places handcuffs on the Spider-Man.

"That's like the third Spider-Man they've arrested this week," says Corey.

Standing, you shout so the officers can hear you. "The other guy swung first!"

The policeman who isn't arresting the Spider-man turns back to you. "We're just keeping the area safe from assault," he says smugly.

You aren't satisfied with this response. "And yet, an entirely different Spider-Man assaulted Broadway dancers down the street for *two years* and you did *nothing*!"

Looking baffled by your accusation, the policemen escort the Spider-Man out of Times Square.

Corey shakes his head. "I swear *we* could do a better job solving crimes than these people."

"That would be a great SNL sketch," you joke.

"If someone pulled a gun on us, we could just rond de jamb it out of their hand!" Corey starts laughing.

You stand. "Good. You're happy now. Can we leave? That Dora is freaking me out." You gesture with your eyes toward a costumed Dora the Explorer, who waves at you creepily.

Corey remains seated. "I don't want to go back yet. Zach could still be there."

"Don't you want him back in your life?"

"Yeah," Corey says quietly. "But it's not going to happen."

You sit back down. This might take some convincing. "Well, if we go back, maybe you can try talking to him again."

Corey stays quiet for a few seconds, and then scoffs, "No. I told you. He'll never talk to me. It would take a grand gesture of ridiculously epic proportions for that to happen."

Ugh. This is going nowhere. You could keep trying to get Corey to attempt opening up a new dialogue with his brother, but he is far too restrained to be the active one at this point, so you might as well give up this approach. The definition of insanity is, "trying the same thing and expecting different results and/or pursuing a career in the theatre." You want your friend to be happy, and if it means mending his broken family, you're going to have to create some circumstances where his douchey brother is forced to pull his head out his ass. A "grand gesture of ridiculously epic proportions."

A light bulb goes off in your head. It's either that, or a minor stroke. Perhaps both.

"What if we solved it?" You ask.

Corey looks at you strangely. "Solve what?"

"The murder," you say, without a drop of irony in your voice. It's possible you're crazy.

"Are you crazy?" Corey asks.

You ignore him. "Wouldn't it be funny if we did?"

"It'd be wildly unrealistic."

"We're swings. Our job is to pick up on details," you say convincingly. You're really trying to sell this.

Corey hasn't looked this confused since the time he had to go on after sixty shows off. "Oh. You're actually serious."

"I'm also really bored, and shockingly good at Google. We could figure it out!"

"I…"

It's clear that Corey is not on board with your idea…Yet. I'm on the fence myself, tbh. I wouldn't even know how you'd begin to investigate the murder of a random person you know nothing about, without any of the usual things detectives have, like files, forensics departments, and magnifying glasses. However, you did ask for something to fill all your backstage time with, and we all know the universe has a sick sense of humor — take a look at duckbilled platypuses and Constantine Maroulis as Jekyll *and* Hyde. You asked for this, and in many ways, you know Corey has been begging for something to eliminate the monotony in his life as well. You need to convince him that becoming detectives and solving random mysteries is totally the answer.

You stand. "Corey," you smile, shaking your head. "Corey, Corey, Corey. Dream. The impossible dream. This is the moment. This is the day! When we send all our doubts and demons on their way!"

340

The intensity in your voice grows with every thought. You're really laying it on thick.

"It's our time. Breathe it in! We got a lot of livin' to do. I've got a goal again! I've got a drive again! I want to feel my life coming alive again! Just because you find that life's not fair, it doesn't mean that you just have to grin and bear it."

You crouch down to the seated Corey, and look passionately into his eyes.

"You'll never walk alone. I'll always be there, as frightened as you, to help us survive. Being alive. Being alive. Being. Alive."

Corey leaps to his feet, nearly knocking you over. "I'll do it!" He screams with Peggy Sawyer enthusiasm, throwing his fist in the air like the end of *The Breakfast Club*.

Normally, this would be when you would "smash cut" to the two of you outside the theatre, but that doesn't happen irl.

After an awkward few seconds of silence, Corey puts his arm back to his side and asks, "So, what do we do now?"

You shrug. "I guess go back to the theatre?"

***

As you and Corey approach your theatre, you see Barkowitz exiting out of the stage door. Normally, you'd suggest here that Corey talk to his brother and give one final attempt to make amends. Now that the two of you are official detectives, you want to instead find a way to use their more extensive knowledge of the crime scene, and other stuff, to your advantage.

You need to find out the victim's name and as many other details possible. Barkowitz seems like the idiot of the two, and therefore the person more likely to accidentally spill information. You're going to have to act fast. One of you needs to distract Zach while the other talks to Barkowitz – but which one of you? Zach could ignore Corey and leave you without the opportunity to grill Barkowitz. However, even if you're able to distract Zach, what if Corey isn't successful at manipulating Barkowitz? Do you...

Talk to Zach...? (page 345)

Talk to Barkowitz...? (page 347)

*

Ellyn agrees to read your script, provided you promise to go to her solo concert at Feinstein's/54 Below, Birdland, Joe's Pub, or wherever the kids are flocking to these days in order to secure the least expensive drink minimum that their poor actor friends will be forced to pay while fulfilling their friendship obligations by going to a show they'd otherwise not attend.

Given the money you'll spend on Ellyn's concert, you could have just hired someone to read your script—but they might not understand your sensibility, and at least you're getting to see a show out of it. Hopefully this won't be an uneven trade. I say that because your script may suck, and Ellyn is one of those rare solo performers who actually puts on an entertaining (if random) show, instead of the usual "let me tell you about my life" concerts that plague the New York City cabaret scene. Ninety percent of all solo acts these days are about someone between the ages of 25 and 40, stretching their brief career into *Elaine Stritch At Liberty*.

They say "third time's the charm," but Ellyn is your fourth attempt to get your script read, so I call bullshit. Furthermore, that trite idiom still has yet to apply to the one show you've auditioned for sixteen times, so if that's any hint at how many friends you'll have to ask before one of them finally follows through with their promise, you might as well give up, and throw your script at Jordan Roth, because by that point, why not?

After a week of waiting on Ellyn to get back to you (come on girl, *stop* focusing on your concert), you finally receive a much-anticipated email:

Yo!

props to u for writing an entire musical! so badass. couple of notes… the show seems a little bit like *American Idiot* funneled through an episode of *The Hills*. is that what you were going for? if so, GREAT. if not, then it's a little whiny… and privileged. but, if that's the point, cool! I don't know anything about Hilary Duff… but other than that, it's great, and awesome, and can I play the lead pleeeeeeeaaaaaaaseeee.

still coming to my show?

Ellyn

Sent from my iPhone

Well, that was certainly *not* what you were going for. You were trying to write deeply layered meta-commentary on Millennial culture, but if it's coming off as *sincere*, then that's the antithesis of what you're trying to trying to say. This is horrible! Ellyn was supposed to tell you that your script is perfect, but this is a major setback. If you don't receive positive encouragement every step of the way, then what are you even doing here? There's no way you can continue working on *Metamorphosis: the Hilary Duff Musical* with this kind of negative feedback. Your lack of likes makes it impossible to stay motivated and active.

THE END.

*

"I'll divert Zach," you whisper to Corey, "You talk to Krupke."

"About what?"

"Anything," you say, shoving Corey ahead of you, "Find out what you can."

Corey heads off toward Barkowitz, who is packing a bunch of random shit in the trunk of a car parked outside the stage door. You lag a bit behind and wait for Zach to exit the theatre.

The stage door swings open, and Zach breezes through, nearly knocking you over in the process.

"Sorry," says Zach, unconvincingly.

"You're good," you respond, "We're all good. It's all good, man." Wow. Way to not be awkward.

"OK, then," mutters Zach, as he scoots around you and off to the car, looking down at his phone.

"Wait!" you cry.

Zach turns around. "Yes?" he asks, diverting his eyes from his phone and focusing all of his attention on you.

You're at a complete loss for what to do or say. You were never very good at improv. To you, improv is something a choreographer makes you do when they're too effing lazy to do their job. Because of your disdain for shit like that, you've hated improv in all its forms, and have never been quick when it comes to thinking on your feet. Furthermore, improv is also used to induce anxiety during every commercial audition you've ever had, so right now, as Zach stares at you waiting for you're to say something, you start having toxic flashbacks to some of the most trying moments in your life.

Zach looks back down at his phone. "OK, then."

Shit. That was your moment, and now it's gone.

Zach turns around and looks to Barkowitz. "Dick. Let's roll."

Barkowitz (who has been talking to Corey for the brief amount of time it took for you to blow this entire plan) hops into the passenger seat as Zach makes his way to the driver's side.

"Catch yah later, Corey." Zach says, with little care in his voice.

The car doors slam, and the vehicle peels off.

"What happened?" Corey asks.

You hang your head. "I froze."

"He was just about to start talking to me. Now we got nothing. And this was *your* idea!" Corey is pissed. You effed up.

"I don't do improv!" you shout.

"That was our one chance," Corey bemoans. "I haven't seen Zach in four years. I don't have his number. He's not on social media. He basically doesn't exist. There's no way we can solve this murder now, because we literally know nothing."

Corey is right. You can't go further with this case because you never respected the importance of "yes, and." It's a shame. You were excited to have something to fill your time backstage. Now Corey is never going to reconnect with his brother, and you have to go back to playing Candy Crush.

THE END.

"When Zach comes out, divert him," you whisper to Corey, "I'll talk to Krupke."

"No," Corey urges. "Other way around."

"I know exactly what to ask him," you insist. "You'll have a better chance of detaining Zach than me. Get in an argument, or something."

"I can't do this."

You grab Corey by the shoulders, as if you're about to shake him. "You are Corey Michael Cooper. You are fearless! I once saw you cover five tracks in one night, after accidentally getting day drunk. Be the Corey I know!"

"You're right!" Corey states with pride, "I'm not going to let him hurt me anymore!"

Corey marches up to the stage door. It swings open and smacks him in the face, knocking him to the ground.

Zach stands in the doorway, looking down. "Corey?" He moves to help his brother off the ground.

"I'm fine!" Corey scoffs. "I was practicing floor work for the show."

You take this happy accident as an opportunity to talk to Barkowitz, who is packing some things in the trunk of a car.

"Detective Barkowitz?"

"Hey," he smiles. "You're that swinger from earlier."

"Sure." This guy seems dumber than you remember. "Sorry about making that joke about detectives dying. I didn't know you lost one of your own."

"You didn't mean it," he says. "Charlie probably would have found it funny."

"Charlie. Yeah… Charlie…? What was his last name again?"

347

Barkowitz blurts out, "Noone," without any hesitation. "Zach wasn't even supposed to be on the case because it's too personal. It was mine first. Should still be. Zach's too emotional. A hot head."

He sure likes to talk. This is going to be easier than you thought.

"Was he shot in the theatre?" you ask.

"No," he says. "Definitely carried in. We don't know how, or why."

"Interesting," you ponder aloud, looking over at Corey and Zach, who appear to be finishing up their altercation. You don't have a lot of time. "Who would go through all that trouble?"

"Classic serial killer technique. Set the body in an elaborate staging. Ironic, since it was actually backstage—but, serial killers love irony." It's strange how much Barkowitz is willing to tell you, and yet, he doesn't stop there. "Charlie was always digging around where he shouldn't. Problem is we don't know if he was the first in this killer's streak."

Figuring that Barkowitz really doesn't understand his job, you start to press your luck. "Any suspects?"

Barkowitz pauses for a moment. "You ask a lot of questions."

He's onto you. Maybe. It's hard to tell through his vacant expression. It doesn't matter anyway, because you see Zach speeding toward you with great intensity.

"Dick!" he yells. "We have to go."

"Nice alking' to yah," Barkowitz says, as he hops into the passenger seat and slams the door.

Zach moves around to the driver's side, gets in the car, and hits the gas. You turn to find Corey seated sadly up against the wall of the theatre.

"Everything OK?" you ask, as you approach Corey.

"Yeah," he sighs. "Zach's still mad at me. He say's his job is to draw blame back to its origin point."

Corey starts mocking Zach's voice in between his own. "He was all, 'There are a hundred cold cases out there. Our parents aren't one of them,' and I was like, 'Ugh. How long are you going to hold onto that?' and then he got all pissed and told me to stay away from him, and I said, 'You are at *my* place of business. And don't you find it weird that your partner showed up dead at your brother's theatre?' That's when he stormed off."

You nod your head. "So, it went well."

After recounting to Corey everything you learned from Barkowitz, the two of you open the stage door and breeze past Sammy Fusco, a curt doorman who's been working at that desk since before this theater was born. You head up to your dressing rooms to spend half hour doing research on the World Wide Web. Sadly, your service backstage is limited, and the best place to grab a wifi signal for your iPad is in Bernadette's dressing room. Unfortunately, it's occupied. Normally she spends the show invasively shadowing backstage. Not tonight.

It's crazy that Bernadette doesn't seem at all fazed by the fact that not three hours ago, there was a dead body where she is sitting proudly in front of her mirror, applying a third coat of makeup. Under the assumption she'll leave, you consider creeping her out by bringing up the murder, but you're too concerned with why she is putting on full beat when she isn't going to be performing.

"You're not on tonight," you remind Bernadette, as you and Corey stand in her doorway.

Bernadette pulls her eyelid down and sketches on heavy dark liner. "When you've been in the business as long as I have, you can smell approaching opportunity in the wind."

"What does that even mean?" Corey asks. Bernadette ignores.

This is getting ridiculous. You just can't with her anymore, so you finally ask a question that's been bugging you for three years. "Why did you choose to add your middle initial when you joined Equity?"

Bernadette moves to darken her other eye. "What do you mean?"

Corey joins in. "Like... Why stick with such a well-known name? It's... confusing. I mean if I didn't change mine, I'd be Corey Feldman."

Bernadette deflects. "There's room for more than one Bernadette Peters in show business."

"I don't think there is," you laugh.

"There are two Michelle Williams'," she says, piling on blush. This woman really is delusional. She could talk herself into believing anything.

"They're both famous," Corey says dryly.

"One of these days, the other Bernadette and I will do a show together and you'll see." She drops her blush on the floor. You take her distraction as an opportunity to scare her out of her own dressing room.

"See what?" you ask, as you inconspicuously pull a photo off her mirror and forcefully throw it to the floor.

Bernadette looks up and gasps. "Did you see that?! My picture with Elaine Stritch just leapt off my mirror!"

"Maybe it's a ghost," you suggest. "I mean, there was a dead guy in here earlier."

Bernadette stands anxiously. "Then I can't be in this dressing room anymore. It'll mess with my process!"

Upon making this declaration, Bernadette rushes out of her room, presumably to complain to Mark.

"Score," you smile, "We got the room now."

The two of you sit down in the middle of the floor and start tapping away on your multiple Apple devices. After about four minutes, you have assembled a presentation to show Corey.

"OK, look," you say, holding up your iPad that currently shows a bad Facebook photo of Charlie Noone, drinking a Guinness. "Victim: Detective Charles Noone."

"Where did you get that?" Corey asks.

"I told you, I'm really good at Google," you say with pride.

"What else did you find?"

"Male... Older.... Not alive," you say with false confidence.

Corey raises and eyebrow. "You suck at Google."

You shrug. "There's not much more on him. Just this blocked Facebook page, and a blog about marathon running. What a weirdo."

"I think we're getting ahead of ourselves," Corey cautions.

You step back and think. "Yeah. We should start at the very beginning."

Corey starts singing, "*A very good place to* –

"Nope."

Corey stops.

You continue. "OK. The body. Why was it here?"

"Maybe the killer was trying to send a message to my brother. It being my theatre?"

"Or, maybe that's a huge coincidence," you say. A true detective plays devil's advocate.

"Huh." Corey scratches his head. "This is hard."

"So, the body. He was in a costume."

"Looked a bit like me when I did *Guys & Dolls* in high school – except I wasn't that jacked. Or that dead."

"Why would he be in a costume?" you wonder, feeling this detail is key to figuring it all out.

"We need to find out how he got in here first," Corey says.

He's right. You think. "Sammy guards the door. Wouldn't he have seen *something*?"

"Unless the killer came in a different way," Corey ponders aloud. "There's all sorts of secret shit in, around, and below Broadway. I read all about it in *The Untold Stories of Broadway: Volume XI* by Jennifer Ashley Tepper." Corey starts swiping feverously on his iPad. "I have it on my Kindle app –

Bernadette reenters the dressing room with Mark. She points to the photo on the floor.

"See?"

"See what?" Mark asks, with zero fucks of a care.

"There's a ghost in my dressing room," Bernadette says, shaking her head in disgust.

Mark rolls his eyes. "I have to call the show."

"This dressing room isn't made for more than one person."

Mark gestures to her name on the door. "It's just you."

"And the ghost."

"I can't talk to you right now," Mark says as he turns and walks back down the hall.

"I'm not staying in here alone." Bernadette says with fear in her voice as she looks longingly into your eyes. "You two can't leave me."

There's a greater chance of a literal ghost hanging out in this dressing room before you or Corey voluntarily choose to babysit Bernadette.

"Oh, we're supposed to watch from the house tonight, byeee," you say as you head to the door.

"Then I'll have to shadow backstage again," Bernadette decides, as she looks around the room, trying to lock eyes with a spirit from beyond. "And hope the one in this room stops shadowing *me*."

Bernadette starts waving her arms around and saying some weird witch crap while mentioning she did a guest spot on *Charmed* once, so she knows. Corey and you walk out of the room quickly and reconvene in the hallway.

"Should we wait until she leaves?" he asks.

"No," you decide, "We need to talk to Sammy to see if he noticed anything suspicious today."

"Cool!" Corey smiles for the first genuine time today.

"This is fun. I think we make great detectives!" you say as the two of you walk downstairs.

When you arrive at the front desk, you see that Sammy has nodded off. Corey is more afraid of him than you are, so it's your job to try and wake him up. You hesitate for a moment, because even though he means well, Sammy still has that old school Italian intimidation thing going on. As you lean over his desk to tap him on the shoulder, you notice an old framed black and white photo of a father and a young boy outside the Shubert Theatre. You can't tell what the show is, but the block looks completely different than it does today. It looks even older than those #tbt Broadway pics Craig Burns posts on Instagram. Sammy and his family have been in the business so long, they've become part of its history.

Your first try to politely shake Sammy awake doesn't land. Your second take isn't very grounded either. It isn't until your third attempt that you finally commit to the objective and get Sammy to wake up.

Sammy looks at you, disoriented. "What the –

"Hey, man!" you say confidently, "So... Remember earlier? You know... When the dead thing happened?"

"Why are you kids bugging me?" Sammy mutters. "I've got over two hours left to sleep before I have to deal with bringing D-Listers backstage to tweet pics with the cast."

You continue on. "We were just wondering if you saw anything suspicious when the murder happened."

"Because we didn't," adds Corey.

"I told the guys earlier. No," groans Sammy, still half asleep. "Why do you care?"

Huh. This seems weird to you. If Sammy told Zach and Barkowitz that he didn't see anything, then what was their next step?

"Just interested in how the body got back here," you say.

Sammy motions to a takeout bag in the wastebasket next to his desk. "I leave every day at the same time to pick up lunch from Yum Yum Bangkok IV. They got a delivery charge. Takes twelve minutes, or so."

There's the answer. That's a small window for the killer to make it in and out of the backstage area undetected, but it's doable. Still, you think there's more to all of this. You bid Sammy goodbye, and head quietly back to your dressing room with Corey.

"If the killer got past Sammy," you say. "Then they had to have been casing the theatre and known his routine."

"Or," Corey says, pulling out his iPad, "They got in another way."

"How?"

Corey taps around on his iPad. "I told you. There's all kinds of shit in *The Untold Stories of Broadway: Volume XI*." He stops tapping and quietly whispers, "I solemnly swear that I am up to no good."

"What was that for?" you ask, peering over his shoulder. He's looking at a complicated map.

"Nothing. I've just always wanted to do that."

You study the hand-drawn map for a moment. It's a section of Broadway theatres, yours included, all interconnected by what appears to be some sort of underground alleyway.

"See?" Corey states proudly, "If the killer used that, there's no way of knowing where he came from or where he went."

Chills envelop your entire body. Even though you've made no headway in this case, you haven't felt this excited in three years.

"Should we check it out?" you ask.

Corey stares at you blankly. "Um. Duh."

Following the cryptic directions on the map, you and Corey find the staircase that leads to the hidden underground passageway – which is really just the same staircase you take up to the dressing rooms, but instead, you go one level down.

You open up a large industrial door into the alleyway to find that it's fairly tame. Deep down, you were kind of hoping it would be like that scene in *The Last Crusade*, where Indiana Jones and Elsa go underneath a library and have to swim away from a bunch of rats on fire. That sequence always seemed like a metaphor for an open call. Moreover, you've always identified as Elsa. It doesn't matter which Elsa, actually. Your personality is pretty much a combination of the one from *Indiana Jones*, *Frozen*, *American Horror Story: Freak Show*, and Laura Benanti.

Sadly, the passageway excursion is feeling fairly uneventful, mainly because there's nothing down here but boring theatre equipment. You can't dust for fingerprints, because you don't know how to, and even if you did, you'd have no resources to connect them to a suspect. You don't have any actual training in this field, so right now, the two of you aren't really doing anything constructive. It's at this moment when you realize that two Broadway swings might be slightly under-qualified to investigate a murder. However, since you grew up with your extended family constantly asking you at Thanksgiving why you didn't go to college for "something to fall back on," you're used to the fear of failure—and you combat it with blissful unawareness.

Corey stops. "This is pointless."

"No it isn't. There's got to be something down here."

There's a long stretch of empty hallway up ahead.

Corey shakes his head. "Look. There's nothing."

"Please," you plead, "Just a little further."

Corey reluctantly continues on behind you. After a few minutes, you reach another section cluttered with similar unused equipment: empty costume racks, wooden planks, broken down boxes, a stack of old Playbills, a *High Fidelity* poster signed twice by Will Chase. You're about to give up and turn around, until your eyes land on three trunks.

"Hey," you say, motioning to the trunks, "See how they were antiqued to look really old?"

"Yeah," Corey agrees. "They're probably old props."

"Those two are." You point to the trunk on the left. "But that one looks different. More real."

"Huh." Corey tries to open the trunk, but it's locked.

"Damn."

Corey grabs a coat hanger off the empty costume rack, and deconstructs it into a long, pointy thing. He sticks it into the lock, and starts jiggling it around.

"Do you know how to pick locks?"

"Of course," Corey smirks, "There's a lot you can learn backstage in a long run, besides how to knit an afghan."

CLICK. The trunk swings open.

Corey peers in and then turns back at you. "We're dealing with someone much more sick and twisted than we thought."

You run over and look inside. Small spots of blood stain the bottom of the trunk, and a large, pink feather boa rests delicately in the upper right corner, next to a single black button.

You're speechless. Almost. "What the actual fuck."

"Do you think this is how the body got in?" Corey asks.

"Yes," you say with certainty.

Corey looks at you concerned. "Should we… Call someone?"

If you call the cops, they'll come down here and take all your evidence. You'll also risk people finding out that you were amateur sleuthing, and the last thing you want is to be perceived as the non-Equity version of a detective. However, alerting the proper authorities is the right thing to do. Perhaps you'll find out more about the case, and what this weird-ass pink boa means. But, on the other hand again… non-Equity. Do you…

Keep the boa to yourselves…? (page 366)

Alert the authorities…? (page 368)

*

I SAID YOU PLAY TO WIN! What kind of bullshit is this?! How else do you expect to get *Metamorphosis: the Hilary Duff Musical* produced? You don't know anyone besides actors and parents still paying off student loans! What are you going to do, redefine the theatrical landscape with the important work of Hilary Duff via crowdfunding…? You missed your chance here. Broadway is no place to be bashful. BOOO. Bye.

THE END.

*

Hopping on the 101 again, you drive to the 405 and head north to the other side of the Valley where you merge onto the 118 East and take that to the 5 South for a few short miles before arriving at your destination.

As you wait to audition for *Evener Stevens*, you scroll through Twitter and see that there was some sort of alpaca situation blocking traffic on the southbound 5 around an hour ago. Had you not spent so much time looking for parking in Santa Monica, you probably would have been stuck in it. You remember this feeling of gratitude as you give a thoughtful audition for *Evener Stevens*.

Next, it's on to Universal City for *This Will Get Cancelled*, and that means taking the 5 South to the 170 and restraining yourself from making a detour to The Wizarding World of Harry Potter (you do, however, remember to stop for gas). You think that your audition went well, but you honestly can't remember much about it because you were too excited about being in front of the production company that brought you *Smash*.

Now, it's back in the car for a quick jaunt up to Burbank by taking Lankershim to Cahuenga to Magnolia.

Strolling into your last audition, you couldn't feel more proud of yourself for making it through the day. No matter what the outcome is, you made it to six different locations in a strange town without getting lost, or even being late once.

"Oh," frowns the casting assistant who greets you, "didn't your agent tell you?"

"Tell me what?" you ask.

"That audition was moved to the primary casting office below Wilshire," she explains. "This is the studio office."

"So, what are you saying? I have to go downtown? I'll never make it!"

"Well," she says, looking at her watch, "I'll take your name and give them a call. It's only forty minutes away. You should get there right before they finish!"

Normally in this circumstance you'd be frustrated as fuck. Everything has been going so smoothly, however, that there's really no reason to curse the Universe for giving you one tiny hiccup in what could have been a truly disastrous day.

You politely thank the lady and race out of the building and into your car where you turn south on Olive, right on Cahuenga, right 101 South, and into West Hollywood, where you turn on a couple of other streets that you remember from the score of *City of Angels*.

Magically, you succeed in arriving at your final audition for the second time. With all of the stress that the last hour could have brought, you're surprised to discover how calm you feel during your audition for *My Eight-Year-Old Son*.

Unable to get a true read on how it went, you leave the building and hope for the best. It's out of your hands now. If nothing comes from any of this, you'll always have the self-gratification of knowing that you made it through a marathon audition day during your first pilot season, and if nobody wants to hire you, then they can suck it! I mean do you really want to work with people who don't want to work with you? This question bounces around your brain as you drive home in bumper-to-bumper traffic, wondering if maybe LA is not the place for you, and if you should just call it quits and move back home to—

Your phone rings.

"Hello?" you answer through the Bluetooth hands-free car thing that you had installed.

"So, this day, huh?" It's your agent. "Kinda crazy!"

"Yeah, thanks for letting me know they moved that audition."

"Don't know what you're talking about," he says smugly. "I just got off the phone with some people, and I've got great news... *2 Friends & Their Job. This Will Get Canceled*."

"Huh?"

Your agent laughs. "They both want you to test."

This news comes as such a shock; you'd probably slam on your breaks if your car weren't already standing still.

"What does this mean?!"

"It means," he explains, "that we gotta talk contract. Salary. Billing. The whole nine yards."

"But I didn't book it yet."

Your agent laughs again. "Some of you New Yorkers can be so green."

He goes on to clarify that before you test for either show, your entire contract for both series' has to be agreed upon. Furthermore, because *This Will Get Canceled* moved you on to test first, they have position over *2 Friends & Their Job*. If you get hired for both shows, you're going to have to take *This Will Get Canceled*, even though you like the script for *2 Friends & Their Job* more.

It's super cool to have a popular pilot season, but you know deep down that NBC is going to fuck up *This Will Get Canceled*, and *2 Friends & Their Job* is a CBS show, so the only way it won't run for ten seasons is if it's *How I Met Your Dad*. It's kind of imperative that you get released from your hold with NBC, so *2 Friends & Their Job* can move from second position to first.

"Don't get ahead of yourself," says your agent, "you've still got to do work sessions with the director and producer and shit, so they can tell you what they want, and what they're looking for."

"Sounds like they're looking for me. Shouldn't that be enough?"

"So," your agent continues, "it's pretty late in the season, and I'm thinking this might be one of those situations where they just need to give up and pick someone. As long as you don't royally suck, one of these pilots should be in the bag."

Wonderful. They need you. You're the star they're looking for. There's no reason you shouldn't walk into either of these screen tests like you're a mother-fucking celebrity. You keep all of this is in mind at both work sessions, and as you sit in the waiting area before your studio round test. If you impress them, you'll be passed on to the network, and then hopefully to the Emmys.

The actors up against you for *This Will Get Canceled* are basically the same five people you see whenever you're in for a drama. The folks you're in competition with for *2 Friends & Their Job* are a mix of those you've seen at your average audition for a comedy.

At one point, an actor in the *This Will Get Canceled* waiting area gets up to leave because their deal didn't go through with NBC, and someone at *2 Friends & Their Job* departs because they got a call that they'd booked their first position pilot that they'd already tested for. This is great. You haven't even gone in for either yet, and they are already dropping like flies.

Both tests seem to go pretty much the same way. You walk into a giant screening room with around twenty people in it staring at you with cold and unreceptive faces. You stand in front of a blank movie screen with lights shining on your face. You sit down, do your thing, and then leave without anyone talking to you. It's a lot like dating in New York.

Once you're back in the waiting room, you're told to hang around for everyone else to finish, on the off chance they need to see anything from you, or anyone else, again.

They don't.

When you're on the way home, you get another call from your agent, informing you that both shows have moved you on to the network test.

"This is all happening so fast!" you think.

Welcome to Hollywood.

The network tests feel pretty much the same, except there are now just two other actors against you for *2 Friends & Their Job*, and you're the only one testing for *This Will Get Canceled*. All signs are pointing to you landing a pilot on your first season out the gate. You've never felt more Michigan than at this very moment.

Both tests go extremely well, and you couldn't be more thrilled with how amazing your life is at this very—

"We got a problem," your agent sighs over the phone the day after your tests.

"What…?"

"CBS is interested, but NBC has you under contract."

"So, tell them I used to write hate blogs about *Smash* and they'll release me," you suggest.

"It's not as simple as that," he explains, "they're legally allowed to hold you for seven to ten days."

"And then…?"

"If they don't decide to use you, *2 Friends & Their Job* will move to first position."

"That's good then, right?" you ask.

"CBS wants to lock this down," urges your agent. "NBC has to decide by end of the day, or you're screwed."

Shit. If NBC chooses to pass on you, but waits until tomorrow to actually articulate that decision, you could potentially lose *two pilots*.

Ultimately, NBC doesn't make up their mind about you before the end of the day (or even the end of week) and you find out on Deadline that your role in *2 Friends & Their Job* went to someone else. To add insult to injury, NBC surpasses the allotted seven to ten day holding period, and has to pay you out for keeping you under a contract that hasn't even gone into effect yet. The insult here is that they never actually give the role to anyone! *This Will Get Canceled* not only doesn't get picked up, it doesn't even get made! Instead, the network publicly announces that the show will not be produced because of a "depleted talent pool."

"*Excuse me?!*" you scream to your agent. "They're blaming the actors?!"

"This happens all the time," your agent says in a fabricated attempt at being sincere.

"I mean let's be real, though!" you screlt. "The script was shit, and they didn't want to make it—but instead of admitting to that, they had to go and tell the world that none of us have any talent? Did they need to pick literally *the only people* in pilot season who have zero control, and blame it on them?!"

After having your heart ripped out of its chest by Hollywood, and then told that it's "too round" or "red" or "full of dreams," you decide that you've had it with this city. During your brief time in LA, you've been forced to memorize material for shows that you have a greater chance of booking than they'd have of finding an audience. Seriously. Some of these scripts were truly poopy, but you learned them anyway! You brought your soul to every page of sides, and how are you repaid? By being indirectly told in a national trade paper that you're untalented! It's like Hollywood is one big publicly-published Broadway World chat board!

Feeling fulfilled by everything LA has to offer, you decide that New York is the lesser of two evils, and after March is over and you aren't brought in to audition to replace anyone who was fired from their pilot, you pack up your things to move back east and…

Embrace who you've become… (page 454)

You take several photos of the inside of the trunk with your iPhone and then tell Corey to take the boa.

"Why me?"

"Because I am photographing the scene, and I want to get a shot of the trunk without it."

Corey reaches inside the trunk. This isn't the first time you've seen him try to steal a boa in a dark alley, but it's certainly the strangest. He drapes it dramatically around his neck as you snap a few more pictures.

"Now what?" Corey asks. "Do we Instagram it or something…?"

You're stumped. "I don't know."

The two of you start speculating what this all means. Then, you spend about fifteen minutes arguing if whether or not the boa was in *Kinky Boots*, *Priscilla*, or the second *La Cage* revival. That leads to you both debating which *La Cage* revival was better, even though neither of you saw either. After that, you spiral into post 2000 *Gypsy* revivals, and before you know it, an hour has past and you still don't know what the boa means.

SLAM! The sound of a door shutting rings down the alleyway. The lights flicker.

"What was that?" Corey whispers, his eyes widening.

"I don't know," you say, peering back toward where you entered. You don't see anything suspicious.

The lights go to black.

You grab Corey's hand. This is some real weird shit, and you're not OK with it. You try to feel your way around in the darkness together, but it's pretty difficult.

Corey's voice is shaky. "You think the power went out?"

"I hope so."

The two of you attempt to guide yourselves back toward your theatre, but it's difficult to tell if you're even going in the right direction—

Your foot hits something. Damn it. You place your palm out in front of you to feel your way around the wall, but you're greeted instead by soft fabric. You must have hit a costume rack or a pile of old garments. The only problem is, you don't remember passing any costumes – just empty hangers. As you feel around more, you realize this is no discarded William Ivey Long original, it's a living, breathing, person. A cold chill runs down your spine.

CLANG!

It's the deafening sound of metal hitting skull. Corey's hand goes limp, and falls from yours.

THUD. Corey hits the deck.

"Corey!" you scream, pulling out your iPhone to use as a flashlight. Why didn't you try that before? It's too late now.

As you fumble with the phone, you can see Corey sprawled out on the floor, blood pouring from his head. You look up at the attacker. The dim backlight reveals a face, and before you can scream, you see the head of a shovel swinging toward you. There is a brief moment of searing pain at your temple. Then darkness.

THE END.

"We should call the police," you say, while pulling out your phone.

Corey has already been looking at his. "We don't have service down here."

"I know," you reply, opening up your camera app. "I'm taking pictures. We won't get near this scene again."

Once you are finished with your photo shoot of the trunk and its contents, you and Corey race back down the alleyway, and safely to a zone where you can check your social media notifications and call the police.

***

Zach and Barkowitz arrive shortly before intermission. They speak to you briefly. Their primary concern is with why you and Corey were in the underground alleyway to begin with. You're able to deflect the question by explaining that swings typically get so bored, they start exploring random shit. They seem to buy it, and spend the rest of act two downstairs with the trunk, leaving you and Corey time to debrief.

Since Bernadette is still backstage shadowing, you and Corey take advantage of her dressing room's wifi. However, at the moment you have nothing to google because you're still trying to come up with an answer for what you've just seen in the alleyway.

"A boa, and a button," you repeat a few times, while straining to understand.

"Serial killers have trophies, right?" Corey asks, rhetorically.

"In *Dexter* he did," you say. "And irl, I think they do, too."

"So, let's assume the button belonged to Charlie's costume. Clearly, the boa didn't."

"That would mean it's from another murder," you say, as you pull out your iPad. "If someone is killing people and dressing them up in costumes, that has to have made news, right?"

"Yeah, maybe."

You type into Google aloud. "Murder. Costume. New York."

Corey laughs condescendingly, "You're just going to get a bunch of Halloween costume shops."

"Wait for it!" you insist, and continue typing. "Body. Found."

Corey looks at you expressionless. "Whoa. Mind blown."

You laugh when you see the first article that pops up. Holding the iPad up to Corey, you smirk and say, "I know you don't eat much, but you're about to eat your words."

Corey grabs the iPad and reads the headline emblazoned across the screen.

"*NEWS: Girl Found Strangled in Central Park Dressed as a Vintage Prostitute in What Witnesses First Thought Was a Halloween Prank.*"

"Holy shit," Corey gasps. "This was from two weeks ago."

You take the iPad back, click the link, and read the article.

"The body of Zoe Summers, 26, was found by two tourists taking a walk through Central Park's Ramble Saturday morning. Karen Waters and Barbara Greenberg, visiting from Iowa, stumbled upon the scene after getting lost on the way to brunch at the Boathouse.

'We were very inconvenienced by this,' noted Waters, 'The sight was somewhat upsetting, and ruined our plans for the day.'

"Greenberg was more disturbed by the misrepresentation of New York City. 'A body dressed

369

like a vintage French prostitute?' she commented. 'This was nothing like the Central Park in *Enchanted*.'

"Summers was working as assistant to Warren Snyder, hedge fund billionaire, at the time of her death. There are no suspects in her murder at this time."

You put the iPad down.

Corey looks at you in shock. "We've walked into a serial killer investigation."

"Cool."

The dressing room door swings open. Jenn, your assistant stage manager, stands in the doorframe, panting.

"Corey! We've been looking everywhere for you!" Jenn is breathing heavier than you do when you finally have to go on and are too de-conditioned to execute any of the big numbers.

"What's wrong?" Corey asks.

"Bernadette was in the way backstage and Alvin ran into her. He rolled his ankle, or something. You need to finish his show!"

Corey shrugs to you apologetically and races out of the room with Jenn. There's not a lot about this case that you think you can figure out on your own, and in about twenty minutes, you'll be free to leave early. So, you retreat to your dressing room and pack up your things.

Should you wait for Corey to finish so you can continue the investigation? This wasn't your average Thursday, so maybe it's a better idea to call it a day. You might get burnt out, and if you blur the lines between work and your personal life, you'll never know the difference anymore. However, you don't want to lose headway in the case. Do you...

Wait for Corey...? (page 372)
Go home...? (page 377)

*

You shoot a message off to David, requesting if he'll give *Metamorphosis: the Hilary Duff Musical* a quick pass and some notes. He doesn't respond immediately, and that gives you pause. David always responds. He's also one of those rare entities who uses the "Send Read Receipts" option, so you always know when he's opened a text. Your message is still marked as "delivered," so he's either not opened it, or stopped using that function. Either way, since it's been an hour since you sent it, all signs point to him being dead.

Alas, David is not dead. You randomly remember that he was just put into *Finding Neverland* after a long stint in *Chicago*, and has been finding himself in the process. After indulging heavily in the Kool-Aid at the Lunt-Fontanne, it'll be some time before he gets to your text. Onto the understudies and swings...

Send your script to Corey....? (page 25)

Send your script to Paige....? (page 232)

When Corey gets backstage, you notice something different about him—like he's riding a crazy high. It's weird seeing Corey with post-show endorphins, because you've never seen him with post-show endorphins. Usually when Corey goes on, he treats it like a job, but it looks like he actually enjoyed himself out there tonight. Maybe the stress of the day, combined with the unexpected thrill of being thrown on last minute, has caused some sort of chemical change in his DNA makeup that made him remember why he loves performing again. Ugh. That's so inconvenient for you right now.

You gather from the buzz on Twitter that Corey's mid-act replacement was raved about by no less than three people. Clearly Corey is having a moment, but it's far more important to you that you both get back to work on the case. Unfortunately, Corey appears to feel somewhat indifferent about it. He agrees to discuss the new evidence over drinks, and by discussing the new evidence, I mean, talk a lot about himself. This is so not like Corey.

Maybe he needed time for the adrenaline to die down. It probably would have been a better plan to keep discussion of the case confined to your office hours at the theater. Sadly, you didn't, and now there's tension between the two of you because Corey doesn't want to talk about serial killers right now, and also, you just told him he is being a "major douche."

I'd explain this all more thoroughly, but your friendship with Corey is so important, it's hard for me to go into too much detail without upsetting you. Basically, after you call Corey a "major douche" for not wanting to work on the case after work is over, it gets really ugly and he decides to call the whole thing off. This stops your investigation cold, and now you don't have anything to fill your time with backstage. Furthermore, you think you've lost a friend. In fact, you know this, because as you lie in bed playing sadly on your phone, you see that he just favorited a bunch of tweets and none of them were yours. You should probably kill yourself.

THE END.

*

You die.

LOL. Jk. Our choices in life are never so random that the teeny decision to physically better oneself could end in death—or *could* it? Nope. This is not a day to wish death upon yourself, because you're heading out the door to work out at Mark Fisher Fitness.

You decide to walk to the gym, because it's a nice day, and Mark Fisher Fitness (MFF) is a quick jaunt down the street from your apartment. The New York Sports Club next to the Nederlander (which was briefly renamed Paper Mill Playhouse a while back) is closer, but you go to MFF because you heard Telsey goes there. You aren't sure if someone from Telsey actually goes there, or if it's just the general essence of the casting office. Other notable members include: half your Twitter feed, that guy from that thing, and any girl who is currently forced to wear a bikini on Broadway that is not already going to Physique 57.

MFF is Broadway's gym for Broadway people who don't want to pay for Equinox—which is weird because at least at Equinox, the group fitness mirror-mugging comes free with your membership. MFF specializes in being crazy during classes. Like, certifiably insane. On your first day, the instructor used a Pride-month playbill of *Cabaret* as a megaphone to scream along to the original cast recording of *Seesaw* while shooting glitter out of her vagina. And that was just the warm-up.

You arrive at the Clubhouse and open the front door. It is GAYHEM in there and it's not even happy hour yet. They have this thing where they call their members "ninjas," but today must be a theme day, because everyone is dressed as actual ninjas and doing across-the-floor routines. The disco ball is turning, and Liza Minelli is riding a real, live unicorn. You know that scene in *Wayne's World* where he opens the door to a bunch of literal ninjas? This is just like that, except shot with a Balanchine filter, directed by Conan the Barbarian, and styled by the entire cast of My Little Ponies.

Assessing the scene, it occurs to you that you must have missed the memo because you left your costume bag at home. It's fight or flight right now, and you're not sure if you literally can with this right now. Do you...

Leave, because you literally can't even....? (page 26)

Stay, because you literally can...? (page 135)

Deep down, these fans are your people, and they can't possibly hurt you after all of the backstage tours you've given in your life. Believing that you can find a way to reason with this gaggle of disgruntled theatre lovers, you firmly stand your ground and calmly place your hands up.

"Whoa," you smile, "surely this is all some kind of misunderstanding."

The three fans with old Elphaba brooms scowl at you, their eyes red. A fourth one hops on the stage and barks at you like Mary Sanderson. Meanwhile, the *Once* fan has climbed up behind you when you weren't paying attention. She grabs your shoulder, whips you around, and beats you across the face with a rolled up playbill from *The Adventures of Tom Sawyer*, causing you to fall backwards onto the ground.

Lying down in a vulnerable position makes it impossible for you to take on the herd alone. They begin to smother you from all angles. No matter how hard you fight, you're unable to free your arms and legs from the six men in *Bombshell* t-shirts who are holding them down. You try to scream, but a fan stifles it by yanking Aaron Tveit's ditty bag from *Saved* over your head, and tying a *Legally Blonde* jump rope around your neck, making it nearly impossible to breathe. While gasping for air, the sudden unwelcome invitation of incomparable searing pain shoots to the back of your head as Audra McDonald's heel from *Lady Day at Emerson's Bar and Grill* stabs you in the eye.

The crowd continues to repeat, "Soundtrack is whack!" as you're wrapped in curtains from *Rebecca* and set on fire. Flames envelop your body, causing you to shriek horrifically, hoping that it's not too late for someone to save you—but nobody can hear your cry over the deafening chant of the enraged mob... FIN.

*

This day has been a lot, and while you're interested in this new activity you've found to fill your time at the show and combat your boredom, you're certainly not going to take your work home with you. Not when *Gilmore Girls* is available on Netflix.

You shoot a text to Corey, telling him you're going to head out and the two of you can talk more about this tomorrow. It's probably for the best, because the murder in your theater has made your show relevant again, and you gather from three people on Twitter that Corey's mid-act put-in was pretty kickass. He's probably getting a lot of much needed attention, and wouldn't want to focus on the case right now, anyway. You've seen Corey get self-congratulatory, and it's not pretty.

After binging on three episodes of *Gilmore Girls* (the ones where Rory and Lorelai drink coffee), your brain is still not relaxed enough to fall asleep. You're either too distracted by the dead body and bloody trunk you saw earlier today, or the fact that re-watching *Gilmore Girls* from the beginning can't undo the fact that season seven happened. It's all just too much.

Still unable to wrap your head around why all of this tragedy took place where you work, you switch off the TV and grab your iPad. There has to be something you're missing. Your theater is rich in history, and it wasn't until today when you realized how little you know about it. Fortunately, there *is* someone who knows all of the history about everything theatre related, and they've made it easily available to the world. Her name is Jennifer Ashley Tepper, and you can access her rich knowledge of the American Theatre in her book series, *The Untold Stories of Broadway*, and also, in all of her Facebook posts.

When Corey mentioned Tepper's book earlier, you couldn't believe there were already eleven volumes, and yet, you've read none of them. Like any good friend, you'll get to them eventually. Things have just been so crazy now! Anyway, you're familiar enough to know that for *The Untold Stories of Broadway* series, Tepper spent a shit ton of time interviewing everyone alive who has ever worked in a Broadway theater. She literally got to all of them. She even interviewed you. Each book focuses on a group of theaters, and each theater is given its own chapter. Within those chapters, the history of the theatre is told chronologically through interviews and Tepper's own narrative. It's a really great series, and now that I've said that, I can collect my check.

Thinking this is the perfect time to at least read about your own theater, you click open Amazon and search for the appropriate volume (the map to the underground alleyway is in volume eleven, but the chapter about your theater is actually in volume ten.) Once you've downloaded the book, you turn off all the lights in your apartment and start reading it lit only by the backlight of your iPad, because it's more mysterious and Harry Pottery that way.

As you read, you learn that the theater opened November 16th, 1912, and has been home to many notable productions, with the prestigious honor of "longest running" belonging to your show. A four-year run is great, but in this day and age, it's fairly short to hold a record like that. It turns out that you're working in an epic flophouse—one that rivals the Marriott Marquee, the August Wilson before *Jersey Boys*, and the Neil Simon after *Hairspray*.

There's a lot of interesting information in this chapter that you'll have to go back and read about later, because right now you're combing through it for any detail that even remotely connects to what you've seen today: Bullet wounds in heads, bloody trunks, pink feather boas—anything. Sadly, you've made it all the way to the 1980s and you still haven't gotten a break. Then, as if all of Facebook sent you positive vibes at once, you come across a passage that might turn into a lead…

1984. The Play that Almost Killed Me

Robert Morrison, Playwright

"My debut flopped there, and I haven't been back since. *I Dunnit!* was a murder mystery, but it quite literally almost murdered my career. I was young. It was crap. And some producer lost a lot of money. Everything about it sucked worse than the title. It was the Eighties, so shit was weird, but this was so weird that it closed in tech. When you're a kid, there's so much at stake. So much fear about what a flop can do to you. I needed to make people forget it happened, so I rounded up every copy of the script I could find and burned them. I was afraid I'd never work again! Now that I have an EGOT, I'm cool talking about it. I wish I had a script now. I'd love to see how shitty it was, and then do a revival. Unfortunately, I've gone to great lengths to make sure that nothing from the show survived – not even a Playbill. The only thing I remember about it was this truly ghastly scene they could never stage without it being comical, where one of the leading ladies had to be strangled with a feather boa."

Chills run through your body. "This is a game changer," you say aloud to yourself, unironically.

You move to text Corey, but it's four in the morning and the only person awake right now is Louis Peitzman from the AfterSmash podcast, and he just wouldn't get this. Instead, you decide to google the shit out of "Robert Morrison" and "*I Dunnit!*" There's plenty on Morrison's illustrious career, but nothing about this one play—not even a mention of it on Broadway World's message board. He really did make *I Dunnit!* disappear.

Throwing a classic "Hail Mary," you go as far as posting on All That Chat (under the screen name you made six years ago for purposes like this), but again, it's four in the morning, and while this is the only demo that would have knowledge of a play that was almost on Broadway last century, they probably all went to bed before your last half hour call. Hopefully by morning, you'll have a response.

Since your adrenaline is at an all time high, you pop a handful of audition Xanax, down a glass of rosé, and pass out. Around one in the afternoon, you awaken fully refreshed, and refresh the All That Chat screen that you've had open on your iPad since the wee hours of the morning. Unfortunately, your request for more information about *I Dunnit!* has been completely ignored, and instead, the dominating topics on the board are that potential Barbra Streisand *Gypsy* movie and How Much Better Things Used to Be. Hopefully when you tell Corey about your discovery, he'll have an idea of what to do next.

When you arrive at the theatre, you're thrilled to see that Corey doesn't have to go on tonight. Alvin, the guy he covered for last night, didn't break anything, and is comfortable performing on a sprain because dancers have a pain tolerance that regular people could never understand. Seriously. I have a dancer friend who took some time off for her pregnancy, and near the end she was having a lot of back pain, so she started foam rolling and later found out she'd been in labor for twelve hours. It's crazy what we performers consider normal. One time, I was impaled by a Samuri sword and didn't even know it until I couldn't fit into my costume.

"I think he's recreating murders from that play," you say to Corey as he reads.

"Why didn't you show this to me earlier?" Corey asks, looking up from your iPad.

"I wasn't going to see you until just now."

"You could have screen capped it and texted it to me," claims Corey.

"That's like bootlegging but with books!"

"Who are you, the Andy Mientus of the literary world?" Corey hands you back your iPad. "We've got to talk to Robert Morrison's mom."

"Wait, what?"

"Moms keep everything. This was going to be his Broadway debut as a playwright. If his mom is still alive, and there's anything left from this production on the face of the planet, she'll have it. Moms find a way."

He's right. You need to find Robert Morrison's mother.

For the majority of the performance, you and Corey google the shit out of Robert Morrison and his family in Bernadette's dressing room. She's still trying to talk herself into getting moved, so there's a good chance you'll have this office space for the remainder of the weekend because Bernadette does not know when to quit.

You learn quickly that Morrison was raised on the Upper East Side and came from a wealthy, well-connected family. His Wikipedia lists the names of his parents, but no information on whether or not they are deceased. After finding this out, you lose most of act two to a Wikipedia wormhole that started on Robert Morrison's page and ended at the one dedicated to the lineup of shows in the 1997-98 season of TGIF – and somewhere in between all of that, you watched six different Elphaba-riff supercuts on YouTube. By curtain call, Corey finally turns to you, and confirms that Robert

Morrison's mother, Estelle, is still alive, widowed, and living in her penthouse on East 71st Street and Madison Avenue.

Showing up uninvited to a rich old lady's residence, late at night, seems like an abrasive way to make a first impression, so you and Corey decide to wait until morning. Like, you literally agree to wakeup early on Saturday, a two show day, to pretend to fan out over a playwright you don't know a lot about, in the hopes that gushing to his mom will yield a clue. Well, it's not any crazier than anything in the next announcement we'll hear regarding *Rebecca*.

When you and Corey finally make it to the Upper East Side, after traveling via a combination of crosstown bus, UberCopter, and floo powder, you see that the block Estelle Morrison lives on has turned into a closed film set. They must be shooting a movie or an episode of *Blue Bloods*. Nine times out of ten, if there is a filming crew blocking traffic in Manhattan, it's for *Blue Bloods*. *Orange is the New Black* dominates Queens, and pretty much everything else shoots in Brooklyn. You know this because you pay careful attention to all of the jobs you don't book.

Two guys from the production block the sidewalk where you need to go. The best thing to do in circumstances like this is to say you live in one of the buildings. You'd be surprised how few people will check to see if the address on your I.D. matches that of the building you're sneaking into, let alone the same city or state. I'm assuming this is how the majority of New Yorkers watch the Macy's Thanksgiving Day Parade when they aren't in it.

After explaining that you live in a building down the street, the two guys say that the crew is shooting right outside and you'll have to wait until in between shots to go inside. Being the respectful actors you and Corey are, you politely agree to adhere to their request and wait patiently outside the building, well out of view of the camera and the crew's way. However, the Upper East Side matriarch you spy about to head straight through the shot from the other side of the building does not provide the same respect. As the two actors delve into their meaty scene, this woman (easily eight-five, and looking fabulous in jewels, scarves, and a pearl colored cane) walks straight into the shot.

The actors acknowledge her presence but refuse to break character. It's essentially a standoff. The woman, unable to get around them to the door, looks to one of the actors and very casually says, "I'd like to get to my home, please."

"Cut!" the director yells, and you and Corey are allowed to follow the woman into the building.

"Wow," you comment to Corey. "I wish I could go through my life with that utter lack of giving a shit."

"Seriously," Corey laughs in disbelief. "It's crazy how, to some people, acting isn't a big deal?"

Once inside, you and Corey find yourselves right near the woman, who is talking to the doorman.

"I'm telling you, Crosby, I've been walking through sets for years!" She laughs, "It's hysterical!"

Crosby, a friendly looking man, shakes his head and smirks. "Estelle, one of these days, your literal walk on roles are going to turn into a series regular."

"Estelle," Corey whispers to you.

Estelle throws her arms up, cane and all, and doesn't fall. "Why do you think I've been doing them?"

"Estelle Morrison?" You ask, approaching the woman.

"Yes," she says. "Do I know you?"

"We're huge fans of your son —

Corey steps in. "And what you just did out there. Seriously. Genius."

"Disrespectful," you think to yourself, but entertaining nonetheless.

Estelle smiles. "Well, life's too short not to laugh, or say motivational crap like 'life's too short.' How do you know my son?"

"We don't," Corey says. "We just do a lot of Broadway, and have a lot of mutual friends. I'm sure."

"Well, mutual friends of Robby are mutual friends of mine," says Estelle.

You decide now is as good time as any to ask, "We were wondering if we could ask you some questions about his work?"

"I've an hour before Pilates, want to come upstairs?" asks Estelle. "I can show you all the Broadway.com Audience Choice Awards that Robby refuses to keep at his place."

Well, this is almost as great a stroke of luck as the time you booked your Broadway debut five minutes out of college. In mere moments, you and Corey find yourselves in a swanky Upper East Side penthouse that is so Rich Old New York that while Estelle was in the kitchen having her maid pour iced teas, you almost broke into a chorus of "If My Friends Could See Me Now," but you didn't because you aren't a fucking loser.

"So, what about Robby did you want to discuss?" asks Estelle, sipping from her iced tea. "How he never calls anymore?"

You might as well cut to the chase. "Do you remember a play he wrote called, *I Dunnit!?*"

"Oh, of course! I loved that one."

Corey raises a brow in disbelief. "You did?"

"Didn't it flop?" you ask.

"It was dreadful! But I loved it because my son made it. My son made a hat."

"That's sweet," smiles Corey.

"Actually, it was more of a shat," Estelle says, shaking her head. "Boy, did it suck."

Corey crosses his legs and drinks casually from his iced tea. "Did you get to see it?"

"I saw a studio rehearsal."

"What do you remember from it?" you ask.

Estelle thinks for a moment. "Nothing. Other than it being terrible. You want to believe your children can do anything—and I believe that now, given Robby's success. But, at the time, I thought he was done. I'm happy he was able to put it behind him, but more happy I get to ground his ego occasionally by reminding him that he's written a lot of crap."

"Is it true that no copy of the script exist?" Corey asks.

"Not that I know of."

This might be a dead end. "So, you don't even have a playbill?"

"Well, of course I have a playbill. I have every damn program Robby's name has been in."

This is really surprising. The show didn't even make it to previews and yet she has a playbill? Corey was right; Moms find a way.

"Wow. That's great!" Corey blurts out with excitement. "Could we see it?"

"Sure." Estelle stands. "I'll only be a minute. I keep all of Robby's most embarrassing things at easy access."

Estelle walks out of the room, and down the hall, at a pace fairly quick for her age. You check the time on your phone.

"Shit," you say, "We have to get to work, like, soon."

"We won't have any time to look through it," Corey moans. "If only she'd let us borrow it."

"You can't borrow it," Estelle says as she magically appears back in the room. This woman is stealth. Maybe she's the killer. "You can have it," she smiles, handing it to you.

"Are you sure?" you ask. "Isn't it extremely rare?"

"Of course it is," Estelle assures you both, "But I have boxes of them. I leave one around the house every time Robby visits. Drives him nuts. It's hysterical."

Corey and you politely thank Estelle for her help, and then casually make plans to get bottomless brunch next weekend. After making it back across town and down to the theatre district barely on time for the matinee, you rush through your stage door and up to Bernadette's dressing room. Over the past few performances, you've grown fairly accustomed to this being your detective office. It provides you with privacy from the other swings, whom you know would ask too many questions about what the two of you are doing, and then feel free to give you their input.

Regretfully, upon flinging open the door to her dressing room, you find Bernadette sulking sadly in front of the mirror. Ugh. This sucks. Why is she throwing herself a pity party privately in her room? Normally she finds a group for occasions such as this.

"Are you OK?" you ask.

"Sorry," Bernadette says, looking down in an attempt to hide her puffy eyes. "Allergies. I'll be right back."

Bernadette leaves the room in a huff, but you have a feeling it isn't for good, because you hear the restroom door slam loudly down the hall. Crap. I was afraid this would happen. You sympathized with Bernadette, and thus, have fed her monster. You must *never* feed the monster. Monsters live deep inside many unstable actors, and once their insecurities or tantrums are paid any attention, the monster rears its ugly head. The best thing to do with people such as Bernadette is ignore their monster when it appears. If the monster isn't fed, it usually goes away. Unfortunately, Bernadette's monster is off growing stronger and it will be back for more. You need to find a way to defeat it.

Thinking on your feet, you pop next door to your dressing room, grab the yarn you've been using to knit that beanie you intend to give to someone random who didn't ask for it, and return to the scene of the crime.

"What are you doing?" Corey asks, confused.

"Don't worry about it," you say, as you tie the yarn around one leg of the end table next to Bernadette's makeup station. You then take the other end of the yarn and trail it along the floor and across the room. Luckily, the yarn is dark enough to blend in with the carpet. You then sit down, covering your end of the yarn with your feet.

"Come here," you demand to Corey, "I have a plan, just stay cool."

Corey sits next to you and you both start playing on your phones, real chill like.

Bernadette mopes back into the room. Uh-oh. This is a powerful monster she's morphed into in such a short amount of time. The Mopey Monster is so much harder to deal with than the Loud Erratic Diva Monster. If you ignore the Mopey Monster, you might be perceived as a dick because what if the Mopey Monster is actually a truly depressed person who needs your help? I mean, they aren't, but it's much easier to use your indifference to their monster against you when the offender is acting sad. To be honest, when Bernadette unleashes one of her various monsters, it's usually the best acting you ever see her do.

"Hey, babe. Everything OK?" you ask, turning on the false honesty. She can't accuse you of being unsympathetic now!

"I'm fine," she whines. Ugh. She's acting so put-upon right now.

"Don't worry," you say with encouragement, "You'll go on again sometime soon."

Bernadette sits in her chair and faces her mirror. "It's not that," she says, gazing longingly up at the photo of herself from the last time she performed the starring role. "It's this room."

"How come Mark didn't move you?" Corey asks.

"Apparently, I don't have enough of a case for this room being haunted."

Bernadette drops her head into her hands and slams it on the table. This is your moment. It's now or never.

With brute force, you yank your end of the yarn and pull the end table over onto its side, crashing the lamp to the floor, where it smashes into pieces.

Bernadette throws her head up. "Holy Mary Martin!"

"Looks like you have a case now," you say curtly.

Leaping to her feet, Bernadette screams, "Mark!" as she runs out of the room.

"That was literally the dumbest thing I've ever seen," comments Corey.

"But she's gone," you say, pulling the *I Dunnit!* playbill out of your bag.

Corey and you immediately start flipping through it, searching for anything that catches your eye. Unfortunately, you don't exactly know what that would be.

"Anything look suspect?" you ask.

Corey eyes the pages closely. "Just these eighties headshots."

The two of you spend the matinee poring over every detail in the playbill, in an attempt to find a name that looks familiar. When that proves uneventful, you try to decipher anything from the list of characters that could yield a clue. No wonder Robert Morrison is embarrassed about this play, all of the characters are named crap like Victim #1, Victim #2, and –

"Victim #3," reads Corey. "There's a third."

You look at the names of the actors who played the roles. Victim #1, a woman. Victim #2, a man. Victim #3, a man.

"You think the character of the first victim was the prostitute?" you ask.

Corey nods. "And the second a cop, or a detective, probably."

"What about the third?" you wonder.

Corey starts pacing slowly. "We either have to find Robert Morrison and ask him, or track down all of these actors."

"That could take forever," you say.

"Ugh. I wish this were simpler."

The finale music rings through the monitors.

You stand. "We should take a break."

"I could try calling Estelle in between shows," offers Corey, "Maybe she could set up a meeting with her son."

"Not yet," you urge, "In the book, he explains that he doesn't remember anything, and he seems really touchy about this play, so the last thing we need to do right now is annoy him and get blacklisted by one of the most powerful playwrights in the business."

I find it kind of interesting that now you all of a sudden care about the future of your career on Broadway, when two days ago you were contemplating

389

quitting. I suppose it's best to keep your options open, and I appreciate that performing has now become the job you're prepared to fall back on, should the entire detective thing not work out.

Corey agrees that maybe it's a better idea to leave contacting Robert Morrison for when there are no other options. You both decide to reconvene at the evening show and find a way to contact all of the actors and find out what they remember about *I Dunnit!*.

On your way out of the stage door, it hits you that you have one of the industry's greatest informational resources right in your own theatre, and you have yet to use it.

"Hey, Sammy?" you ask, as you pass the front desk.

"Yeah, kid?" Sammy responds, kindly.

"Do you remember a play called, *I Dunnit!* that was here in the early Eighties?"

"No," Sammy responds regretfully. "But, I wasn't the doorman in the Eighties. I was across the street until about '82. Don't remember much about the decade, anyway."

Corey nods his head in understanding. "Oh yeah, because cocaine."

Sammy shoots Corey a look, and then, "Well, yes, as a matter of fact."

You force a smile. "Thanks, Sammy." Finding any information on this play is going to be close to impossible.

Sammy turns back to his newspaper. "Take care, kid."

Corey and you decide to rest in between shows and not think about this case. Some people take work so seriously. You need time to relax! This isn't life or death right now—wait, no, this literally is life or death. Whatever. It's a two-show day and you need your nap!

When the evening show rolls around, you see on the callboard that Bernadette has called out. The good news is you have the room again. The bad news is Mark clearly didn't play into her demands to be reassigned to another dressing room and she has taken her monster to a new level. Good thing Sunday is a "one and done" situation, and then you'll have a day off. You're hoping that by Tuesday you'll have solved the case and won't have to worry about tricking Bernadette. You'll still trick her occasionally, but not out of necessity.

As you sit down with Corey and the playbill, your first plan of action is to make a list of every name involved in the production. Cast, crew, producers, etc. Once you've done that, you'll start the painstaking googling process. As Corey reads off the names, you type them into a document on your iPad. The longer the list becomes, the more discouraged you get. You don't recognize a single one of these Eighties names. There's not even a Chip Zien.

Corey continues reading from a list of producers. "Roda Vallens, Kristoff Jenson, Carol McGallagher, Warren Snyder, Bill Steinbergerstein, Andrew –

"Say that again."

"Steinbergerstein."

"Before that."

"Warren Snyder." Corey looks at your notepad. "Aren't you writing them down?"

"I zoned out," you say while quickly opening your Internet browser. "But I know I've heard that name before."

"Where?"

You type profusely. "Holy shit. If I'm right –

"About what?!"

The page you're looking for pops up and you quickly flip the iPad around so Corey can see the headline.

Corey's eyes widen as he looks down at:

NEWS: Girl Found Strangled in Central Park Dressed as a Vintage Prostitute in What Witnesses First Thought Was a Halloween Prank.

You see the shock on his face. "I know, right?"

"No! I don't know!"

Frustrated, you scroll down to the bottom of the article and read aloud: "Summers was working as assistant to Warren Snyder, hedge fund billionaire, at the time of her death."

Corey grabs the iPad from you and reads the last sentence. "There are no suspects in her murder at this time."

You jump up gleefully. "There are *now*!"

"This is better than callbacks!" exclaims Corey.

"We've got to get this playbill to Zach."

"What!? No!" screams Corey.

"What else are we going to do?!" you firmly state. "If Warren Snyder is the killer, we solved it! Case closed! You want to *arrest* him, too?"

"Maybe?"

"You're crazy. I'm calling the police." You pull out your phone.

"No!" Corey slaps the phone out of your hands. "What if they send someone else to pick it up? I want to hand it to Zach myself."

"How are you going to find him without loitering at the station?"

Corey starts typing on his phone. "I know where he's going to be."

After a few seconds, Corey shows you a news article announcing the time and location of Detective Charles Noone's public memorial service: 10:00 a.m. tomorrow morning.

***

Due to unforeseen, but consistent, shittiness from the MTA, you and Corey arrive at the memorial service fairly late. As you sneak in the back of the packed church, you see Zach approach the podium next to a closed casket and a large portrait of Charles Noone. So much attention the past few days has been placed on Corey's family drama, or the thrill of the case, but as you focus in on the kind face of Charlie Noone, it finally hits you that this entire thing is real—that the expressionless body in Bernadette's dressing room was a person. For the first time in your life, you experience a moment that genuinely doesn't need to be about you.

"This is Charlie," Zach says, looking at the casket beside him. "Lying down. Charlie's first words to me were, 'We ain't going to get the bastard lying down.' And here we are. It happens. Crap happens. And it sucks. There's no other way to put it. Nothing happens for a reason. How do you explain why a guy can win the Lotto, while some kid gets shot for being on the wrong side of the street? That was our first case together. It was random. But I was lucky to have been placed with the man beside me. You have to think about the people you get. We don't get to choose a lot in this life, so when you get a guy like Charlie, you take note. And you thank whoever it is you need to thank. For giving you that family. Because you need to thank someone."

Zach stops and clears his throat. He's kept remarkable composure throughout this eulogy. Seeing such subtle vulnerability has nearly humanized him.

"You need to hold someone accountable," he continues, "For their actions. Good or bad. Life is random. And I won the lottery with this guy."

The execution of Zach's speech is quite good, despite its indirect dig about "holding people accountable for their actions." You get anxiety anytime non-theatrical folk dabble in public speaking. When it comes to moments in life that you find most uncomfortable, it's right up there with audience participation. So, props to Zach for not sucking, and also managing to present himself as a somewhat sympathetic person.

After the service concludes, you and Corey approach Zach outside the church. The expression on his face is that of conflict—like he's fighting between being mad and deeply touched by the presence of you both.

Corey looks up at Zach. "I'm sorry for your loss."

"You didn't need to come," says Zach.

Corey pulls the playbill out of his bag and hands it to Zach. "I want you to have this."

Feeling that this random playbill might need an explanation, you think it's appropriate to step in. "We learned about this play that flopped at our theatre, and—

"I know," Zach says, feverishly flipping through the playbill. "Dick and I figured out the connection last night and met with the playwright this morning. He had nothing to tell us – how did you find this!?"

Corey smiles. "Never underestimate an artist's mother."

"Why are you helping me?" he asks.

"I wanted to," Corey says, looking down.

"Give me your phone," demands Zach. Corey obliges. "This is my number," he says, typing into the phone. "If you're going to randomly find shit like this, you have to keep me in the loop."

Zach hands back the phone and directs his focus back to the playbill.

"Page 32," you offer, in an attempt to speed things along.

Zach flips to the back of the playbill and scans the page. After a moment, his eyes land on the name he's looking for. "Boom."

"Right?" Corey laughs.

"I have to go," Zach says quickly, as he storms past you.

"You're welcome!" you holler back at him, knowing full well that he is too far gone to hear you. "Still think he's a dick," you sigh.

Corey looks down at the iPhone clutched in his hand that now carries Zach's phone number. "Baby steps."

***

Back at the theater, you and Corey catch Bernadette carrying a box out of her dressing room.

"Where are you going?" asks Corey.

Bernadette raises her head proudly. "Mark finally sees that an artist can not work on her craft with supernatural distractions."

"But literally, where are you going?" Corey asks again.

"There's a cubby on the stage level," explains Bernadette. "An old broom closest, or something. They've converted it for me."

You don't bother asking if she's going to feel cramped. Whatever power play Bernadette was trying to make, in her mind, it worked.

"You'll be so far away now," Corey sighs, "I'll miss your stories."

"Who's moving into your old room?" you ask.

"Nobody," says Bernadette. "Surely the other swings have told you that everyone in the cast believes it's haunted."

"We don't talk to the other swings," you say dryly.

"Take care," Bernadette smiles proudly, and walks down the stairs.

Corey glances at you. "Well, if we get another case, it looks like we have an office now."

Taking advantage of the newly available space, you and Corey lounge around during the matinee. You reminisce about the excitement of the last four days, and the boundless opportunities the universe can bring you if you just look up the sky and say, "Hey, Universe, you rock! But, I'm bored as shit. Give me something to do!" You're both so grateful that your request was heard, and you were able to flex new creative muscles and share your gifts as detectives with the world. Solving this case was exactly the thing you needed to feel…well… needed again.

"You know Nineties Nostalgia?" you ask Corey, lying back on the floor, staring up at the flickering florescent lights. "I have Ninety Minutes Ago Nostalgia."

"Me too," agrees Corey. "That was so cool. I wish we could do it again."

"We make a great team."

"We work together so easily."

"Huh," you think, "Don't you wonder if that's the problem, though? This shouldn't have been so easy. I mean, we rock and all, but we aren't actual detectives."

"Yeah." Corey thinks for a moment, "We were pretty successful right out the gate. Is this what it feels like to have gone to Michigan?"

"I think we're missing something."

Corey shrugs. "Well, if Warren Snyder isn't the killer, we'll find that out soon enough."

"I just don't understand why a hedge fund billionaire would bother with all these theatrics," you ponder aloud, "Wouldn't he save a lot of time by having them whacked?"

It's possible you're thinking too hard about this, but you're a swing, and you're trying to consider all details. Now, in an effort to be objective, you've managed to talk yourself into believing there's something missing from the big picture.

"We need to see a script," you insist.

Corey rolls his eyes. "They. Don't. Exist."

"But if there's one left on the face of the planet, I know where it'll be."

SMASH CUT TO:

The outside of a building on West 40th Street. Early evening. You and Corey stare up at a sign that reads: "The Drama Book Shop." The location of this New York City treasure doesn't really get any more Borgin and Burkes. It's not that the Drama Book Shop specializes in sinister antiques, (although, it does remind you of a time when you had to scour their walls for monologues to present to potential agents, and that does represent a rather dark period in your life) it's the very off-the-beaten-path vibe, kitschy Diagon Alley shop sign, and quirky customers that combine for a mystical and mysterious experience.

Corey motions bluntly to the front door with his hand. "*Here?* You think they're going to have it at the Drama Book Shop?! It wasn't published!"

"Calm down and follow me," you say coolly.

As you enter the store, you feel somewhat confident. Be it either the natural poise you carry with you daily, or the penny you found on the street that was facing heads up, you're positive something will come from this.

You approach the woman at the front desk. Her nametag reads, "Gladys." She has a sweetness about her, and resembles Melissa McCarthy from when she was on *Gilmore Girls* (you seriously have to find a new Netflix show).

"Hi, Gladys!" you say in the friendliest way possible. "You wouldn't happen to have a copy of the script for a flop called *I Dunnit!* by Robert Morrison, would you?"

Gladys smiles. "Let me check!" She types for a moment on her computer and then shakes her head. "Hmm. I'm afraid not. Looks like it's out of print or was never published."

"Surely," you say, leaning in, "there's a secret archives or something you got here."

Gladys remains quiet, her poker face strong. After a moment of silence, she looks down at Corey's messenger bag (the one you've been giving him shit about for years because it's embroidered with your show logo) and back up at you—she knows you're in the business now.

"OK," Gladys whispers, leaning in so only you and Corey can hear her. "I'll let you see the secret Broadway archives, if you get me Bernadette Peters' autograph."

You're completely taken aback by the offhanded joke about "secret archives" being real, but you still manage to get out, "We don't know Bernadette Peters."

Gladys' mysterious glance changes to that of confusion. "Isn't she in your show?" she asks, motioning to Corey's bag.

Corey's mouth drops open. "*That one!?*"

Corey and you retreat back to the street to figure out what to do next. It's Sunday evening, and you're off until Tuesday night. Dare you try to contact Bernadette before the time during which you're obligated to be in the same building as her? You've never seen her in the "wild" before, and the idea of confronting Bernadette in real life is very disconcerting. What if she eats you? Or worse, invites you to her place for a game night, or something? The answer seems clear: wait until Tuesday. However, you need to access these "secret Broadway archives" as soon as possible. Do you...

Find Bernadette now....? (page 406)

Wait until Tuesday....? (page 433)

Memorizing your material with LineLearner proves to be easier than anticipated, and you're able to accomplish so many other activities while listening to the smooth sounds of your own voice. You go for a run, wash the dishes, do your laundry, and map out how you're going to navigate six different audition locations for tomorrow.

Siri says this entire trip will have you traversing over eighty-three miles. This means you'll need to stop for fuel at least once, and it's at this moment that you maybe regret buying the LineLearner app, because you're broke, and it cost about as much as a gallon of gas. With all of the complaining you did about the rate of a monthly Metrocard, it was nothing compared to the amount of money you're currently hemorrhaging on transportation alone.

Your remorse for purchasing a product designed to help you do something you've been capable of accomplishing yourself for years quickly fades when you awake after falling asleep to LineLearner to discover that all of your sides were permanently etched in your brain over night. Not only did you get some solid sleep, you managed to learn each script flawlessly, so you won't have any stress accompanying you as embark on your auditions that will take you from Studio City to Santa Monica to Glendale to Sherman Oaks back to the Valley and onto Universal City and Burbank. This day is going to be a breeze.

Hopping in your car, you head west toward Laurel Canyon Boulevard, where you merge onto the 101 West and then take the 405 South to the 10 West, and arrive in Santa Monica fifteen minutes early. Amazing. Now all you have to do is find parking.

Forty-five minutes later, you make it to your appointment. After years of living in New York City, you're still not quite accustomed to having to locate a place to put the four thousand pound piece of metal you brought to your audition. Luckily, the casting director for *2 Friends & Their Job* was running behind as well, and you're able to waltz right in and slay your first audition of the day.

With *2 Friends & Their Job* down, you jump in your car and take the 10 East to the 405 North, where you merge onto the 101 South and take the 134 East to the other side of the fucking Valley, where you arrive in Glendale and nail your audition for *This Won't Get Picked Up*. After that, it's on to Sherman Oaks for *That Show's Still On?* which means going back through the Valley by taking the 134 West to the 101 North and getting off on Van Nuys Boulevard to kick ass at yet another audition. You're halfway through the day and three for three.

Up until now, traffic has only been its usual dickish self, so while you've wanted to kill yourself the entire day, nothing has prevented you from making it to your auditions on time. The next stop is going to require you to go straight through the Valley, and there are two routes you can use to get to it from here: the 405 or the 170. Both freeways are showing red congestion lines on iMaps and the same expected arrival time. As you know by now, traffic in LA can change faster than NBC can make a horrible decision. Don't you do the same. Which freeway do you take to your next audition?

The 405. (page 359)

The 170. (page 91)

Success is all about discipline, discipline, discipline, and you're going to apply the strong work ethic you learned in your BFA program to this callback, in the hopes that it will reap major rewards. Since your student loans are still decades away from being paid off, you decide that the only way to feel OK with that is to put to use what you learned at the fine establishment that provided you with a degree—along with severe PTSD and weekly emails from the alumni association requesting more money.

One of the many things you learned in college is the art of spending a scrupulous amount of time marking beats and thinking very hard. After analyzing every line of text in your sides, you feel confident about the backstory you've constructed for the character you're being called in for. You've decided their objective in every scene is colored by the personal need to come to peace with ancestors who were Nazi sympathizers during World War II, and that your character is a direct descendant of Rolf Gruber from *The Sound of Music*. You think this is just the right bold choice to bring to "USC College Kid #3."

When it gets dangerously close to the time of your appointment, you hop into the shower, rinse yourself off, throw on something clean, and race down to one of the Pearl Studios—making it there just in time for your appointment, plus a moment to check yourself in the restroom mirror.

As you gaze into your reflection, you start to second-guess your choice to spend so much time learning your sides. You hope it doesn't work against you. I'd describe your "look" as "decidedly disheveled," but when it comes to the callback material, you couldn't be more prepared if you were PrEP.

Upon entering the room, you try to remember all the subtle nuances of your character that you worked on so diligently earlier. They manage to stay fresh in your mind as you sing through the "song of your choice" that the music director requests you bang out first. Vocally, things go smoothly enough here for the director to invite you to move on to the sides.

"Which ones first?" you ask.

"Um," says the director as he rifles through papers on the table. "How about the last one."

"Shit," you think. That's literally the one you prepared the least!

As you perform the scene opposite the reader, the only thing going through your head is:

Why God? Why these sides?
Confidence changes, with the tides.
The other scenes, I knew much more.
Now I'm confused, down to the core.
Why God? Why –

"Thank you so much for coming in today," says the director once you finish stumbling tragically through the scene.

"No, thank *you*," you assure him.

Feeling blasé about the experience, you try to keep it from eating your soul from the inside out, by eating food from the outside in.

After sobbing over a sensible snack that is a bit too calorically dense for me to mention here, you vow to no longer dwell on the miniscule details of the callback. You tried your hardest, and if that's not good enough for them, they can sit on a rolled up playbill and spin.

You're able to confidently carry yourself through the next few days without hearing anything (your callback fell before a weekend, and then there was a

Monday holiday, followed by a hurricane, so it's possible the creative team took their time deliberating) but after a week, you decide it's best to send your agent a "hey you up" email:

Hey Agent!
Did you hear anything from that callback I had?
-- Your Favorite Client

***

Client,
no sorry
-- Agent

***

can u check
-- Client

***

They went another direction.
-- Agent

***

Is there any feedback?
-- Client

***

Your type didn't fit into the world of the show,
but I got you an appointment for an NYU student film.
Can you confirm?
-- Agent

***

Well, that's unfortunate. It looks like all of the hard work you dedicated to your sides didn't pay off. Not only did they choose the one you worked on the least, but all of that time spent preparing could have been devoted to refining your look – a look that would more aptly fit into the world of the show. Ah well, you live, you learn. I think it was Sydney Lucas who once said, "I have not failed. I've just found 10,000 ways to not book." You've come to discover that this is one of the ways.

THE END.

*

To spare you from the tediousness of the process it was to acquire Bernadette P. Peters' autograph, I'll give you the quick, eight bar cut version of the story:

BAR 1.) You don't have her number, so you have to get it from Mark.

BAR 2.) Bernadette insists upon meeting at Bar Centrale.

BAR 3.) When you can't get in, you go to Blockheads.

BAR 4.) The wait at Blockheads is way too long, so you go to Mother Burger, which is Blockheads with burgers.

BAR 5.) Bernadette demands to know whom the autograph is for, so you lie and say it's for BC/EFA.

BAR 6.) You feel guilty about using BC/EFA to get what you want, so you change it to your dying grandmother and Bernadette doesn't even notice.

BAR 7.) Bernadette signs a menu and then you each slam a round of frozen margs with beers wedged inside them.

BAR 8.) Bernadette passes out because she doesn't normally drink in an effort to protect the vocé (pronounced "vo-chay") so you leave her there under the false hopes she forgets this entire thing ever happened.

Making it back to the Drama Book Shop just before closing, you hand the signed menu off to Gladys and explain the importance of such an item because Bernadette P. Peters does not eat carbs, and therefore a signed Mother Burger menu suggests that the autograph was completed while she was indulging in a forbidden luxury—adding to its rarity.

Gladys is more psyched than Paul Wontorek was when Aaron Tveit joined Twitter. She immediately guides you to a back room, down a spiral staircase and through a tiny door that leads you into a small room, crammed with bookshelves that burst with manuscripts and cast recordings on both vinyl *and* compact disc.

"We close in fifteen minutes," Gladys warns. "I can maybe let you stretch it to twenty."

Gladys smiles and exits the room. You turn to the multitudes of text before you and begin to feel the kind of overwhelming anxiety that you haven't experienced since you first started to learn all the tracks you cover. There's no way you can look through all of these titles before closing.

"Holy shit!" Corey exclaims, pulling a manuscript off of a high shelf.

"No way!" you scream in excitement at how quickly Corey found the script.

"I always heard this existed, but nobody has ever seen it," Corey grins, flipping through what appears to be sheet music.

"That's not the script!"

"No," Corey shrugs. "It's the score to that *Groundhog Day* musical that Sondheim was rumored to be writing. Do you know how rare and magical this is!? It's like the one piece of sheet music Michael Lavine doesn't have!"

Corey continues eyeing what very well might be the Holy Grail, Sivalinga Stone, and Ark of the Covenant rolled into one, but you don't have time to geek out over this discovery.

"We can't take that out of here," you insist, "We don't know its power. If we take that score past the threshold of the doorway, the entire building might collapse and we could decay to dust. Find the *script*."

Corey reluctantly returns the score to the shelf from whence it came. The two of you then begin systematically combing the room for the script to *I Dunnit!*. As the minutes tick by, all hope begins to swiftly dwindle. Until—

"Found it," you announce proudly, as you pull a dusty script out from underneath the score for Adam Guettel's *The Princess Bride*, the budget for the opening night party of *Rebecca*, and Jason Robert Brown's treatment for *A League of their Own*.

Corey runs to your side and you begin furiously flipping through the script, looking for details about the victims in the play. The first, a woman, syncs perfectly with the killer's first victim, Zoe Summers—except in the play, she isn't a French prostitute, she's the killer's girlfriend who likes wearing feather boas. You don't know why the press chose to get so misogynistic about it. Like, a woman can't look sassy without being slutty?

The second victim (a cop) was shot in the head after the killer discovered he had been sleeping with Victim #1. Wow. This plot is horrible. No wonder it flopped. The third victim, a friend of Victim #2, was killed with a shovel. There's even a fourth and fifth victim, but you don't have time to read about them because it's almost closing and you now have reasonable evidence that Warren Snyder was recreating murders from a play he invested in over thirty years ago.

"Call Zach," you say, slamming the script shut, "We've only connected two murders. If there are more out there with no suspect, then these details could help prove Snyder responsible."

Corey dials his phone, and waits for it to pickup. You're honestly shocked he has service down here. The

Secret Broadway Archives really do have powers you don't understand.

"Zach!" Corey shouts out. "We have to tell you about something—wait, what?" Corey looks at you with concern in his eyes. "No, I haven't," he responds into the phone.

Something is wrong. Corey silently listens to Zach, but doesn't articulate anything that he's hearing. Come on, Corey! Mouth words or use simple hand gestures, or something! This would be so much easier if either of you had booked the *Spring Awakening* revival.

Corey continues exchanging indecipherable small talk for about a minute and then hangs up. "That was Barkowitz."

"Why? What did he say?"

"He wanted to know if Zach was with me," reveals Corey. "I guess he stormed out of the funeral after we were there and arrested Warren Snyder without proper evidence. Snyder provided an ironclad alibi, and Zach was suspended."

"Why did Barkowitz have his phone?"

Corey tries to recount all the details he learned in that short amount of time. "Apparently Zach went to some bar, got drunk alone, and invited Barkowitz to join him. When he got there, Zach was gone and had left his phone. The bartender said he started hanging out with some weird guy and they left together."

"This is bad."

Corey huffs. "I don't know his life! Who cares if he's picking up weird guys in bars?"

"No!" You open the script again, flip to the end of act one, and point to a line midway down the page. "Victim #3. *Friend of Victim #2*."

Corey gasps and starts pacing around the cramped quarters, clearly having an anxiety attack. The door swings open and Gladys cheerfully chimes, "We're closed!"

"My brother is getting murdered!"

Gladys turns around quickly. "Five more minutes is fine."

Corey continues pacing. You grab him by the arm. "Pull it together! We have to stay calm! What do we do when we have to go on for someone in the show, but we've forgotten their entire track?"

"We make it up!"

You nod. "Based off what we *do* know. We know the Snyder lead is wrong. Someone else connected to the play is recreating these murders. What *else* do we know?"

Corey starts to calm down and think. "OK. OK... There was a body in the dressing room."

"How did it get there?"

Corey throws his hands up in the air. "I don't know!"

"We need to look at security tapes."

"Zach would have checked them."

You agree. "Then they would have seen."

"Which means the killer had to have accessed the theater through the underground alleyway," ponders Corey.

"But how did the trunk get past the security tapes?" you wonder.

"They were doctored," suggests Corey.

"Who'd have access to that?" You're getting nowhere.

Corey starts pacing again. "Someone who works there. Someone familiar with the facility. And our rehearsal schedule."

"Someone who could move around unnoticed," you add.

"Someone who knows theatre history."

410

This thought makes your mind drift away for a minute. Theatre history… Someone with a vast knowledge of that theater's history. The killer is clearly not Jennifer Ashley Tepper, so who is it? You think back to the previous week. Pictures flash rapidly through your mind. A body in a dressing room, Zach and Barkowitz questioning you, Bernadette drunk, Gladys' laugh, Rory Gilmore drinking coffee, iPads, iPhones, hours on Google, Charlie's smiling face in his portrait, a boy outside a theater, a costumed Spider-Man, two children playing with a Bootleg Elmo, a boy outside a theater with his dad, a boy with his dad outside an old theater… your theater.

You snap out of your spiral. "Oh my God."

Corey stops pacing. "What?"

"It's Sammy. The killer is Sammy Fusco."

"That's crazy!" Corey scoffs.

"It was there right in front of us. How could we miss this?"

Corey shakes his head. "I don't believe it."

"The picture on Sammy's desk! It's outside our theatre! Sammy may not have been the doorman at the time, but his dad was, and I didn't see it."

"This is really out there, you know that, right?"

You make for the door. "We don't have any other option right now."

Corey follows. You zip past Gladys on the way out, thank her for her kindness, and race to the exit.

In your final Google trick of the evening, you manage to find Sammy's address on West 90th by the time you make it outside—using this crazy website called "The White Pages."

Now, what's the fastest way to the Upper West Side? It's a Sunday, which means there are no trains, so it's either a cab or Uber. Which do you think is the better option?

Do you…

Uber it to Sammy's…? (page 419)

Cab it to Sammy's…? (page 424)

*

Hopping on the 101 again, you drive to the 405 and head north to the other side of the Valley. Once you've merged onto the 118 East, you're almost within reach of your destination. All you have to do is get onto the 5 South for a few short miles and –

FUCK.

Gridlock on the 5.

For most of the day you've been running lines in the car instead of listening to the radio. Upon switching it on, you learn that a handful of alpacas from a farm just outside of Sun Valley have escaped and are running up and down the 5 freeway, grinding traffic to a halt. Since you're now stuck in a parking lot, you open up Twitter to follow the alpaca chase in real time. After fifteen minutes, the animals have still not been apprehended, #LAlpacas is trending nationally, and you have no firm estimate of when you'll be able to make it to your next audition, so you phone your agent to figure out some sort of plan.

"Alpacas are in," your agent tells you. "Lot's of people are breeding them out here. Matt Weiner's working on a pilot for next season. Should be big. Anyway, I'll make a few calls, and I'm sure you'll be fine. Lots of people are probably dealing with the same thing."

After an hour and a half of screaming in frustration on the 5, the alpacas are safely recovered, a few of your #Lalpacas tweets go viral, and traffic finally resumes, allowing you to make it to your audition for *Evener Stevens*, which you bomb because you've just spent the last ninety minutes in a fit of rage with veins you didn't know you had popping out of your temple. This day went south really fast.

The next audition doesn't even register because all you can focus on is the traffic on the 5, and the 170, and on Lankershim, Cahuenga, and Magnolia. Somewhere in the middle of all of that, you made a fool of yourself at *This Will Get Canceled*. By the time your car crawls up to your last audition, all you can think about is that you forgot to stop for gas, and now you're out, and you'll have to call AAA for the first time in your life.

As you limp into the building, you pray that this entire day was some sort of test, or way for the Universe to make you emotionally available to bring the type of depth required of the role you're auditioning for in *My Eight-Year-Old Son*. There's simply no other reason to explain why anyone should be subjected to that kind of torture from LA traffic.

"Oh," frowns the casting assistant who greets you, "didn't your agent tell you?"

"Tell. Me. What."

"You're at the studio. That audition was moved to the primary casting office below Wilshire," she explains.

"So, what are you saying? I have to go downtown? I… I'm… out of gas!"

This is horrible. And you thought that going to the wrong Pearl Studios was inconvenient.

"Well," she says, looking at her watch, "they'll be long finished by the time you get down—

Something inside your brain snaps, causing you to get dangerously close to this poor woman's face.

"I have been awake for almost sixty hours," you spit. "I'm tired and I'm dirty. I have been from Santa Monica to Glendale to Sherman Oaks to… where the hell am I?"

"Burbank."

"I am trying to get seen for *My Eight-Year-Old Son*. And now that I'm this close, you're telling me it's hopeless?! No, no, no, no, no, wait. This is Hollywood. In the season of perpetual hope! And I don't care if I have to go outside your studio and hitchhike. If it costs me everything I own. If I have to sell my soul to the devil himself, I am going to get seen for this show."

The casting assistant picks up the receptionist's phone and dials a number.

"Security?"

***

After getting thrown out of an audition following what might have very well been a nervous breakdown, I think it's best that you take that as a sign to cut your losses and move back to New York, else risk being committed the next time you have a nasty run-in with LA traffic.

Move back to New York... (page 4)

*

Even I, a jaded New Yorker, am somewhat judgmental of your decision to use your emotionally unstable friend as an unpaid reader during her moment of need. You really must be a Broadway Freshman if you want a job that badly! Hopefully you have the linguistic skills needed to spin your fabricated empathy into an opportunity.

In a calculated move of pure inspiration, you place your hand on your friend's shoulder and gently say, "Oh, Carol. Put down the vodka sauce. It's cream-based."

Carol looks up at you with doughy, carb-loaded eyes. You take a moment to assess her features. She's aged since college. Gone is the girl who brought a youthful, idealistic layer that only a seasoned twenty-one year old can bring to Carlotta in *Follies*. Unfortunately, she's not still here. She's gone.

"I don't care about anything anymore," she sighs, and spoons another heaping serving into her perpetually gaping hole of sadness and regret.

The worst part about all of this is that Carol hasn't even bothered to dignify herself by using the fine utensils the two of you purchased from IKEA. She's using the plastic "silverware" that came with the delivery, and that's pretty much a lateral move from using your own hands. Someone should put this girl out of her misery or give her a final callback for something. Even just moderate attention from a creative team can keep a floundering gypsy mentally stable for at least six months.

"This isn't the Broadway we were promised as kids," you say, trying to offer some friendly advice. "Michael Bennett is dead. Bob Fosse is dead. Times Square is a theme park. Some-other-line-from-*Camp-*

that-helps-articulate-what-I-mean. Do you really want to pursue this anymore? I don't. We deserve better."

"That's easy to say when you work all the time," Carol groans.

Ignoring her passive aggressive assessment of your success, you pull out your iPad and open up the .PDF of your sides. While scrolling through them, you lament the loss of artistry in the American Theatre:

"I mean look at this dialogue. It's terrible. Read it with me. You'll see just how stupid the people in charge are. It'll make you feel better."

You drop the iPad in Carol's lap and stand up to read opposite her. Your skills are so solid that you're already off book after only scrolling through the sides once, like three seconds ago.

"Take it from the top," you say.

In a manipulative effort to appear caring and concerned for Carol, you're certain she will agree to help you with your material.

"Are these callback sides?" Carol asks.

"No. I mean yes, but – "

"Are you literally for real?"

"Carol, you gave up saying 'literally' for Lent."

"It's October, and fuck you."

"I'm just trying to help."

"If we had a kitchen table, or any flat surface for me to eat this penne alla vodka on besides your bed, I'd flip it."

Carol heaves the tray of pasta across the room and it splats against the wall two feet away. As you watch the vodka sauce drip to the floor, Carol stands in front of you, white-knuckling the plastic flatware.

"You continue to break new ground in douchery-masquerading-as-friendship," she spats. "You could teach a master class in how to make something about you. I really needed your empathy right now, and you couldn't even give it to me for one second."

"Carol – "

"I'm *constantly* there for you. I like all of your tweets, but that's not good enough, because only retweets count. You text *me* when you book something, because whomever you're dating gets jealous, and you need someone to celebrate with. I *donated to your Kickstarter*. Well, I am not going to be that person anymore. And I don't think anyone else should have to be either."

Carol takes the hand with the plastic knife and strikes quickly, slicing just below your chin, causing a searing pain to envelop your neck. Warm wetness runs down your chest. You grab your throat to stop the blood, but you're choking on it. The pain is indescribable. No, really. I can't describe it to you, because my neck has never been sliced open by a disposable plastic knife before.

You fall to your knees. Blood is gushing everywhere. It's gushing worse than your parents at your stage door. Keeling over, you grab Carol's ankles but she kicks you over onto your back. You look up, and just before everything goes black, you gaze into Carol's cold eyes and then focus over to the faint blur of her hand holding a plastic knife soaked in your blood. And vodka sauce.

Carol leans down and whispers into your ear, "The world is a whole lot bigger than you."

Fade to black.

Carol was a fine actor, but never really committed to a performance. I guess today you could say she "killed it."

Well, between Carol's need to feed her face, and your need to feed your ego, it was a full day of eating for both… THE END.

*

There's an Uber within two minutes of your location outside the Drama Book Shop. This is great! You're going to be there in no time.

When the black car arrives, you and Corey slide comfortably into the backseat and speed off toward West 90th Street. The driver bypasses heading up Eighth Avenue, probably because of traffic. He then skips going north on Tenth Avenue, causing you concern.

You lean forward. "What route are you taking? Because I think it would have been better if we went up Central Park West and turned left on –

"I know where I'm going," the driver barks. Shit. He's one of *those* Uber drivers.

There's no fixing this now. You're stuck sixteen avenues out of the way, flying up West Side Highway. When you finally arrive at Sammy's brownstone, what seems like hours later, you run to the front door where Corey starts picking the lock with a spare bobby pin (why he has one, you've no idea) while you leave a horrible rating for your Uber driver. Once inside the dark house, you both run upstairs to the only lit room you could see from the car when you pulled up.

Corey swings open the door to reveal Sammy, pushing Zach's limp body into a trunk. It's too late.

Sammy turns to you, his eyes fiery with rage. "What are you kids doing here?"

Corey freezes in horror. You're speechless. It looks like the deed was done not moments before. You would have made it if you had another Uber driver. How could technology fail you now?!

Without warning, Corey races to attack Sammy. Even at, like, sixty years old, Sammy's reflexes are quick. Corey tries to swing at him, but Sammy grabs his wrist and buries a knife into his chest. Your stomach turns. Corey drops to the floor.

419

It all happened so fast. There was nothing you could have done. As Corey bleeds out on the ground, you remain motionless.

"Whataya gonna do, kid?" Sammy laughs.

There isn't a choice here. You have to run. Turning, in what feels like slow motion, you make for the door.

BANG! The deafening shot rings from behind you. You feel it hit the back of your head, but only for a moment. Then silence.

THE END.

*

"Mary? Mary Testa?!" exclaims Yourself.

Wow. That name popped out of your mouth easier than a Michigan alum can get an appointment from Telsey. Even *I'm* impressed.

You slip out of line and saunter over to Mary Testa. She looks a little confused, but you know that once you mention that you were both in the reading of *Nineties Movie: the musical*, she'll recognize you.

"Cat?" asks Mary Testa.

"No, we didn't do *Cats*. We did a reading together last —

"Meow," she whispers, and then puts her hands on her face, like she's making whiskers with her fingers.

It's in this moment that you realize that this is not Mary Testa. This is a homeless person. OK, my bad. I'm sorry. Mary Testa played the Homeless Lady in *A New Brain*, so like, it's easy for me to make a mistake like this. I'm only human.

You decide to just go with it and continue pretending this homeless lady is Mary Testa, but she continues to speak gibberish to you and smells like the Broadway Flea Market, so the second the opportunity presents itself, you move to leave before you and Not Mary Testa end up developing a web series together.

"Great seeing you, *Mary Testa*!" you smile. "Hope we get a chance to work together, *again*, real soon!"

Since you are a giving person, you slide a gift card to Broadway.com into Not Mary Testa's hand, and slip out the door.

Well done! I'd say what you just did to your exes was the real life equivalent of that emoji where the girl is flipping her hair. Now it's time to rush home and study all of those new sides. You better book it so you can *book it*.

421

As you race back downtown, you can't help but feel a little guilty for using that seemingly sweet homeless lady for a fairly petty reason. Hopefully you can find a way to pay it forward in the future. Think of all the philanthropic work you could do for the non-Equity. There are plenty of humanitarian opportunities at the New England Theatre Conference, StrawHats, and Ellen's Stardust Diner. Or, maybe you could start a foundation for Career Transition for Aspiring Actors Who Don't Know They Should Transition Careers. These are all great ideas, but, before you can save others, you have to save yourself—and the only way to survive right now is by turning your unemployment contract into a production contract.

All of those good thoughts about wanting to help others really took the focus off your commute home. You should think about doing selfless acts more often, because before you know it, you're swinging open the door of your apartment, tossing the gym bag you didn't use to the side, and reaching for your iPad to start rehearsing your—

"Oh. Hi, Carol," you say to your roommate, who is sprawled out on the couch-slash-your-bed, eating a tray of penne alla vodka that's been freshly delivered from Carmine's on 44th Street.

"Hi. How was the gym?" She asks in the typical gloom-laden tone that you've grown accustomed to ever since she ended up in the *If/Then* of her life where she didn't book the tour of *If/Then*.

"Gym?" You ask.

You look at your gym bag and then remember that you switched up your workout today with Schmackary's, but Carol doesn't need to know that.

"Oh, yeah. It was great. The new trainer at Mark Fisher Fitness really rode us hard, but I think that's because he's literally a gay porn star. Anyway, it was effective."

"That's nice," Carol responds with the kind of sadness that can only be filled with vodka or carbs—or in the case of Carol's pasta, both.

"Cool," she sighs, shoving another forkful of penne into her mouth.

Carol has good days and bad days. It's rough for her because her career is moving perpendicular to yours. After months of depression, missed opportunities, and bad luck, Carol has turned into a 2006 Snow Patrol album. You want to save her, but you're also on a time crunch, and selfless acts can be surprisingly inconvenient. Perhaps if you approach the conversation in a way that safely redirects the focus to you, you'll be able to cheer her up and she'll agree to help you work on your sides. Or you could just talk to her like a human being…But, like I said, this callback is really important, and helping Carol could set you back an hour or seven. Do you…

Talk to Carol…? (page 104)

Ask Carol for help on your sides…? (page 416)

Finding 40th Street to be a dark, barren wasteland, you hightail it to Eighth Avenue to grab a cab and—FML… It's that Port Authority bullshit where every northbound cab is either taken, or in line to pick up commuters coming into the city. You don't have time to piss away waiting for your turn, so the only option is to cut the line and pray that you're able to dig deep within your actor toolbox and finally use some of that acting crap you learned in your BFA program in an effort to sway the emotions of the people waiting.

"Excuse me, miss," you stammer as you approach an elderly lady at the front of the line with her husband. "Our dog is very sick, and we need to get him to the vet right away."

The old lady looks at you questionably, and then you remember that time you didn't book that one job, and had to find out about it on social media. This causes you to burst into the Oprah Ugly Cry.

The old lady clasps her mouth, sympathetically, "Your poor dog!"

Her husband opens the door of the cab for you. "Go right ahead!"

Corey and you slide into the backseat, quickly fire off the address of Sammy's to the driver, and speed away.

Wiping your tears away, you smile at Corey. "Thank you, Stanislavski."

Woof, dude. That was some hardcore bamboozling you just pulled off. You bamboozled that poor couple almost as good as half the working actors on Broadway have bamboozled the industry.

When you arrive at Sammy's brownstone (apparently IATSE Local 306 is where the dollars are at) you see that all the lights are off, save one, upstairs.

"How do we get in?" you ask Corey.

Corey pulls a small bobby pin out of thin air and starts picking the lock. You're not even going to ask why he carries around a random bobby pin, just like I'm not going to ask why you've neglected to call the police, and have instead chosen to handle the capture of a serial killer yourselves. I understand an actor's hubris is at play here, but I also understand that there is zero evidence implicating Sammy Fusco in these murders, therefore nothing to merit a warrant to search his place, thus making breaking and entering the only option here.

CLICK. Corey slowly creaks open the door and the two of you quietly sift, stealth-like, through the darkness of Sammy's house, up the stairs, and down the hall, searching for the room with the light on.

Years of experience in having to be silent backstage (or while on stage goofing off during a quiet scene) have prepared you for this moment. It's as if you and Corey are invisible as you approach the closed door at the end of the hallway.

"You're really annoying," says the voice of Sammy Fusco.

"I get that a lot," responds Zach.

Corey tries to communicate with his eyes that he wants to go in. You're able to gesture that it isn't the right time, and that you need to figure out a plan. Sammy continues talking to Zach. You listen.

"It's been fun watching you torment Snyder. I think I'll leave you in his garden with his shovel."

"Why are you framing him?" asks Zach.

"Oh! I finally get my big monologue, huh?" Sammy laughs. "Snyder invested in a play. My dad was the doorman. Snyder offered to help him in the stock market. It was a boiler room. A con. Pop lost his savings, Snyder became a billionaire, and I got a dad with a bullet in his head."

"Why don't you just kill Snyder?"

"Loads more fun killing his mistress and the cops suspecting him. He'll be ruined. Don't kill the man. Kill the legacy."

This is not going to end well if you don't do something now. You need to go in, but you also need backup. Using text-9-1-1 (a real thing you discovered when you had an emergency, but were on vocal rest) you send an SOS message with your coordinates.

Zach guffaws. "Why haven't you killed me yet?" He's never seemed more cavalier than in this moment.

"I have a system." Sammy reveals. "You think this is my first spree? I've been killing since before you were born, and every single one of you gets to hear how good I am."

Corey quietly nudges the door open.

"Three decades listening to actors gripe for attention," Sammy's voice is slowly progressing to rage, "When all the while I was doing my thing and never getting credit. I'm the best."

Slipping into the room silently, you see Sammy, back turned to you, holding a shovel and standing over Zach, who is on his knees with his hands tied behind him.

"When I kill, it's art." Sammy raises the shovel. "I'm the Stephen Sondheim of psychopaths, and I'd like a little recognition!"

Corey races across the room and grabs the shovel by the handle as it swings upwards. Sammy turns, shock and fury in his eyes. They wrestle for a beat, allowing you the opportunity to "battement" your foot right into Sammy's face. He stumbles backwards and drops the shovel. You run to untie Zach as Sammy pulls a knife from his pocket.

Corey steps back. "Jesus, Sammy. You're like sixty."

Sammy scowls. "How'd you find me?"

"You think we don't notice you?" Corey asks, still in disbelief.

Sammy charges at Corey with the knife. You're too far away to help, and Zach's hands are nearly impossible to untie. Corey preps into a rond erse, leaping high, turning in mid-air, and swinging his right foot into Sammy's jaw, forcing him to the ground. Corey then picks up the shovel and beats it across Sammy's face, knocking him out cold.

You finally free Zach. He sits backwards, stunned. "How the—? Who the—? What just happened?!"

Breathing heavily, Corey manages to chuckle. "You're welcome."

Sirens blare in the distance.

Sensing that it would be better in the long run to get out now and allow Zach to claim responsibility for capturing Sammy, you turn to Corey and say. "We should go… or we'll be late for that Feinstein's/54 Below show we're in tonight."

Before anyone can see you, the two of you race out of the brownstone and into the night.

***

"You were right," Corey says, as you dive into your favorite late night entrée at Westway Diner. Still pumped with adrenaline and ravenous from the recent brush with death, neither of you were ready to go to bed.

"Right about what?" you manage to ask through a stuffed mouth.

"Making up that excuse to get out of there. I think Zach needed to claim that victory to get reinstated. Can you imagine how embarrassing it'd have been for him if it got out he was saved by two Broadway chorus kids who figured out the case before he did?"

You nod and laugh. "For real."

Corey looks out the window. "You know that feeling you got when you booked your first big job?"

Uh-oh. Corey is getting sincere again. However, while it feels like it was a hundred years ago, you've never forgotten the thrill of landing your first big job. The phone call that made you tense your body up so tight with excitement, it hurt whenever you inhaled, as if you had punctured a lung, and that delightful pain lingered with you for weeks. You never forget that.

"Yeah," you smile, "I feel like that now."

"Me too."

If only there were a way the two of you could continue consulting on cases with Zach. On paper, it's a ludicrous idea, but so was *Sweeney Todd*. It's worth a try, and you know just the way to make it happen.

"Zach would be dead without us," you say, "We're going to his station tomorrow to have a few words with him. I have an idea."

Corey doesn't even debate you. Like yourself, he's far too addicted to the endorphins provided by the novel idea of doing something you love. This kind of happiness has been gone from both of you for far too long, and now that it's back, you need it more. Add to this the fact that neither of you can share your experience on social media because there's a chance that some of what you did was illegal—also, it's probably not something you should be openly talking about if you want to continue doing it. This rare, self-imposed filter set in place to keep you from bragging online is providing an oddly educational moment right now, because you realize that probably nobody gives a shit that you just took your serial killer doorman out with a shovel, because it doesn't have to do with them.

You and Corey meet the next morning to accost Zach outside his place of business. You're exhausted from the night before. Since today is your day off, you thought there was a good chance you could sleep, but you were unceremoniously woken early by the epic full cast text thread that began when the news broke that Sammy was first arrested for killing Charles Noone, and then admitted to being responsible for over a hundred cold-case murders. Apparently he was a legend, and you and Corey caught him.

Of course, you kept this information to yourself, and just casually texted the group, "oh wow," with that emoji of a monkey holding his mouth. You then rolled out of bed and realized that to be able to function today, you needed two Beroccas. (Berocca is an effervescent vitamin tablet that is rich in vitamin B, C, and cocaine level caffeine. It can get you through a morning press event, rehearsal, put-in, show, and late-night concert without batting an eyelash. You learned about them from Lesli Margherita—it explains why she's like that.)

When you arrive at the building where Zach works, Corey texts him to request he come outside. After a little back-and-forth, Zach agrees and meets you—somewhat reluctantly I might add, for someone whose life you just saved.

"I can't stay out here long," says Zach, "You want a thank you? Thank you."

Corey smirks. "I don't need a thank you."

You step in. "We want a job."

"We've been talking," Corey adds, "We're a great team, and we saved your life."

Zach looks confused. "What are you getting at?"

"I want to be your partner," Corey says, coolly.

Zach laughs. "You're crazy. No."

"Where was Barkowitz during all of this?" you ask. "You need us."

"Besides," Corey confidently smiles, "What would happen if everyone found out that a couple of chorus kids caught New York's most elusive serial killer? You'd be finished."

Zach stares Corey down. "When did you get this good at blackmail and manipulation?"

Corey stares right back. "I'm in theatre."

Zach pauses for a moment. Corey got him good. "You get to help with one case."

You think, "Wait, what?!" but you say, "One case. A week."

"I can't pay you."

"We already get paid to do nothing," notes Corey. #Truth.

"I won't work around show schedules."

"We'll figure it out," you say.

"You have to lie low. Stay out of my way. Nobody can know. Just you two."

Corey looks at you. Is this stunt actually being pulled off? I mean, as excited as you were about the very theatre-centric case you stumbled upon and solved, you never imagined Zach would actually go for bringing the two of you on board to investigate crimes outside your bubble of expertise.

"Deal?" Corey asks.

Zach shrugs. "Looks like I have a new partner."

Corey moves to hug Zach, but he deflects with a handshake.

"We're like Fred and Ginger: SVU," laughs Corey.

"I don't know what that means, but I better not be Ginger."

Corey shakes his head. "You could never be Ginger. Ginger did everything Fred did—except backwards, and in high heels."

Zach points his finger sternly at Corey. "No heels. Unless you're undercover."

430

"People think she came up with that line, but actually, it originated—

Zach puts up his hand up. "Save it."

Corey smiles, a tear glazing his eyes. "I missed this."

It's at this moment when you realize the bigger picture here. Sure, your objective was always to eliminate the mundane in your life—to change your attitude and discover a way to find your purpose. But, through your process of self-fulfillment, you stumbled into selflessly bringing two estranged family members back together. Through literal blood, and literal sweat—but, mostly, literal blood, especially at the end there—you saved your friend—in every way that a person can be saved.

As you watch Corey laugh with Zach, you feel optimistic for the first time in ages. Well... cautiously optimistic. Like, you're not going to post online about your sudden positive change in attitude, because the last time you were this ecstatic about the future, it was still acceptable to use social media that way, and you know better now. Instead, you're going to revel in all the exciting possibilities this new chapter in your life is going to bring. You're going to reflect upon how it is possible to redirect your unhappiness, but only when you're active about it. You never imagined the road to figuring out all of this would involve murder, but sometimes the universe has to speak a little louder when you're that jaded.

The next time you enter your stage door, your head will be a little higher knowing you'll be filling your swing "office hours" solving random mysteries and becoming a better detective for however long, and even if someday it all ends, you'll be able to pitch this entire story as a series for Netflix, or Hulu, or, at the very least, as a web series or something for NBC. You think you'll call it: *Shubert Alley*.

"Well, shit," Zach says, breaking your daydreaming.

"What?" you ask.

"A body was found in the dumpster outside Buffalo Wild Wings," says Zach, gazing down at his phone. "That's smack in the middle of your jurisdiction."

"Holy shit," says Corey.

Zach shrugs. "Looks like you kids are up."

Corey turns to you and smiles.

EPILOGUE (page 465)

*

Deciding to take your Equity-mandated day off, you and Corey agree not to bother with this next step in the case until Tuesday, because it involves Bernadette, and anything with Bernadette can wait. Instead, you head to Corey's to watch one of the fourteen shows that air on Sunday nights or, depending on the season, football (because like Patti Murin and Sam Strickland, you will not be defined solely by your involvement in theatre.)

Midway through your viewing party, Corey receives a call from Zach—except it isn't Zach. It's Barkowitz on Zach's phone. Apparently Zach tried to arrest Snyder without enough evidence and was suspended, causing him to embark on a bender and leave his phone at a bar. Nobody can find him, and Barkowitz was hoping Corey would know where he is. Unable to offer any assistance, you and Corey try to continue watching TV, but the ominous feeling of doom colors the remainder of the evening.

The next day, you and Corey text on-and-off, but still no word from Zach. Corey doesn't seem too concerned because when they were younger, Zach had been known to slip into self-indulgent shame spirals where he'd disappear for a few days. While that could be the case here, you're still not feeling great about it, but you don't want to worry Corey.

Tuesday rolls along, and you and Corey are starting to feel a little guilty about doing nothing about Zach's disappearance. You agree to meet for lunch to open your own missing person's case at Chipotle on 44th and Ninth (because you're hoping for ultimate positive vibes due to this location's close proximity to Telsey and the fact that it's Chipotle).

As you sit down with your burrito bowls, Corey receives a call from Zach's phone. Your stomach somersaults, like when you see your agent is calling, but you don't know if it's because you booked that big job or they're just phoning to tell you about some other appointment for a busted gig you don't want.

Corey takes a deep breath and answers. "Hello?"

He remains silent and expressionless for what feels like an eternity. Then, slowly, he puts the phone down on the table. The Fray's "How to Save a Life" starts playing through the restaurant's speakers.

"That was Barkowitz," Corey says, looking straight through your eyes—not into them, but straight through them, out the door, and across the street to somewhere safe... far away. "He's gone."

"What? No. Gone where?" This can't be.

"A gardener found him buried in the backyard of Warren Snyder's estate in Westchester."

"But," You're so confused, "No. They let him go. They let Snyder go and..." It's all too much to register.

"I... *We* failed him," Corey whispers, nearly catatonic.

"We didn't fail him," you say. But, you know you did. You gave an already over-emotional hothead unsolicited evidence moments after speaking at his best friend's funeral. Sure, you didn't have control over what he would do with that information, but ultimately you failed him by stepping into a complicated investigation and delivering the right puzzle piece, at the wrong time.

When a swing goes on in a show, should anything in that performance feel out of place to the rest of the cast, they must sometimes be prepared to take the blame, whether it's their fault or not. In this case, because of you and Corey, something happened out of place, and you must shoulder that blame.

You went into this case with the best intentions, but then fell flat when it came to getting Bernadette's autograph so you could work your way into those archives that you believe held the missing piece to all of this. You lacked commitment when commitment was needed most. You marked when you needed to hit the back of the house. In short, you failed because you didn't play to win.

THE END.

*

I'm impressed that you've committed to drinking before half hour. In theory, most of us would love to live life like Elaine Stritch in the Seventies, but the only people who've come close to that are in the touring cast of *Newsies*. It's pretty acceptable to drink in this moment. You've had a rough day. Your best friend just revealed to you that his parents died in a horrific car wreck, he's estranged from his brother, and is still clearly in major shock from seeing a dead body. This is some half-priced-drinks-drama you're dealing with, and you know just the place to go: Gyu Kaku.

Nestled quietly on 44th Street, between Eighth and Ninth Avenues, this Midtown jewel goes fairly unnoticed because it is located next to Jay Binder Casting and not Telsey. With half off the entire bar, all day, every day, Gyu Kaku is a day drinking game changer that few know about, and I gather talking about it openly right now is seriously going to fuck shit up for me.

"Follow me," you say, placing your arm around Corey, as you walk him out of Shubert Alley, and in the direction of Eighth Avenue.

"Where are we going?" he asks.

"Don't worry about it," you say, and make small talk with Corey until you've reached the pearly gates of Gyu Kaku.

"No. We can't drink this close to the show" urges Corey.

You roll your eyes. Corey occasionally likes to have morals at truly inconvenient times. "I think for today, we can make an exception." And with that, you head to the bar and order four martinis for twelve dollars—this place would blow Eileen Rand's mind.

As you drink the first round, you mostly try to amuse Corey by talking about how difficult your life is.

It's not clear if he wants to listen or not, but a good friend knows their audience, and even though your problems don't begin to compare to Corey's, you plow on because, at the very least, you're offering him a distraction. By the second round, Corey begins to loosen up and unload all of his drama with his brother, and you're only mildly annoyed he's interrupted you.

"Yeah. He was a cool brother. For like *five minutes*. Whatever, Zach! You're a douche now. Detective Douche!" There's a chance that after four years of hopping on and off a Broadway Bares diet, Corey can't hold his liquor.

"Maybe you should save that second drink for me," you suggest with care, "Why don't you try opening another dialogue with him?"

"My brother is gone. It's like, *Fun Home*, you know? What happened to those brothers? Why is nobody talking about the middle one? He was so chill! What. Happened. To. The. Brothers."

You pull out your phone, trying to stop this from escalating too far. "I'm sure if we look at Alison Bechdel's Wikipedia, we can figure it –

"I saw Sydney Lucas. Yeah. I saw her. I should have told her: Listen Syd, Tony Shmony. It's family. It's all about family. *Fun Home* is about *family*." Corey's eyes widen. "Whoa. I think I just got *Fun Home*. I gotta go tell Sydney Lucas. Do you think she knows what it's all about?!"

Corey abruptly stands, causing the messenger bag that is attached to his bar stool to tip over and slam to the ground. I hate when that happens. It makes you look like you're the drunk one at the bar, when you're not. Yet, in this case, Corey is totally the drunk one at the bar, and he's about to storm out and give Sydney Lucas a piece of his mind. This can't end well.

You chase after him. "Corey, stop!"

Corey stops, but only because he can't get through the onslaught of normal business people clogging up the doorway. Ugh. It's Thursday after 6:00 p.m., New Yorker's night out. You pray that's the case, and not the possibility that other people have found your hidden treasure. Where will you go if you can't go to Gyu Kaku? Not Blockheads. No, you can't go back there. Literally. They won't let you back after Cinco De Mayo, 2014.

Corey mumbles to you, "I can't stop-s when-s there's s-people."

"OK," you say in a comforting voice. "Let's go sit back down then?"

"This place used to mean something!" Corey yells. "I'm not staying, there's muggles." He looks at a businessman with all the disdain and judgment usually reserved for talking behind someone's back at an audition. "*Muggles.*"

Clearly Corey shouldn't be drinking anymore. Maybe it's best to take him back to the theater for a nap on the Equity Cot. However, now that it appears the place is being overrun by people who don't belong, this could be your last time at Gyu Kaku for a while, and you still have two solid bar seats. Should you leave, or take advantage of your favorite hangout one last time?

Stay at Gyu Kaku… (page 443)

Leave Gyu Kaku… (page 451)

"I… think," you continue, with mild trepidation, "I would like to write the lyrics. After all, it's my concept, and the show is called *Pieces of Me* because the words being spoken are all colored with little pieces of, well… me."

Daniel squints in confusion. "I thought you said it would be based on the two of us, and our friends—

"Well, yeah, but like… the tone, you know? I want the language between spoken and sung to be cohesive."

"Then I'm going to have to pass," sighs Daniel. "I'm really only interested in writing both music and lyrics."

"Well," you continue, in an effort to sway Daniel back, "Stephen Sondheim wanted to write both music and lyrics for *West Side Story*, and can you imagine where he'd be had he turned down that job?"

"Something tells me Stephen Sondheim would have figured it out."

"Are you equating yourself to Stephen Sondheim?" you ask.

"Are you equating *Pieces of Me* to *West Side Story*?" asks Daniel.

"Yes," you state. "Yes, I am."

"I wish you the best of luck."

And with that, your lunch meeting with Daniel comes to an unsatisfying conclusion. It's a shame it didn't work out, because Daniel could have proved to be a tremendous amount of help. Now you're going to have to…

Write the book, music, and lyrics yourself… (page 137)

*

There's an age old saying in the theatre that goes, "It doesn't matter if you make strong acting choices, as long as you make *attractive* ones."

Keeping this sage advice in mind, you race home and spend the remainder of the time before your callback making yourself look on fleek af so all of the casting people will scream, "YAAAAASSSSSSS" when you walk into the room thriving. By the time you're finished getting ready, there isn't a moment for you to look over any of the new material – but who cares? You're a walking spank bank.

When you enter the studio at one of the Pearls, you hear a subtle, but audible gasp from the creative team that assures you that you've already nailed this callback. As long as you're moderately capable of reading words off of a piece of paper, this job is all but yours.

"What would you like to sing for us?" asks a man who must be the music director.

You smile. "Would you like something from the show?"

"No," he shrugs, "we want you to do what you do best."

"Well, clearly it's these jeans," you think to yourself as you hand your music to the accompanist and rip into thirty-two bars of complete and utter ecstasy in the form of notes emanating from chords deep within your perfectly toned neck.

"Great!" says the MD. "That's all I need!"

The director looks up from your resume and eyes you from head to toe before asking, "Can you read the sides?"

"Sure!" you giggle. "Which ones?"

"Try the one you prepared the least."

OK, that's not exactly what he said, but it might as well have been, because the sides he requests are most definitely the shittiest of the bunch. Had you poured over the material during the hours before this callback, there's no way you'd have devoted any time to the pages he's asked you to read.

After awkwardly navigating your way through the scene with a reader who essentially carries you, the creative team makes some friendly small talk and then politely sends you on your way.

"Well," you think, "that couldn't have gone any better had I actually prepared for it."

Since there's not much else you can do right now but wait (Wait to die. Wait to live. Wait for another callback... which may never come) you decide to go about life normally, by falling victim to an anxiety-spiral that causes you to text a bunch of friends and recount the entire process to them in hopes they'll talk you off the ledge by assuring you you'll book.

Once you've been moderately satisfied by your friends' feigned attempts at sympathy and support (which took somewhere between a few hours to several days), you are ready to integrate yourself back into society to live a normal life—

An intense vibration rumbles from your phone. It continues on for a while, which means it's a ring, and a ring usually means "Broadway" is calling, and when Broadway calls, you answer it.

"Hello, Broadway?" you say into your phone.

The call is from your agent informing you that the creative team loved your audition, and wants to have sex with you in the form of offering you a role in the show, because you have a look that fits perfectly into the world they are trying to create for this new project.

Boom! Good thing you didn't waste time learning all of that material! This decision allowed you an ample amount of hours to prepare your physical presentation, and it didn't backfire because you ended up being asked to read the one side you probably would have practiced the least! Being so damned efficient gave you a leg up, and you should feel very proud of yourself.

EPILOGUE (page 465)

The businessman, who just got sassed *"muggles"* by Corey, turns and scowls at the two of you. This could get ugly.

You step between Corey and the muggle. "You'll have to excuse my friend. He's in the theatre."

The businessman nods, and you immediately guide Corey back to your bar stools.

"I could have taken him," insists Corey.

"To where? Brunch?" you ask, and then pause for the sitcom laugh track that follows you around.

Once you are both safely seated back at the bar, you order a third round for yourself, and allow Corey to nurse his second drink. True friendship is all about proper supervision and understanding which one of you is more likely to blow chunks on Eighth Avenue in broad daylight.

As you slam back the rest of your third martini, Corey casually mentions that it is five minutes until half hour. Shit! You quickly settle your tab and race out the door with Corey trailing closely behind. The only thing worse than running through Midtown thirty-five minutes before curtain is nothing. Why. Are. There. So. Many. Lines. Don't people know that if they get there two minutes before, they can just walk to their seat? The only people who seem to know about this are theatre people, which is why when you're attending a performance that's been heavily papered, there is a line around the block at five *after* curtain.

Miraculously, you and Corey manage to make it backstage on time. Everything seems OK, except for the fact that as you stumble to your dressing room, you realize there's a small to definite chance you are completely blasted. Who cares? You never go on! Everything is going to be –

CRASH!

You knock over a costume rack and it falls hard on top of two of the ensemble members you cover. Well shit. You're on. In a split track you'd probably fuck up sober. Merde!

So, like, you know how sometimes you think that third drink is a good idea because the second one didn't hit you? And then the second one hits you after you've finished the third? That's what is happening here. You were moderately functional when you injured your cast mates, but as you get into your costume, you realize you're about two minutes away from not being able to form sentences. I'm confused how taking Corey out to commiserate over his family life led to you getting blackout drunk. I'm kind of inspired by how you continue to break new ground in making shit about you. Bravo!

I think it was Sydney Lucas who once said, "Beer before liquor, never been sicker. Liquor before curtain, you gonna face plant in the middle of the stage." And that's essentially what you believe to have happened as you open your eyes and find yourself laying on your back with Norbert Leo Butz glaring down at you with a look on his face that's like, "The fuck?"

The last thing you remember is getting your places call, but judging by the costume you're in now, you managed to make it to the act one finale without killing anyone or stopping the show—until now. The lights go to black and two members of the ensemble help you to your feet and guide you off stage.

Needless to say, you're fired for this severe lack of judgment. You don't even get to storm out of the stage door in costume with your mic on and dance around in Times Square. Moreover, your stunt has gone viral on Broadway Internet, which means it is now your legacy. There is no coming back from this. Broadway Internet never forgets... THE END.

*

"Katie," you say into Voxer, "can you design a strong social media marketing plan?"

"Sure," she says, "it's called: 'making good content and putting it online.'"

"Oh."

For the next week, you and your creative team blast social media with crazy teasers and funny graphics. The engagement on Twitter and Instagram is pretty great, but Facebook is lacking—and that's the platform that holds your key demographic of Older Family Friends with Money.

"It's the algorithms," you scoff. "Facebook hates me."

Andy assures you that, "maybe it's people that hate you."

Joey pipes into Voxer after going M.I.A. for twenty-four hours. "You guys are posting the show graphics to Facebook from Instagram. That'll fuck you. And you need to manually upload the videos instead of using the YouTube links. If Facebook isn't the main platform for what you share, anything you try to post is going to get stiff-handed harder than *Finding Neverland*."

Taking Joey's advice, you upload everything directly to Facebook and the likes and shares immediately come rolling in, causing your show to sell out an entire month before curtain.

"EEEK!" you exclaim. "We have so much to rehearse!"

In the month preceding your debut concert at Feinstein's/54 Below, you practice your material whenever and wherever you have a chance. On the subway, in your apartment, dressing room, friend's dressing room, in your head at other people's Feinstein's/54 Below concerts. For thirty days straight, your life revolves around you even more than it normally does.

After several work sessions and music rehearsals with Andy at one of those janky Ripley Grier studios up on 56th Street, Katie and Joey join you for run-throughs (where you spend the bulk of the time asking if they think what you're doing is funny, if they think people who know you will find it funny, if people who don't know you will think you're funny, if people watching the concert back on YouTube by accident will find it funny, etc.). Once the show is set, the only thing left to do is roll into your upstairs dressing room at Feinstein's/54 Above with your hot outfit for the show and your humidifier (because obviously you got sick on the day of the show).

Sound check goes smoothly, and before you know it, evening is upon you, and you're back upstairs being photographed at the smallest and most fluorescently-lit step and repeat ever to be crammed into an office break room, while Andy hastily applies last minute cuts to music, and Katie and Joey drink vodka out of a paper cup. You're officially part of the New York City Cabaret Elite.

Five minutes to start, you get your call to places, so you hop in the elevator, snag a selfie, and make your way to the eager crowd that awaits your arrival.

As you hover in the kitchen house left, a server brings you a cup of chamomile tea that you politely sip on until Katie races over with a glass of wine of the drink-ticket-varietal, which you promptly chug as you hear your name ring through the speakers. This is it... Don't get scared now.

***

I feel like I'm going to say what any other person who's done a solo cabaret for the first time says, but the entire thing was a tunnel-visioned blur. Nothing from it registered in the moment. In hindsight, you remember spending a lot of the performance hyper-aware of what was landing and what wasn't. While you were being a committed performer, you were also an objective critic. It was important that you made mental notes during, because even after the stress involved with putting this show together, the moment the lights went up, you knew you wanted to do it all again.

The stakes were really high tonight. Not because you were putting yourself out there, but because so many close friends and family members came from *outside of the five boroughs* to see you. There was pressure to live up to some kind of expectation, even though everyone was there because they love you and were positive you'd be good. This overwhelming support came from not just your central social circle, but from the tertiary friends you'd never expect to spend forty bucks to see you flop around on a stage. You kept thinking, "Who the fuck am I? You're all willing to give up an hour and a half for *this*? <u>Thank you</u>."

The words "thank you" are so trite, and never feel sincere enough to say in response to someone when they show you this kind of support. There needs to be a small collection of words that mean more than what you utter to your barista. Words that say, "You could be doing anything right now, and you chose to see me. Like, what are you doing?" It's overwhelming to look out an audience and see so many people care deeply enough about you to physically show up." Saying "thank you" is not nearly enough.

Now that all is said and done, you're really proud of yourself for stepping out of your comfort zone and into a new genre of performing, even though it's not necessarily one that you always enjoy. The art of cabaret is so easy to do poorly and anyone thinks they can do it.

What many cabaret performers typically imagine other people want to see usually turns into a boring mess. Cabaret is a combination of knowing your audience, being accessible to a wider audience, and not giving a shit. You feel what you did tonight achieved that goal, and as someone who was in the audience, I must agree. Thank you.

EPILOGUE (page 465)

*

"One Funfetti, please," you respectfully request from the Schmackary's employee. The men and women who work at Schmackary's really are the heroes of Broadway. True heroes. Like IATSE members, or anyone who has ever made it through an eight-show week with Tovah Feldshuh.

"We're just about to take a warm batch out of the oven," responds the Schmackary's employee. "Would you like to wait?"

"Was Laura Osnes adapted from the first fifteen minutes of *Enchanted*? Hell yes, I'll wait!" You exclaim eagerly. Nothing gets you hotter than a warm batch from Schmackary's.

While waiting for your fresh Funfetti, you pull your audition materials out of your bag and give them a quick glance-over. You could have played it subtle by reading them on your phone, but then nobody around you would be able to see that.

After about seven minutes, your Funfetti is ready, and boy you can't wait to run your tongue along it. After a few seconds of taking in the aroma by teasing it on your lips, you thrust the Funfetti deep within your mouth, and savor the gooey, warm, magical goodness. The cookie is gone within a matter of moments.

Thrilled with your life choices, you strut through the door and back out onto the New York City streets that seem to hold so much more hope than they did when you awoke this morning. Overcome with satisfaction and refined sugar, you feel compelled to tweet to the world how happy you are.

You pull out your phone, open the Twitter application, and –

BAM!

Something hits you. You don't know what, but it was big. It could have been a bus. Possibly it was a street

449

cleaner. Most likely, it was whatever killed Kyle Bishop on *Smash*—and just like his character, (and 100% of the audience) you'll never know what the hell it was. Who gives a shit? You've been hit. Everything is moving in slow-motion on an iPhone 6, and you're being thrown through the air like half the cast of *Bring it On*, the *Pippin* revival, or whatever Broadway show is currently representing basket tosses.

Thoughts are processing quicker than time.

How did you get here? How the hell? Maybe you should have stayed at the gym. Maybe you should have gone to Juice Generation. Maybe you shouldn't have gone to the ball. Maybe you just weren't meant to have children. Don't say that, of course you don't have any children. Yes, maybe you shouldn't have.

Maybe you shouldn't have chosen your standby cookie. Who likes standbys, anyway? If you had chosen the Chocolate Telsey + Co-Coa Cream, you wouldn't have waited the seven minutes like you did for Funfetti, thus allowing you to make it out the door and safely out of harm's way before whatever hit you, hit you. You should have chosen Telsey. YOU ALWAYS CHOOSE TELSEY.

The light is getting dimmer. There is no glimmer. It's funny. It doesn't hurt at all. It's just as if whatever hit you, had kissed you.

"Is it possible for something to hit you hard like that – real loud and hard, and it not hurt you at all?" You ask.

"It is possible dear, for something to hit you, hit you hard, and it not hurt at all," responds the soft voice of Shirley Jones.

Just before it all fades to black, you hear the sound of an unresolved chord play ten blocks away by a mediocre accompanist at Nola Studios. Then, darkness.

THE END.

In an effort not to engage any longer with the unsuspecting victim of Corey's muggle-hate-speak, you grab your inebriated friend's arm, and yank him through the crowd, and out the door of Gyu Kaku—completely forgetting to close out your tab, which is OK, because you'll be back soon enough… like after the show.

Corey is pissed. "Where are we going?" he asks in a huff.

"Back to the theater. You need to sleep this off," you say, dragging him down 44th Street.

The majority of your journey through Midtown is spent trying to stop Corey from swinging around street signs while singing "Chandelier"—mainly because he only knows his sixteen bar cut. When you arrive at your theater, you see Zach and Barkowitz exiting the stage door. By now, the second drink has hit Corey hard and he is belligerent.

"Wait here," you urge him, as you block his chest with your arm.

Corey pushes your hand away. "You want me to 'open up a dialogue?' I'll open up a dialogue." And with that, Corey storms off towards Zach.

Shocked by this sudden action from your obliterated mess of a friend, you take a beat to understand what just happened before chasing after him. When you catch up to Corey, he is already giving a surprisingly calm Zach a piece of his mind—Barkowitz looks dumbfounded.

"Like, you think you can walk in my theater and ignore me?" Corey screams. "After four years? You know how many times I've offered you comps when I've been on? Why don't you support me!?"

Zach keeps his cool. "Are you drunk?" he asks.

"Is it a day ending in 'day'?" Corey retorts.

This is more awkward than trying to carry on a convincing conversation with a friend after seeing them in a shitty show.

Barkowitz steps in. "I'm going to have to ask you to calm down, sir."

"Shut up, twunk," spats Corey.

Having been verbally provoked, Barkowitz shoves Corey. "Who you calling twunk, twink—

Corey takes a swing at Barkowitz... Except he doesn't really know how to punch, and delivers more of a flying straight-armed throw with a fist—like he's clotheslining someone. Corey must have failed stage combat in college.

Barkowitz is out cold. Zach places handcuffs on Corey.

You know this shit is wrong. "Officer Krupke swung first," you insist, "Come on, he's your brother!"

Zach shoots a look at you. "Stay out of this, or you're going with him."

"Like hell, I am!" You yell defiantly. When did you and Corey get so badass? Usually you save this kind of passionate behavior for social media campaigns.

"You were warned," says Zach, as he slaps a pair of cuffs on you, too.

"What the actual fuck." You state, "I promise you this is not how this works."

Zach smirks. He doesn't give a shit. You try to stay chill, even though you have no clue how this could possibly end well. Corey starts yelling Arthur Laurents-psychobabble-Jet-slang at Zach. This is a disaster. What does "Rigga tigga Rum Tum tugger" mean anyway?

While "drunk and disorderly" is definitely one of your special skills, you've never been asked to pull them out at an audition. Now, you're getting arrested for perhaps your finest performance of this ability yet. So, I guess that's a positive way to spin it. Anyway, that's about all I can tell you right now because I don't have time to deal with your drama. I already have enough hot mess friends to police, so you're on your own with this. Sorry 'bout it.

THE END.

BROADWAY SOPHOMORE

The life of a Broadway Sophomore is somewhat problematic. Deep down, you still love the business, but for some reason you put up the façade that you're just a bit too cool for it. The basis of this central conflict is difficult to analyze. Keeping current about what's going on in the industry is important to you, but you're not going to be the first person to share your knowledge about what show is third in line for the Walter Kerr at your next dinner party. You don't jump to participate in events, but you're disappointed if you aren't asked. You'll often go days without being active on social media, and then out of nowhere, you'll be all about some random colleague's Periscope. Why you choose to mask your enthusiasm towards an industry that still brings you great joy is an enigma.

This duplicitous existence you're living could put you in danger of sliding down the slippery slope to jaded Junior territory—which is why you've decided to indulge yourself in a simple Sophomore pastime: creating your own project.

When an actor in the Broadway community is still passionate about the world they work in, but wants to give off the perception that they don't *need* it to feel fulfilled, they typically find something creative over which they can have control. This can take the form of a debut album, web series, solo concert, parody Twitter account, etc.—and all of them involve some form of crowdfunding.

You know it's important for actors to create their own shit, because even if it sucks, at least it's something they have power over in an industry that provides such little opportunity to feel in control—like, literally no opportunity to feel in control.

There are three different types of creative projects that interest you: one that fulfills your budding behind the scenes writer side, one that puts you square in the spotlight (far from the standing-on-twelve-in-the-back-in-the-dark you've grown accustomed to) and one that is more philanthropic. All of them will feed your soul, bring you out of your comfort zone, and show your friends and fans online a side of you they haven't seen—but you can only choose one.

Should you pick the venture that allows you to step out center stage and show the world the kind of multifaceted performer you are? Do you confine your creativity to the page? Or do you go with the one that makes you feel like a humanitarian? What you have in mind for these projects comes with great risks that could reap greater rewards. Which do you choose...?

The performer project. (page 183)

The writer project. (page 128)

The humanitarian project. (page 177)

*

OMG! YOU'RE LENA HALL! You win!

THE END.

*

Social media is a nuanced medium, and finding success in it is like breaking out of jail or writing a hit show: you can't do it the same way twice. Fortunately, you figure out a unique method of marketing yourself as a composer/lyricist using the tools you've developed from years of staring at your phone. It isn't long before you garner a niche following and catch the attention of a Kevin McCollum or Daryl Roth type—whose main objective as a producer is to develop works with distinct voices. The next thing you know, *Pieces of Me* is Off-Broadway, and then on Broadway, and then you're at the Tony Awards where you lose to Lin-Manuel Miranda's third hit show: *Cash Cow* (a loss to Lin-Manuel Miranda is still a win).

It may seem strange how quickly you found success, but like, that's literally how it is for some people.

EPILOGUE (page 465)

BROADWAY JUNIOR

Broadway has been getting you down, but you're not to the point where you want to quit. There isn't anything else you know how to do, or care to learn, so it's easier to put up a front and pretend you love it. This blasé point of view you have towards the industry has begun to color how you behave in your personal life as well. It makes you unable to truly connect with people because there's this deep secret about yourself that nobody knows. As much as you should probably be addressing this issue in therapy at the moment, you can't, because your Broadway Junior status has made you contractually obligated to work the Broadway Flea Market this year.

Now, no matter how little you like to deal with industry traditions, you're always obliged to help out with BC/EFA whenever possible. Be it collecting during Gypsy of the Year and Easter Bonnet seasons, or donating your own money, BC/EFA will always be an organization you feel passionately about and are eager to assist whenever possible—unless it has to do with a large event because some of them give you hives. Broadway Bares is easy to get around by throwing money at your friends' Strip-A-Thon pages, but the Broadway Flea Market is damn near impossible to avoid when you're employed.

Since every show running on Broadway puts together a booth for the Flea (with company members working in rotation throughout the day) you look like a major douche when you neglect to help out. It's not that you don't want to support BC/EFA, it's that you don't know what to do with so many theatre fanatics in an uncontrolled location. While you appreciate their presence when they are following you on Twitter, you feel the same way about most Broadway fans as you do about audience participation…it's just better when the fourth wall remains intact. Individually, fans are great, but if you put enough of the wrong ones together in an open space crammed with access to actors and niche memorabilia, there's bound to be chaos. Chorus calls give you anxiety; how is the Broadway Flea Market going to be any different?

This season's Flea, however, is going to be unlike years past. Normally, you casually pop behind your show's table or booth for an hour or two in the morning, and then clear out of Midtown after your matinee. This year you've been asked to co-host the Live Auction with Ann Harada, and there was just no way you were going to turn down the opportunity to joke around with her in front of thousands of screaming fans, no matter how many Broadway Bowling trophies they might own. You'll be safely positioned on a stage anyway, so it'll be fine.

Choosing when to be jaded about this business is tricky. In other circumstances, perhaps you wouldn't be so willing to accept such a public position at one of the largest Broadway fan events of the year. But hosting the live auction will perpetuate the idea that you care about the business more than anything else possibly could, thus providing you with enough karma to cover a year of backing out of things you're asked to do. This is a fairly inspired plan for someone who doesn't quite know what they want out of life.

As far as Broadway Flea Market Live Auction hosts go, you and Ann Harada are probably the best ever. There is true chemistry between the two of you, and it actually looks like you're having fun. Just because you are literally dying inside doesn't mean you're going to mark it when there are that many iPhones pointed at you. Moreover, the one character trait from your history as an actor that you'll never be able to deny is your unparalleled love of attention.

This specific year's auction has the distinction of being the first one to break all records of moneys raised during a Flea Market before it even comes to an end. This is partly due to your charisma, but more so because of Ann Harada, as well as the truly unique collection of lots available for bidding:

Personal Tour of Billy Porter's Closet…
$12,000
Vial of Ramin Karimloo's Sweat…
$14,000
Watch Patina Miller Work Out…
$13,000
Walk-On Role in *Misery*…
$10,000
Box of Dye Idina Used to Go Blonde for the Last Two Performances of *If/Then*…
$7,000
Signed Christopher Walken Cue Card from *Peter Pan Live*…
$9,000
Mystery Box Containing Something from *Smash*…
$87,000
Anything from *Hamilton*…
$412,000
The Guitar Sting Wrote *The Last Ship* With…
$12

The final lot in the live auction is the cast recording of Bernadette Peters' *Gypsy*, signed by Patti LuPone.

"This rare entity," you explain, "is the only known copy in existence…I give you…and don't forget to bring her back when you are finished with her—

Ann Harada rolls her eyes.

"The Bernadette Peters' revival of *Gypsy* soundtrack, signed by—

A ripple of audible gasps races through the crowd, causing you to pause and stare out at thousands of horrified faces waiting in total silence. It's chilling. You are completely unaware of what just happened to cause this turn. Then, slowly, a woman in her mid-thirties wearing a *Once* t-shirt steps forward…

"It's called a *cast recording*," she spits with rage. "*Not* a *soundtrack*."

A single tear runs down young Iain Armitage's face.

Another woman in a *Bonnie & Clyde* hat shouts from several feet back, "Who *are* you!?"

"Yeah!" screams a man holding a life-size cutout of Cheyenne Jackson from *All Shook Up*.

More people start screeching, "It's a cast recording!" and "You don't deserve your Equity card!" The outcry doesn't show any signs of letting up.

As the throng gains strength, they begin chanting, "Soundtrack is whack!" over and over again as they descend upon the stage.

Ann Harada whispers, "See yah," and quickly disappears.

Three fans in the front row hop on stage, waving old Elphaba brooms as pitchforks. More follow suit, leaving you a mere moment to decide if you can take on this angry mob or not. This is literal fight or flight right now. What do you do!?

Fight! (page 376)

Flight! (page 266)

461

*

Birdland it is!

Shit. Birdland is also booked for the dates you want.

Do you...

*Pray that
Feinstein's/54 Below is available...?* (page 306)

Quit. (page 4)

EPILOGUE

AND—Scene.

I can't believe you made it to the end without dying. That's so crazy. Due to your educated choices and incomparable savvy, you have successfully survived and thrived in show business. There were ups…there were downs…there were five-minute calls, happy hours, late nights, near deaths, deep talks, long walks, dance belts, retweets, likes, and a lot of references to Nineties movies—but throughout it all, your passion and drive endured.

Your journey may have been irritatingly slow, or perhaps it was perplexingly brief. Either way, it is important to remember that it isn't over. Good things don't have to come to an end. Bad things are allowed to stop. In this life, no matter how grand or dire the status quo, you always have the chance to try again—you just have to figure out how.

You're here now because you played to win. But want to know something funny? It was never a game. The only person you're ever playing in this life is yourself. Life has no rules. There is no right path. There isn't a formula. There isn't an answer. Life is just one hauntingly short, yet joyously long, game of Scenes from a Hat, performed with the erratic inconsistency of a high school drama class. And when the game doesn't go your way, you have the power and ability to change the script. Once you accept that you can be in control, your potential opportunities are endless. So, go forth into your life remembering to always follow the first rule of Improv, and instead of accepting "No," demand, "Yes, and—

ACKNOWLEDGEMENTS

THANK YOU to my editor, Ashlee Latimer, who saved this book…in every way that a book can be saved.

THANK YOU to the following people, whose contributions added to the authenticity of *#GRATEFUL* and *#SOBLESSED*: Cameron Adams, Aaron J. Albano, J. David Anderson, Kristen Caesar, Peter Donovan, Nikka Graff Lanzarone, Jamie Grayson, Sarah Marie Jenkins, Stephanie Jump, Ellyn Marie Marsh, Chris McCarrell, Julia Murney, Tim Murray, Katherine Paige, Jacquelyn Piro Donovan, Krysta Rodriguez, Tara Rubin, Kate Shindle, Jennifer Spitulnik, Drew Wutke, and Alex Wyse. I hope I didn't leave anyone out! They only gave me ninety seconds!

THANK YOU to the person who endured so much BS from me during this process. Thank you for your patience and understanding, while I disappeared for hours a day to write sweeping sequences about Schmackary's, Hilary Duff, and Myself. I love you.

THANK YOU for buying this book and supporting live tweeting. Whether you're knew to Annoying Actor Friend, or have been there since the beginning, I am truly, unironically #GRATEFUL for your presence. Without you, I do not exist. So, please go back to Amazon and give this book a five star rating whether you thought it was shit or not.

ABOUT THE AUTHOR

In 2012, anonymous parody Internet personality Annoying Actor Friend (@Actor_Friend) rose to notoriety on Twitter by spoofing the social media behavior of actors. It soon spun off into a blog, where it did everything from recapping season two of NBC's *Smash*, to constructing drinking games for live events such as the Tonys, and even becoming an empowering voice that inspired actors to evoke change within the stage union, Actors' Equity Association as well as ignite the viral movement #Dim4Joan that motivated the Broadway League to reverse their decision not to dim the lights of Broadway in memory of Joan Rivers.

In October of 2013, Annoying Actor Friend released their first book, *#SOBLESSED: the Annoying Actor Friend's Guide to Werking in Show Business* on Amazon, where it became the #1 Best Selling Theater and Parody book on its first day of sale. The audiobook benefits Broadway Cares/Equity Fights AIDS and features the voices of Alan Cumming, Leslie Margherita, Megan Hilty, Julia Murney, Will Swenson, Keala Settle, Tituss Burgess, Krysta Rodriguez, Andrew Keenan-Bolger, and Brian Dennehy.

Annoying Actor Friend was placed on Backstage Magazine's "Future Broadway Power" list, and was a wildcard finalist in the 2015 Shorty Awards—which honor excellence in social media. With over 20,000 followers on Twitter, @Actor_Friend is considered a leading satirical voice and cultural commentator for the Broadway industry.

48297219R00262

Made in the USA
Lexington, KY
26 December 2015